EFFECTIVE

MARKETING

Effective Management
Series Editor: Alan H. Anderson

EFFECTIVE MARKETING

a skills and
activity-based approach

ALAN H. ANDERSON
and
THELMA DOBSON

First published 1994

Blackwell Publishers
108 Cowley Road
Oxford OX4 1JF
UK

238 Main Street
Cambridge, Massachusetts 02142
USA

British Library Cataloguing in Publication Data

A CIP catalogue record for this book is available from the British Library.

Library of Congress Cataloging-in-Publication Data

Anderson, Alan H., 1950-
    Effective Marketing: a skills and activity-based approach / Alan H. Anderson and Thelma Dobson.
        p. cm. – (Effective management)
    Includes bibliographical references and index.
    ISBN 0-631-19118-6 (pbk.: alk. paper)
    1. Marketing–Management. I. Dobson, Thelma. II. Title.
III. Series: Effective management (Oxford, England)
HF5415. 13A52 1994
658.8--dc20

Designed and typeset by VAP Group Ltd., Kidlington, Oxfordshire

Printed in Great Britain by T.J. Press (Padstow) Ltd, Padstow, Cornwall.

This book is printed on acid-free paper

I would like to dedicate my contribution to this book to my wife Maureen whose immense effort and support have sustained me in writing my overall contribution not only to this book, but to the whole series.

Alan Anderson.

Contents

Figures

Boxes

Activities

Introduction to the Series

" He that has done nothing has known nothing. "

Carlyle

The Concept

In this series 'effective' means getting results. By taking an action approach to management, or the stewardship of an organization, the whole series allows people to create and develop their skills of effectiveness. This interrelated series gives the underpinning knowledge base and the application of functional and generic skills of the effective manager who gets results.

Key qualities of the effective manager include:

- **functional expertise** in the various disciplines of management;
- an understanding of the **organizational context**;
- an appreciation of the **external environment**;
- **self-awareness** and the power of **self-development**.

These qualities must fuse in a climate of **enterprise**.

Management is results-oriented so action is at a premium. The basis of this activity is **skills** underpinned by our qualities. In turn these skills can be based on a discipline or a function, and be universal or generic.

The Approach of the Series

These key qualities of effective management are the core of the current twelve books of the series. The areas covered by the series at present are:

People	*Effective Personnel Management*
	Effective Labour Relations
	Effective Organizational Behaviour
Finance	*Effective Financial Management*
	Effective Accounting Management
Marketing and sales	*Effective Marketing*
	Effective International Marketing
	Effective Marketing Communications
Operations/Enterprise	*Effective Enterprise Management*
	Effective Entrepreneurship
Policy/General	*Effective Business Policy*
	Effective General Management

The key attributes of the effective manager are all dealt with in the series, and we will pinpoint where they are emphasized:

- *Functional expertise.* The four main disciplines of management – finance, marketing, operations and personnel management – make up nine books. These meet the needs of specialist disciplines and allow a wider appreciation of other functions.
- *Organizational context.* All the 'people' books – the specialist one on *Effective Organizational Behaviour,* and also *Effective Personnel Management* and *Effective Labour Relations* – cover this area. The resourcing/control issues are met in the 'finance' texts, *Effective Financial Management* and *Effective Accounting Management.* Every case activity is given some organizational context.
- *External environment.* One book, *Effective Business Policy,* is dedicated to this subject. Environmental contexts apply in every book of the series: especially in *Effective Entrepreneurship, Effective General Management,* and in all of the 'marketing' texts – *Effective Marketing, Effective International Marketing* and *Effective Marketing Communications.*
- *Self-awareness/self-development.* To a great extent management development is manager development, so we have one generic skill (see later) devoted to this topic running through each book. The subject is examined in detail in *Effective General Management.*
- *Enterprise.* The *Effective Entrepreneurship* text is allied to *Effective Enterprise Management* to give insights into this whole area through all the developing phases of the firm. The marketing and policy books also revolve around this theme.

Skills

The functional skills are inherent within the discipline-based texts. In addition, running through the series are the following generic skills:
- self-development
- teamwork
- communications
- numeracy/IT
- decisions

These generic skills are universal managerial skills which occur to some degree in every manager's job.

Format/Structure of Each Book

Each book is subdivided into six units. These are self-contained, in order to facilitate learning, but interrelated, in order to give an effective holistic view. Each book also has an introduction with an outline of the book's particular theme.

Each unit has *learning objectives* with an overview/summary of the unit.

Boxes appear in every unit of every book. They allow a different perspective from the main narrative and analysis. Research points, examples, controversy and theory are all expanded upon in these boxes. They are numbered by unit in each book, e.g. 'Box PM1.1' for the first box in Unit One of *Effective Personnel Management*.

Activities, numbered in the same way, permeate the series. These action-oriented forms of learning cover cases, questionnaires, survey results, financial data, market research information, etc. The skills which can be assessed in each one are noted in the code at the top right of the activity by having the square next to them ticked. That is, if we are assuming numeracy then the square beside Numeracy would be ticked (✓), and so on. The weighting given to these skills will depend on the activity, the tutors'/learners' needs, and the overall weighting of the skills as noted in the appendix on 'Generic Skills', with problem solving dominating in most cases.

Common cases run through the series. Functional approaches are added to these core cases to show the same organization from different perspectives. This simulates the complexity of reality.

Workbook

The activities can be written up in the *workbook* which accompanies each book in the series.

Handbook

For each book in the series, there is a *handbook*. This is not quite the 'answers' to the activities, but it does contain some indicative ideas for them (coded accordingly), which will help to stimulate discussion and thought.

Test bank

We are developing a bank of tests in question-and-answer format to accompany the series. This will be geared to the knowledge inputs of the books.

The Audience

The series is for all those who wish to be effective managers. As such, it is a series for management development on an international scale, and embraces both management education and management training. In management education, the emphasis still tends to be on cognitive or knowledge inputs; in management training, it still tends to be on skills and techniques. We need both theory and practice, with the facility to try out these functions and skills through a range of scenarios in a 'safe' learning environment. This series is unique in encompassing these perspectives and bridging the gulf between the academic and vocational sides of business management.

Academically the series is pitched at the DMS/DBA types of qualification, which often lead on to an MA/MBA after the second year. Undergraduates following business degrees or management studies will benefit from the series in their final years. Distance learners will also find the series useful, as will those studying managerial subjects for professional examinations. The competency approach and the movement towards Accredited Prior Learning and National Vocational Qualifications are underpinned by the knowledge inputs, while the activities will provide useful simulations for these approaches to management learning.

This developmental series gives an opportunity for self-improvement. Individuals may wish to enhance their managerial potential by developing themselves without institutional backing by working through the whole series. It can also be used to underpin corporate training programmes, and acts as a useful design vehicle for specialist inputs from organizations. We are happy to pursue these various options with institutions or corporations.

The approach throughout the series combines skills, knowledge and application to create and develop the effective manager. Any comments or thoughts from participants in this interactive process will be welcomed.

Alan H. Anderson
Melbourn, Cambridge

The Series: Learning, Activities, Skills and Compatibility

The emphasis on skills and activities as vehicles of learning makes this series unique. Behavioural change, or learning, is developed through a two-pronged approach.

First, there is the **knowledge-based (cognitive)** approach to learning. This is found in the main text and in the boxes. These cognitive inputs form the traditional method of learning based on the principle of receiving and understanding information. In this series, there are four main knowledge inputs covering the four main managerial functions: marketing/sales, operations/enterprise, people, and accounting/finance. In addition, these disciplines are augmented by a strategic overview covering policy making and general management. An example of this first approach may be illustrative. In the case of marketing, the learner is confronted with a model of the internal and external environments. Thereafter the learner must digest, reflect, and understand the importance of this model to the whole of the subject.

Second, there is the **activity-based** approach to learning, which emphasizes the application of knowledge and skill through techniques. This approach is vital in developing effectiveness. It is seen from two levels of learning:

1 The use and application of *specific skills*. This is the utilization of your cognitive knowledge in a practical manner. These skills emanate from the cognitive aspect of learning, so they are functional skills, specific to the discipline.

   For example, the learner needs to understand the concept of job analysis before he or she tackles an activity that requires the drawing up of a specific job evaluation programme. So knowledge is not seen for its own sake, but is applied and becomes a specific functional skill.

2 The use and application of *generic skills*. These are universal skills which every manager uses irrespective of the wider external environment, the organization, the function and the job. This is seen, for example, in the ability to make clear decisions on the merits of a case. This skill of decision making is found in most of the activities.

There is a relationship between the specific functional skills and the generic skills. The specific functional skills stand alone, but the generic skills cut across them. See figure SK.1.

In this series we use activities to cover both the specific functional and the generic skills. There are five generic skills. We shall examine each of them in turn.

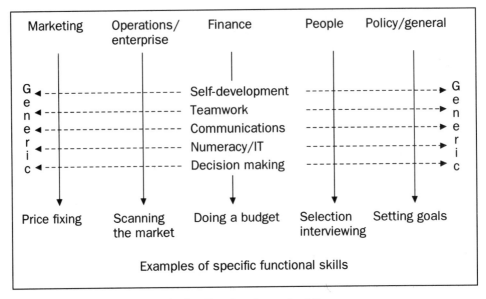

Figure SK.1 Series skills matrix: functional and generic skills.

Self-development

The learner must take responsibility for his or her learning as well as 'learning how to learn'. Time management, work scheduling and organizing the work are involved in the procedural sense. From a learning perspective, sound aspects of learning, from motivation to reward, need to be clarified and understood. The physical process of learning, including changing knowledge, skills and attitudes, may be involved. Individual goals and aspirations need to be recognized alongside the task goals. The ultimate aim of this skill is to facilitate learning transfer to new situations and environments.

Examples of this skill include:

- establishing and clarifying work goals;
- developing procedures and methods of work;
- building key learning characteristics into the process;
- using procedural learning;
- applying insightful learning;
- creating personal developmental plans;
- integrating these personal developmental plans with work goals.

Teamwork

Much of our working lives is concerned with groups. Effective teamwork is thus at a premium. This involves meeting both the task objectives and the socio-emotional processes within the group. This skill can be used for groups in a training or educational context. It can be a bridge between decision making and an awareness of self-development.

Examples of this skill include:

- clarifying the task need of the group;
- receiving, collating, ordering and rendering information;
- discussing, chairing and teamwork within the group;
- identifying the socio-emotional needs and group processes;
- linking these needs and processes to the task goals of the group.

Communications

This covers information and attitude processing within and between individuals. Oral and written communications are important because of the gamut of 'information and attitudinal' processing within the individual. At one level communication may mean writing a report, at another it could involve complex interpersonal relationships.

Examples of this skill include:

- understanding the media, aids, the message and methods;
- overcoming blockages;
- listening;
- presenting a case or commenting on the views of others;
- writing;
- designing material and systems for others to understand your communications.

Numeracy/IT

Managers need a core mastery of numbers and their application. This mastery is critical for planning, control, co-ordination, organization and, above all else, for decision making. Numeracy/IT are not seen as skills for their own sake. Here, they are regarded as the means to an end. These skills enable information and data to be utilized by the effective manager. In particular these skills are seen as an adjunct to decision making.

Examples of this skill include:

- gathering information;
- processing and testing information;

- using measures of accuracy, reliability, probability etc.;
- applying appropriate software packages;
- extrapolating information and trends for problem solving.

Decision making

Management is very much concerned with solving problems and making decisions. As group decisions are covered under teamwork, the emphasis in this decision-making skill is placed on the individual.

Decision making can involve a structured approach to problem solving with appropriate aims and methods. Apart from the 'scientific' approach, we can employ also an imaginative vision towards decision making. One is rational, the other is more like brainstorming.

Examples of this skill include:

- setting objectives and establishing criteria;
- seeking, gathering and processing information;
- deriving alternatives;
- using creative decision making;
- action planning and implementation.

This is *the* skill of management and is given primary importance in the generic skills within the activities as a reflection of everyday reality.

Before we go about learning how to develop into effective managers, it is important to understand the general principles of learning. Both the knowledge-based and the activity-based approaches are set within the environment of these principles. The series has been written to relate to Anderson's sound principles of learning which were developed in *Successful Training Practice*.

- *Motivation* – intrinsic motivation is stimulated by the range and depth of the subject matter and assisted by an action orientation.
- *Knowledge of results* – ongoing feedback is given through the handbook for each book in the series.
- *Scale learning* – each text is divided into six units, which facilitates part learning.
- *Self-pacing* – a map of the unit with objectives, content and an overview helps learners to pace their own progress.
- *Transfer* – realism is enhanced through lifelike simulations which assist learning transfer.
- *Discovery learning* – the series is geared to the learner using self-insight to stimulate learning.
- *Self-development* – self-improvement and an awareness of how we go about learning underpin the series.

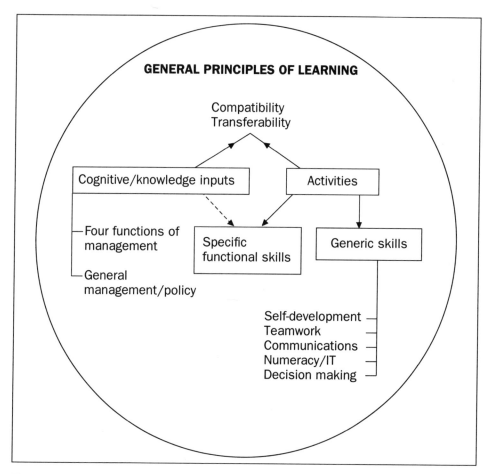

Figure SK.2 Series learning strategy.

● *Active learning* – every activity is based upon this critical component of successful learning.

From what has been said so far, the learning strategy of the series can be outlined in diagrammatic form. (See figure SK.2.)

In figure SK.2, 'compatibility and transferability' are prominent because the learning approach of the series is extremely compatible with the learning approaches of current initiatives in management development. This series is related to a range of learning classification being used in education and training. Consequently it meets the needs of other leading training systems and learning taxonomies. See figures SK.3–SK.6.

Functional knowledge and skills	An educational classification
People: Personnel management Labour relations Organizational behaviour	—— People
Marketing/sales: Marketing Marketing communications International marketing	—— Marketing
Operations/enterprise: Entrepreneurship Enterprise	—— Operations/enterprise
Finance: Accounting management Finance	—— Finance
Policy/management: Policy General management	—— Business environment/ business administration

Generic skills

Self-development	—————— Managing and developing self
Teamwork	Working with and relating to others
Communications	Communications
	Applying design and creativity
Decisions	Managing tasks and solving problems
Numeracy/IT	Applying technology
	Applying numeracy

——————— direct relationship

- - - - - - - - indirect relationship

Figure SK.3 Series knowledge and skills related to an educational classification.

Source: Adapted from Business Technician and Education Council, 'Common skills and experience of BTEC programmes'.

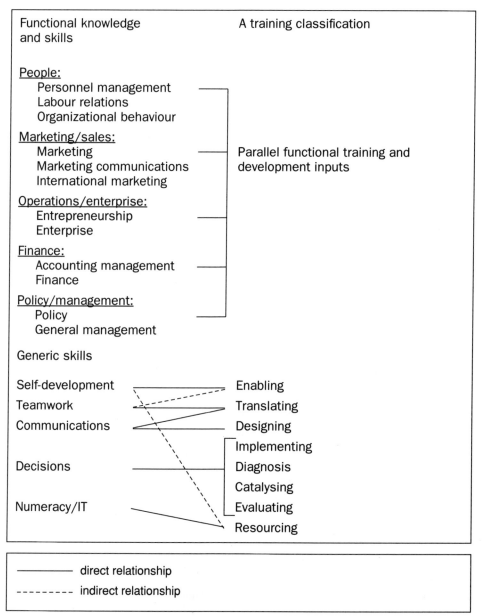

Figure SK.4 Series knowledge and skills related to a training classification.

Source: Adapted from J.A.G. Jones, 'Training intervention strategies' and experience of development programmes.

Functional knowledge and skills	MCI competency
People:	Managing people

Personnel management
    Labour relations
    Organizational behaviour	

Marketing/sales:	Managing operations and managing information (plus new texts pending)

Marketing
    Marketing communications
    International marketing	

Operations/enterprise:	
Entrepreneurship Enterprise	
Finance:	Managing finance
Accounting management Finance	
Policy/management:	Managing context
Policy General management	
Generic skills	
Self-development	Managing oneself
Teamwork	Managing others
Communications	Using intellect
Decisions	Planning
Numeracy/IT	

───── direct relationship

- - - - - indirect relationship

Figure SK.5 Series knowledge and skills related to Management Charter Initiative (MCI) competencies.

Source: Adapted from MCI diploma guidelines.

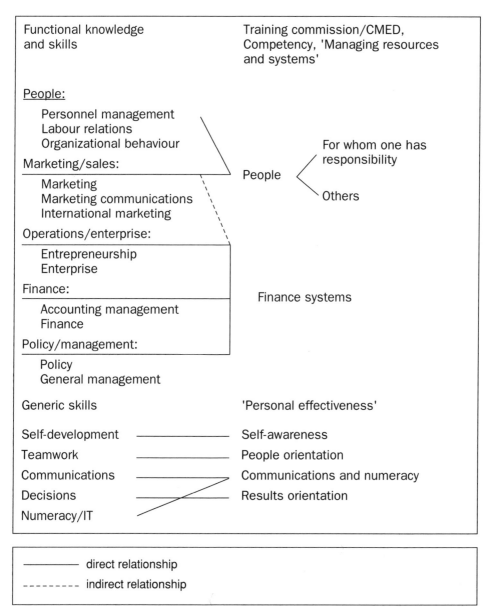

Figure SK.6   Series knowledge and skills related to Training Commission/Council for Management Education (CMED) competencies.

Source: Adapted from Training Commission/CMED, 'Classifying the components of management competencies'.

Preface

❝ The market concept of value, the emphasis on exchange value rather than use value, has led to a similar concept of value with regard to people and particularly oneself. The character orientation which is rooted in the experience of oneself as a commodity and of one's value as an exchange value I call the *marketing orientation* . . . It must be noted that these concepts (marketing orientation and four other character orientations) are 'ideal types', not descriptions of the character of a given individual (which is) usually a blend of all or some of these orientations in which one, however, is dominant. . . . The marketing orientation does not come out of the 18th. or 19th. centuries; it is definitely a modern product. . . . *The whole principle of the marketing orientation implies easy contact, superficial attachment.* ❞

E. *Fromm* Man for Himself: an enquiry into
the psychology of ethics [1]

Without a customer or client there is no business, so marketing with its emphasis on meeting the needs and wants of buyers is critical to the survival and growth of the firm. To a great extent marketing is the business. Fromm's assertion on the 'superficiality' of the relationship between buyer and seller may be debatable but the need for some 'attachment' is less contentious. This concept of 'attachment' between consumer and marketeer runs through this book. Indeed the main theme is as follows: marketing is concerned with **relationships**. In turn, these relationships are based on sound **communications** and an excellent **information** system operating in the context of the firm and its environment. So the marketeer has a unique role in bridging the gap between the organization and its external environment. A systems approach is used in this book. Please refer to Box MKT0.1 'Systems and marketing'.

BOX MKT0.1

Systems and marketing

Any system in business management acts as a frame of reference for users. Systems, if adequately designed and tested, may allow for some predictive validity. Systems are representations of reality which can allow us to make a little more sense of everyday events which can be quite anarchic. They need to be dynamic and must take account of the main variables impacting on an organization within its marketing environment. To this end most systems are 'open' to the environment. In crude terms a system can be seen as:

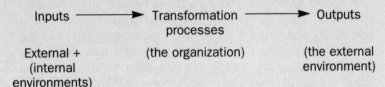

In marketing terms, any system tends to revolve around a relationship between:

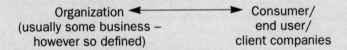

We would complicate the picture by noting middle men, distribution channels and non-business organizations, as well as other industrial users.

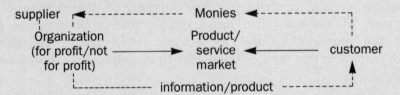

The factors of production tend to manifest themselves in product/service markets and some exchange occurs between the organization giving information and the product/service to the paying customer. The relationship may be guided by state involvement/regulations.

supplier ◄------------- Monies ◄-------------┐
Organization │
(for profit/not ──────► service ◄────── customer
for profit) market ▲
└------------- information/product ---------┘

This system is somewhat static though, for environmental contexts are ever changing and competition is usually lurking around the corner. The political, economic, social and technological realities will thus impact on organizational goals and customer behaviour as in an economic downturn when investment and confidence respectively may be at low ebbs.

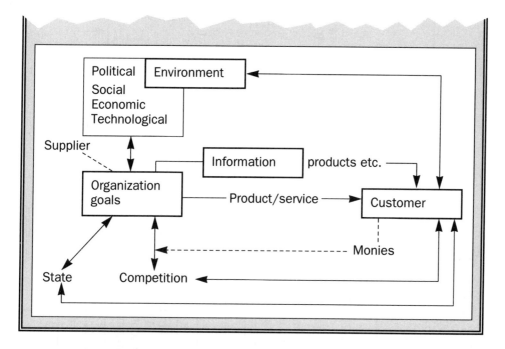

From this box we see the organization in constant interaction with its external environment. Consequently, **information** co-ordination from inside and outside sources, is seen as one of the most important facets of marketing. Without this information, there can be no effective marketing decisions – only 'gut feelings' without any intelligence backup. This is not to decry 'a gut feeling' *per se* for such experience can certainly help the decision-making process but not on its own for it can degenerate into a random and costly affair without real **information** for decision making and forecasting. In turn, this information revolves around **communications** between the firm (and within the firm) and its external environment. The whole marketing **relationship** within and outside of the firm will in turn be supported by the information and communication processes. This is the main theme of the book. Figure 0.1 indicates our views and the route map for this book.

The specific objectives are:

- to promote the 'marketing concept';
- to analyse the external environment in which marketing operates;
- to research industrial and consumer needs;
- to develop the marketing function and process to relate to these external needs;
- to plan a marketing policy strategy;
- to implement these plans through effective policies on price, promotion, place and product;
- to evaluate the role of marketing to the organization, to its customers and to society as a whole;

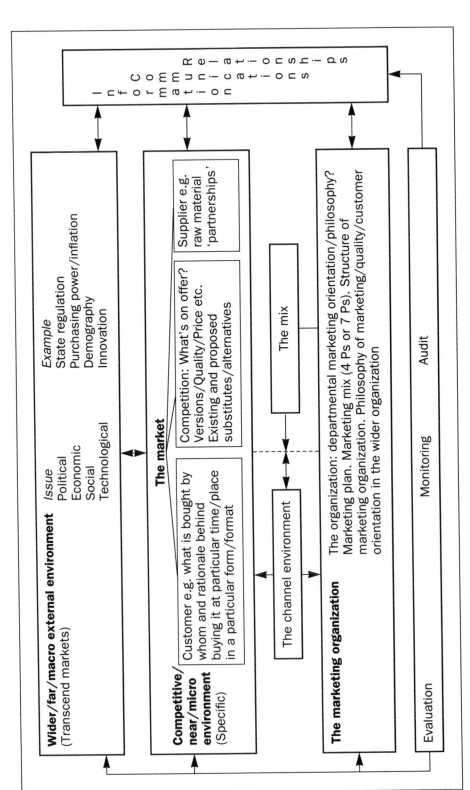

Figure 0.1 A marketing map.

- to meet the generic skills and specific functional skills of marketing;
- to act as the foundation block for the more specialized marketing texts within the series.

The content can be seen as follows.

1 the concept of marketing;
2 marketing management;
3 the analysis of the environment;
4 buyer behaviour;
5 research, forecasting and intelligence;
6 planning and linking needs/wants to internal capacity/resources;
7 products;
8 pricing;
9 distribution (place);
10 promotion-cum-communication;
11 control, audit and evaluation.

The content will now be related to our vision and model for marketing (figure 0.2).

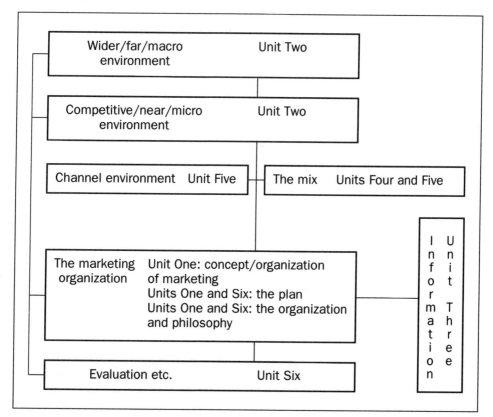

Figure 0.2 The units within the model.

Notes

1 Fromm, *Man for Himself: an enquiry into the psychology of ethics*.

Acknowledgements

The authors would like to thank Blackwell Publishers and VAP for their work assistance, commitment and encouragement.

The authors and publisher would also like to thank Hilary Barnett, Wendy Tury and Andrew Younger for their advice and assistance in the development of this book.

Unit One

The Marketing Context

Learning Objectives

After completing this unit you should be able to:

- distinguish between product, sales and marketing orientated organizations;

- understand the role of marketing and why the marketing department has a high profile in most organizations;

- accept the importance of customer relationships;

- accept the use of the marketing concept in your own organization;

- apply the generic skills.

Contents

Overview

What is Marketing?

How Marketing Has Developed

▶ Product orientated organizations

▶ Sales orientated organizations

▶ Marketing orientated organizations

Beyond Marketing

The Management of Demand

The Marketing Mix

What Does It Mean to Be a Manager of the Marketing Effort?

▶ The task of analysing

▶ The task of planning

▶ The task of organizing

▶ The task of controlling

Relationships with Other Functional Departments

Unit One

❝ No longer is marketing thought of as being limited to personal selling and advertising designed to get rid of the output of the production process. On the contrary, today the concept of marketing held by most successful firms is that (1) marketing must be consumer orientated, and (2) it must have a part in the decision making on all phases of management. Modern marketing begins with the consumer, not with the production department. ❞

W. T. Ryan and R. H. Hermanson, Programmed Learning Aid for Principles of Marketing[1]

Overview

The purpose of this first unit is to analyse what marketing is all about. It starts off by unravelling some common misconceptions about the nature of marketing. Key concepts concerning marketing and the 'mix' are explained. Consistent with the effectiveness aspect of the series, we focus on the work of a marketing manager and the processes involved in managing the marketing effort.

Then we broaden out to consider the relationship between the marketing department and the rest of the organization. We conclude this unit by structuring the concept of marketing and the marketing effort from within the department or function. We return to the 'marketing organization' in the final unit. (See figure 1.1.)

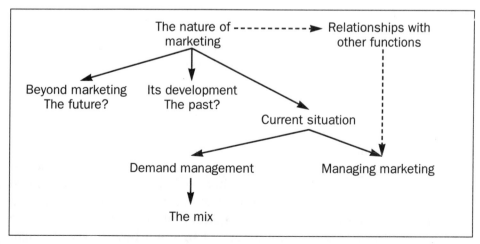

Figure 1.1 Outline diagram of Unit One.

What is Marketing?

As a prelude to looking at what marketing *is* it is a useful exercise to look at what it *is not* and, through this, at some of the many misconceptions which exist in the minds of people not professionally involved in marketing.

Marketing is not just selling, although this is what many people think of when the word marketing is mentioned. If you want to be successful in the highly competitive marketplaces of the 1990s then you do not simply decide to make a product or supply a service and then market it, although the personal selling effort is certainly part of the organization's overall marketing operation.

Marketing is not just the expenditure of vast sums of money on TV advertising campaigns and special offers in local supermarkets although, again, this is what it means to many non-marketing people. Nor does an organization have to have access to a multi-million pound budget to be able to adopt a marketing-based approach to its activities – a plea which small organizations often use as an excuse not to get involved in thinking too much about their customers.

Marketing is not only the junk mail that lands regularly on your door mat offering you all sorts of incentives to purchase that timeshare in Spain, nor is it just the evening telephone call exhorting you to buy double glazing before this month's special offer ends. However, these are both increasingly popular marketing tools and, whatever you might think of them, you can be sure that if these activities did not produce a healthy profit then they would very quickly be abandoned.

Marketing is not just research – the women in your local high street with their clip boards on a Saturday afternoon are just a very tiny part of the whole research operation, as the research project itself is a very small part of the whole marketing operation, albeit one of the most vital parts.

These are all well-tried promotion and information-gathering techniques although they are by no means the whole story. It is not surprising, however, that lay people think that these are what marketing is all about – because this is what they see! This is true even within many organizations that would think of themselves as marketing orientated because individuals from outside the marketing department have very little idea of what goes on inside it, except that the marketing department never seems to do any work – sure proof that there is neglect of what is one of the most important aspects of marketing – the internal effort!

Marketing, in fact, is the whole set of activities which enable an organization to make decisions about what it will offer for sale, how much it will charge, who it will sell to and by what means it will make its offering available. Marketing is concerned with getting the right product or service to the right customer at the right price – at the right time and in the right place. It is not just a fancy word for selling, it is not simply synonymous with advertising or sales promotion, nor is it merely a data-collecting, number-processing and planning activity.

Additionally, marketing is more than a set of techniques or tools, and although it is definitely a management function it is not just the prerogative of managers and others who have the word 'marketing' in their job titles. While functional specialists do exist to fulfil important marketing roles, there are many more people who make significant contributions (often unknowingly) to the effectiveness of their organization's marketing performance.

In its simplest form, marketing is a philosophy of doing business which puts customers and potential customers at the centre of organizational strategy by saying, 'If we don't have any customers (or any clients, or taxpayers, or patients) then we don't have any business (or organization) so it is in our best interests to build up good relationships with them.'

Organizations which think like this do not see marketing simply as another functional activity of management but more as an overall business philosophy, a way of thinking about business and a way of working, which runs through every aspect of their activities. This means that marketing is not thought of as a separate function but rather as a profit orientated approach to business that permeates not just the marketing department but the entire business. However, looking at the customer as the centre of a business does not mean that the company has to bend itself totally to the whims of each individual or organization with which it completes business transactions. Implicit in the concept of marketing there is the concept of *exchange*, that is, *the exchange of something of value (money) for something else of at least equal value (products or services)* so that both parties benefit from the transaction at a level which is satisfactory to them.

You should now refer to Activity MKT1.1 which will help to clarify your conception of the subject.

Sample definitions of marketing include the following:

> *A social process by which individuals and groups obtain what they need and want through creating, and exchanging, products and value with others.*

> *The management process which identifies, anticipates and supplies, customer requirements efficiently and profitably.*

> *Being much broader than selling, it is not a specialised activity at all. It encompasses the entire business. It is the whole business seen from the point of view of its final result, that is, from the customer's point of view. Concern and responsibility for marketing must, therefore, permeate all areas of the enterprise.*[2]

The AMA (American Marketing Association) gives us a working definition of the subject. This gives a perspective perhaps from both a

ACTIVITY MKT1.1

TOWARDS A DEFINITION OF MARKETING

Activity code

- ✓ Self-development
- ✓ Teamwork
- ☐ Communications
- ☐ Numeracy/IT
- ✓ Decisions

Many writers have given us their views of what marketing is all about. Some key views have been extrapolated. You should rank these views on a scale of 1 (totally disagree) to 5 (totally agree) depending on *your* vision of marketing.

	Totally disagree	Disagree	Neutral	Agree	Totally agree
So marketing is:	1	2	3	4	5

A

A1 Assessing and converting customer power into effective demand.

A2 A process whereby goods are exchanged.

A3 A point of view.

B

B1 Directing goods from the producer to the user.

B2 The adoption of the organization to the environment.

B3 The business.

C

C1 Getting the right goods to the right people at the right price.

C2 The basis of a standard of living.

C3 A way of thinking.

D

D1 Stimulating and meeting consumer desires.

D2 The transmission of goods to the wider society.

D3 A business activity adjusted to the needs of customers.

Scoring

Add your total as follows:
    Each 1 in A, B, C and D. 1 Total =
    Each 2 in A, B, C and D. 2 Total =
    Each 3 in A, B, C and D. 3 Total =

See workbook for interpretation.

Source: The initial definitions were collected by Crosier, so the work is adapted from Crosier, 'What exactly is marketing?'

---

functional and organizational base. (See Box MKT1.1.) We will develop this idea.

BOX MKT1.1

Marketing: a definition

❝ Marketing is the process of planning and executing the conception, pricing, promotion, and distribution of ideas, goods, and services to create exchanges that satisfy individual and organisational objectives.❞

Source: AMA Board

The fact that marketing is looked upon as an organizational philosophy as well as a functional activity is one of the reasons why there is so much confusion over what marketing actually is – because the same term is used to describe both the philosophy and the practical activities involved, that is, marketing is both a *basic concept which focuses on customers* and *a set of management techniques*.

So, at this stage, it is useful to look at some of the things which should be happening in a *marketing orientated organization*.

■ Marketing focuses the attention of both the whole organization and of the individuals within it towards the needs and wants of the marketplace.

■ Marketing is concerned with satisfying the genuine needs and wants of specifically designed target markets by creating products or services that satisfy customer requirements.

■ Marketing involves analysis, planning and control.

■ The principle of marketing states that all of an organization's decisions should be made with a careful and systematic consideration of the user of the final product or service.

- The distinguishing feature of a marketing orientated organization is the way it strives to provide customer satisfaction as a way of achieving its own corporate objectives.
- Marketing is dynamic and operational, requiring action as well as planning.
- Marketing requires an improved form of organizational design in order for marketing to be able to lead and catalyse the application of the marketing approach.
- Marketing is both an important functional area of management and an overall business philosophy which recognizes that the identification, satisfaction and retention of customers is the key to long-term prosperity.

This is what the marketing concept is all about! It is epitomized in the marketing strategy of Marks & Spencer. (See Box MKT1.2.)

BOX MKT1.2

A successful marketing package: Marks & Spencer

The brand name St Michael of the leading retailer Marks & Spencer seems to have an image of its own. Service, customer satisfaction and quality are synonymous with this branding policy, in clothing, accessories, home furnishings and food.

The success of this branding policy rests on various premises. The clientele is known and the merchandising dovetails into their needs. Criteria of price, quality, function and 'appropriateness' all seem to be met by the merchandiser.

A strong 'buying mix', the product, quantity, timing, and the vendor all contribute to the success of the operation. The customer orientation is cemented by ongoing research from resident buying offices to a sample of stores, to observation, questionnaires and personal interviews.

Employee evaluation, return policies, promotional impact, price line dominance and cost analysis are all used in this key research area. The whole business is geared towards repeat business and the imagery of the stores and what they stand for reiterate this vision of quality and style at an affordable price.

Branding comes into its own in this context. Product recognition and positive attitudes towards the product are enhanced by the St Michael logo. In turn, the brand helps sales promotion and reinforces one line when another line is being bought. The mark-up is perhaps better owing to this identification process.

Quality control and assurance are both critical components of the 'mix' for the imagery must become reality. The firm purposely has remained a retailer. The production problems are the problems of its supplier while it remains on the High Street.

This means elaborate control mechanisms over its suppliers. Tight specifications must be met and the QC/QA of Marks & Spencer are paralleled in many of their suppliers – who tend to be British.

The whole marketing vision seems to permeate the company, while its staffing policies, albeit relatively paternalistic, reinforce product knowledge, customer care and customer service.

How Marketing Has Developed

At this point, we can look at marketing as being vitally concerned with exchange (or trade) and with keeping customers satisfied. If we could all be totally self-sufficient then there would be no need to establish these important exchange relationships and hence, no need for marketing. As we saw earlier in this unit, exchange is the act of obtaining something of value, usually a product or service, by offering the other party something of equal value. This may have begun simply as barter but nowadays, the medium of exchange is usually money. Having said this, the view of customer 'satisfaction' is very much tested in Box MKT1.3.

BOX MKT1.3

Paying up with a smile?

How would you market income tax? As we have to pay whether we like it or not, is there any need for it to be marketed at all? There is probably no point in trying to 'sell' the concept of paying tax, nor is there any need to because it would make absolutely no difference to the amount of tax collected. However, although income tax itself would not benefit from the application of the marketing concept, the Inland Revenue's system for dealing with its 'customers' can. The service can, and has been, made more accessible, and action can be taken to remove negative feelings, for example, by producing leaflets in plain English.

What the Inland Revenue hoped to achieve was the establishment of a fair and helpful image, with the underlying expectation that if the public believes that the system is fair and efficient then they will be more co-operative and tax will be easier to collect, thus making the job of the department easier and helping to reduce costs. Another promotional initiative was the introduction of a number of mobile advice centres which move from town to town acting as advice bureaux and which are designed specifically to make nervous customers feel at ease.

As with many other public services, one of the main marketing tasks of the Inland Revenue is the simple communication of basic information about the service and how to deal with it. A problem which the Inland Revenue has in common with other similar departments like the Benefits Agency is that members of the public do not understand either their rights or their obligations. The Inland Revenue has therefore translated its forms and its information leaflets into plain English and, in addition, has produced a wide range of free explanatory leaflets. These are available through Citizens' Advice Bureaux as well as from tax offices. This initiative adds to the user friendliness of the department and, along with all the others, helps to make the system more acceptable by promoting the human face of the Inland Revenue.

Source: Adapted from 'Making a virtue out of necessity'

However, more sophisticated relations do exist. Charities ask for donations, offering in exchange the knowledge of having 'done good' plus perhaps a car sticker or lapel badge to make this obvious to the rest of society. Additionally, charities and other organizations such as hospitals make extensive use of volunteers. In this case we have a situation more like barter as no money actually changes hands – the volunteers give time in exchange for the fulfilling of social needs, or the knowledge of helping other individuals in a less fortunate position. Churches too, would be lost without their volunteer labour force. It is only recently that volunteer-using organizations have begun to think of their volunteers as 'customers' and to realize that it is worthwhile keeping them satisfied and fulfilled rather than losing them as they become tired and disillusioned. To this end, training and development programmes are increasingly being established specifically for volunteers.

So, as we can see, the process of exchange actually creates value. The act of production, or delivery of a service, helps to create wealth and its ultimate value is greatly increased via the exchange process by allowing individuals and organizations a greater range of consumption possibilities resulting in greater satisfaction and utility all round.

Product orientated organizations

Before the Industrial Revolution the production and distribution of goods tended to be on a small scale, but, with industrialization in the late eighteenth century, the UK economy shifted from depending mainly on agriculture to an industrial orientation. This meant that areas of production became more and more concentrated as large factories sprang up, centred in appropriate areas. Ship building flourished on the Tyne and Wear close to supplies of coal and steel, while the cotton trade thrived in Lancashire. This new concentration of production permitted enormous economies of scale and brought manufactured goods within the reach of the new middle classes.

At this time, the key to success was thought to be a better product at a keener price and the new large firms concentrated on producing what they were best at, taking full advantage of the fact that they were operating in a sellers' market. This was the stage of **production orientation** epitomized by Henry Ford's attitude to business. (See Box MKT1.4.)

Product orientated organizations, whether businesses or non-profit are inward looking and concentrate on what they want to produce rather than looking outside into the wider environment to see what customers and potential customers actually want and need. In the long term, this situation can only survive while demand exceeds supply!

BOX MKT1.4

Any colour as long as it's black

It is vital to have a good product and equally important to have a good price – for both the seller and the buyer. Some people still believe that the only factor needed for business success is to be an efficient producer, thus enabling the organization to cut its costs and therefore to sell at a lower price than the competition. This concept worked for Henry Ford in America – for a time!

Ford was the pioneer of mass production and had standardization down to a fine art. Everything in the Ford Motor Company was built around the need for production efficiency, a concept which reached its peak in the famous Model T slogan of the 1920s: 'You can have any colour you like as long as it's black.' The plus side of this policy was that, for the first time it brought automobile ownership within the reach of the average American family and Model Ts swept the continent. *But* what this policy did not cater for was the fact that ownership of an automobile might lead to the desire to own something a little larger and more comfortable, nor did it allow for the fact that some people might just want something different.

However, Alfred Sloane at General Motors believed that many individuals wanted more choice, even if it meant paying rather more. He offered cars in a variety of colours plus internal optional extras such as heaters. His prices could not match those of Ford but his sales did, and soon surpassed those of their more basic rivals.

Ford is an ideal example of an inward-looking company. They looked inward into the factory instead of outwards into their marketplace, they ignored their environment instead of moving with it until they lost market share to their biggest competitor. Additionally, they were left with a reputation for producing cheap, basic cars which it took them a very long time to lose, even after their ranges had been extended quite considerably.

Sales orientated organizations

The advent of the depression in the 1930s rapidly forced businesses to become more proactive in the way they promoted their offerings. It was no longer enough just to produce efficiently and cheaply – the product had also to be aggressively promoted and sold. According to the sales concept, the key to success in business is the ability to sell hard and to sell cheaply. In all markets some form of persuasion or at least information offering is essential if sales are to be made in any respectably large volume and this is so even for marketing orientated organizations. The sales orientated organizations make what they want to make or are good at making, then rely on strong sales efforts to shift the merchandise. Please refer to Box

MKT1.5, 'Does this sound familiar?' Box MKT1.6 gives a political dimension to the sales approach.

BOX MKT1.5

Does this sound familiar?

- The sales department has equal seniority with finance and production.
- The sales force is thought to hold the key to business prosperity.
- The most keenly discussed subject in the canteen is last month's sales figures – and next month's!
- Goods and services are things that are 'sold' not 'bought'.
- Getting the sale is the important thing. Customer satisfaction: 'What's that?'
- The sales person's job is to overcome objections and make a sale.
- Consumers can always be induced to buy more through strong sales techniques like time-limited discounts.
- The product is double glazing, fitted kitchens or timeshares.

If any or all of these seem familiar then you are working for, or dealing with, a sales orientated company! If you found yourself on the receiving end of their efforts would you give in and buy, even if just to get yourself out of a difficult situation?

BOX MKT1.6

Would you buy this man?

Political parties also make use of the selling concept. All political parties vigorously sell their candidates to the voters as being a fantastic person for the job – the only one who can be relied on to do it well. The candidate knocks on doors, climbs on soap boxes, kisses babies and makes confident speeches. For the party itself, large sums of money are spent on professional advertising campaigns, posters, mailings and party political broadcasts. Any flaws in the product, that is, the potential prime minister or the local candidate, are carefully hidden (hopefully) because what matters is winning votes and getting elected, not the ongoing satisfaction of the purchaser. After the election even less attention is paid to customer satisfaction. The sales orientation continues, there is little research into whether the public is satisfied or what it wants, and a good deal of hard selling goes on to persuade the public to accept new policies that the politicians and the parties want.

Marketing orientated organizations

Selling focuses on the needs and desires of the seller, marketing focuses on the needs of the buyer. Marketing as a business function emerged in America in the 1950s and spread from there to Europe. Trends towards more equal societies, universal education, the rise of women and young people as consumers in their own right, and improvements in the techniques of communication have all contributed to the more knowledgeable and discriminating buyers of the late twentieth century. Customers are more demanding, more confident and more aware that they have rights. Their expectations of quality and customer service are increasing all the time. Now, the marketing concept is much more relevant than the selling concept.

Please refer to the box on Jaguar Cars (Box MKT1.7), which epitomizes this perspective. Thereafter we need to apply these various perspectives and we do so by referring to Activity MKT1.2.

BOX MKT1.7

Listening to your customers

Outward-looking companies listen to their customers. Try to put yourself in their shoes for, after all, you do know what it is like to be the customer of other companies and none of us likes to be the receiver of bad service. Satisfied customers come back and, even better, they tell other people how good you are, the trouble is that dissatisfied customers probably tell even more people what they think of you!

Back in the 1980s, Sir John Egan of Jaguar said: 'Business is about making money from satisfied customers. Without satisfied customers there can be no future for any commercial organization.' A very simple and basic description of the marketing concept.

In his bid to rescue the company he turned to another marketing tool – research. He put in hand a survey of all recent purchasers of Jaguar cars to see what they thought of the new models. The resulting statements of dissatisfaction were astonishing, but, at least most of them were referring to quite trivial (although annoying) faults. Customers felt that the cars, although of high-quality manufacture, were badly finished and put together. They also considered after-sales service was inadequate. Altogether they felt let down and that they were entitled to expect something better from a company like Jaguar.

Egan then went about putting things right, relieved to find that the cars themselves were not the problem. He concentrated first on a series of small changes intended to demonstrate that Jaguar was a company which cared deeply about its customers. New quality-assurance systems were developed to iron out minor faults like rattles and rust spots, and similar quality standards were imposed on suppliers of components. Egan also made sure that adequate supplies of spare parts were available to dealers and instituted a system whereby all new Jaguar owners were contacted a few weeks after purchase to solve any problems which were being experienced.

This story emphasizes once again the close links between total quality management and marketing and the fact that the marketing approach is one which should permeate the whole organization.

Source: Adapted from N. Hill, *Successful Marketing for Small Businesses*

ACTIVITY MKT1.2

THE PAPER MILL

Activity code
☑ Self-development
☐ Teamwork
☑ Communications
☐ Numeracy/IT
☑ Decisions

The company
The company in question is an independent manufacturer of paper and board, based in Donside, Aberdeenshire. The paper is not high quality and is used for the packaging industry. The board, or chipboard, is predominantly used for the building industry. The firm employs some 400 people on a continuous shift system (6 a.m. – 2 p.m., 2 p.m. – 10 p.m. and 10 p.m. – 6 a.m.) and works all year round, apart from the three weeks maintenance closure in July which coincides with the main vacation of the nearby town. It is an old plant, founded in the late eighteenth century, but with considerable modern machinery recently imported from Germany. There are two board machines and two paper machines with approximately 100 employees to each. In addition, there is a staff white-collar administrative and commercial group of ninety-two.

The market
Although it is well established, the board market is quite fickle, as it is dependent primarily on the building industry – itself a good indicator of the economic wellbeing of the country. The packaging industry is less fickle and is expanding, although there is competition from the plastics industry. However, from milk cartons to chocolate eggs, the company has a growing presence in this market sphere.

Production

Production is a continuous flow process with the raw materials (which are increasing in cost) being mixed at the wet end of the machine and appearing at the dry end as almost the finished product. Printing and coating as necessary are done in the finishing department. Breakages of paper flow through the machines are quite frequent.

Finance

The company is still family owned but increasingly it has opened up to take professional managers in to run the firm. It is highly profitable and much of the money has been ploughed back over the last ten years (at least) to buy more modern machinery. This has trebled the potential output, although the plant is running at only 68 per cent capacity. There are no cash-flow problems, although an over-reliance on the building industry in the past has caused difficulties, particularly over the winter months owing to the construction slump then. Reserves and borrowing power are strong.

Organization structure and personnel

The chart below shows the structure. The rest of the employees are employed in production, catering, finishing and as 'outside' staff. There is an external security firm (400 people).

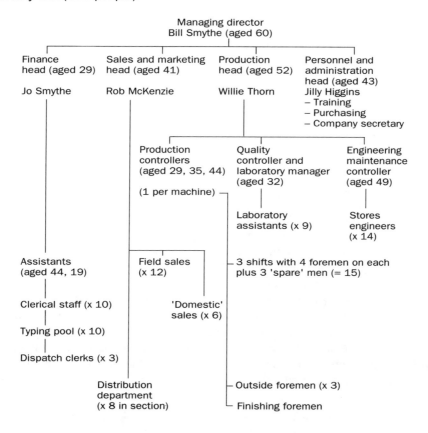

The monthly executive of the Paper Mill was well into its second hour, discussing non-agenda items. Rob McKenzie, the marketeer and William Thorn the operations man, were having a tussle.

McKenzie: I do appreciate the need for longish lead times and standardized products with low 'broke' [waste for repulping] benefits us all. Yet we must get closer to our customers. Marketing …

Thorn: Yes, thanks, I know what marketing is all about, though. Our market is business-to-business or industrial marketing so all this consumer stuff is neither here nor there. The issue here is quality. We can't put on a switch through advertising or whatever and gain more market share. We're not selling chocolate bars.

McKenzie: Precisely. We should not really be selling at all – we should be marketing. Making products and going out to sell them is a dated production philosophy. We could end up like some former eastern bloc country – plenty of tractors with few private cars. Look, I'm not suggesting short production runs with constant product changes. But we have to move away from, firstly, a production mentality and, secondly, a product mentality.

Thorn: I may be an operations man but I do accept the need for a marketing perspective. The point is taken about your tractors. The issue is not about production versus marketing at all. Look, we are like the glass industry, we are a continuous-flow process. It comes in at one end and comes out at the other. I'd rather run at 25 per cent capacity than not at all just to avoid the immense costs of starting up the process, closing it and so on.

McKenzie: Fine, I understand that we still need to go for the middlemen as they are our customers. Our ultimate marketing effort needs to be addressed to them more than to the person buying our plaster board in a house or our packaging for chocolate bars. Yet we need to keep both 'clients' in mind – the middlemen and the ultimate customer.

Thorn: These 'ultimate customers' don't know we exist. Our customers are other businesses full stop. Your role should be to court these businesses with our products. These 'clients' (what the hell next) are interested in quality. All your brochures and ads will not help us if our quality is suspect.

McKenzie: You've moved from a production vision to a product orientation. This is far from ideal and it means that we will never have a true marketing vision about this place.

Smyth: I've listened without interruption and so have the rest of the
(Managing   team. We'll leave this debate for another day and move back to
Director)   the proper agenda.

1 Outline the main themes of both arguments here and critically assess the views of both men.

2 To what extent is McKenzie's parting shot correct: 'This is far from ideal and it means that we will never have a true marketing vision about this place.'

Report on both items.

Beyond Marketing

As we move further into the 1990s the picture is changing yet again – the American dominance of world markets is giving way to that of the Far East and there is growing concern about the fate of the environment and of the third world countries. The question posed by Kotler[3] is whether organizations that do an excellent job of producing satisfied customers and of making profits for their shareholders are actually acting in the best long-term interests of consumers and society as a whole. The marketing concept does not involve itself with the growing conflict between the desire of consumers for immediate gratification and the long-term welfare of society.

The new concept of societal marketing comes again from America and Kotler[4] calls upon marketing people to learn to balance three considerations in setting their policies: company profits, the satisfaction of consumers and the public interest. Originally, companies based their marketing decisions largely on immediate company profit calculations. Then they began to accept the long-run importance of satisfying customer needs and this thinking heralded the introduction of the marketing concept. Now those same companies are beginning to include the interests of society in their decision-making processes, thus adding a new dimension to the producer–customer relationship. This also links strongly to the concept of total quality management and its newer approach to the definition of 'customer', that is, of the customer as anyone (or any group or organization) on the receiving end of what we do.

Alongside these developments, further work is being done on the concept of customer satisfaction. This is taking the overall marketing concept to even greater heights through the pursuit of excellence which focuses on all the extra things that organizations can do to achieve ever-greater levels of customer satisfaction and profit for the organization. The work of Tom Peters[5] in this area supports the marketing concept of customer needs and satisfaction and goes even further in that direction. While acknowledging that it takes a combination of several factors to make a company successful in the long term, he emphasizes the central importance of pointing the business towards researching the needs of, and serving and satisfying customers in a well-defined and understood target market.

Putting this strategy into action is one of the tasks in which marketing management is deeply involved and it leads to the necessity of managing demand to the ultimate advantage of the organization, but with a social-cum-ethical perspective. Societal marketing will run through this book.

The Management of Demand

One of the prime tasks with which an organization charges its marketing manager is that of creating an acceptable level of demand for its offerings. However, the actual task of managing demand goes well beyond this oversimplification of the situation. Please refer to Box MKT1.8.

BOX MKT1.8

Creating or managing demand?

The example of the owners of Vichy, Helena Rubinstein and Lancôme, the perfume company L'Oréal, considers that beauty care and perfume waits for no man (or woman).

An aggressive approach to the marketplace is taken by chairman/chief executive officer, Owen-Jones, and his management team. With pre-tax profits at around £482 million for 1993 the policy seems to be working.

Marketing here seems to be seen as the stimulation of demand. New product development, such as Gio perfume, is critical in sustaining this demand.

The costs of such development may be seen as high (around £36 million) but innovative products are seen as crucial to the creation and maintenance of demand.

Through the interaction of product/service costings, marketing research, sales forecasting and an environmental scan, the organization will come up with what it sees as a desirable, or even just an acceptable, level of demand. But they are still operating in a volatile and highly competitive environment which means that sometimes demand will outstrip supply, for example, as might happen in the case of the availability of rooms in a seafront hotel in a popular holiday resort in the middle of August. At other times, as in the case of the same hotel during November, there may be weak demand or even no demand at all.

This means that marketing managers have the task of developing appropriate methods of dealing with each of these extremes, plus several others in between, and so, of influencing the peaks and troughs, the pattern and the make up of demand in a way which will ensure that the organization is able to reach its marketing and corporate objectives.

Marketing managers deal with these problems and objectives through researching the market, drawing up marketing plans, putting these into action, then monitoring and evaluating the results and making adjustments where necessary. This means that they must (in line with the organization's corporate objectives) be involved in decisions on:

- product/service development and positioning;
- pricing;
- packaging (where appropriate);
- the development of promotional campaigns;
- selling methods and distribution;
- targeting groups of potential customers.

We will develop these activities later. In fact, the marketing manager should be involved in every aspect of an organization's activities and is also likely to be involved at the same time with a variety of products each with a different demand curve. *Different demand levels demand different marketing activities and solutions, and cover all types of organizational design.* These different approaches are well described by Kotler.[6]

- *Maintenance marketing* is the answer when organizations find themselves in the enviable position of experiencing a satisfactory level of demand for their products or services. This is not an excuse to relax, and, in this situation, it is the job of the marketing manager to take action to make sure that demand continues to be high in an ever-changing competitive environment where the preferences of consumers are anything but constant. This is done through continual attention to product/service quality, continually looking outwards into the competitive environment and constantly measuring the satisfaction levels of consumers.

- *Remarketing* is what is needed when demand begins to fall, as will eventually be the case with any type of offering. The marketing manager will need to look for the cause of that decline – perhaps that market has reached saturation point, perhaps a competitor has launched an improved product or perhaps the taste of the public has simply changed. Once the cause has been established, research will need to take place to ascertain whether it will be possible to re-stimulate demand by looking to new market segments, new geographical areas (perhaps on the international scene), repackaging the offering, adding new features or producing a more effective promotional campaign.

  The aim is to reverse the decline through creative remarketing. In recent years social values have changed and churches have seen their congregations dwindling away. Perhaps the advent of women priests – controversial though it may be – will eventually result in a surge in church attendance by women and children and help to promote a more popular image for what might have been seen as an outmoded product.

- *Synchromarketing* comes into play when the marketing task is to try to even out irregular demand whether it be seasonal, as in the holiday trade, or daily, as in the case of public transport or energy, or weekly as in the case of museums and stately homes which are unvisited during the week but overcrowded at weekends and during school holidays. The answer here is to try to alter the pattern of demand through flexible pricing (cheap off-peak travel tickets), strong promotion of quiet times, or other incentives (have central heating installed now but you don't have to pay until after Christmas).

■ *Social marketing* is involved when efforts are organized to re-educate the public away from harmful and anti-social activities like smoking, drink-driving and hard drugs. The effort here is geared up to persuading people to give up something for which they have a need or want: through fear (of death or prison), peer-group pressure, reduced availability and steep price rises or fines.

■ *Demarketing* (or the antidote to too much demand) looks for ways of lessening demand either in the short term or permanently. The National Trust's most popular properties suffer from serious overcrowding on bank holiday weekends so they have put considerable effort into promoting lesser-known sites and areas of countryside in order to reduce both overcrowding and the damage done to irreplaceable monuments.

■ *Benefit marketing* may be used where there seems to be no demand for what appears to be a perfectly good product. Perhaps the underlying reason is the fact that no suitable marketing research was carried out before production began. For example, small builders may not be rushing to buy a simple mixer which promises to take the hard work out of mixing plaster but, the task in marketing terms would be to find links between the benefits of the product and the natural needs of its potential purchasers and then exploit them actively.

■ *Product/service development.* Here the marketing effort would be directed towards estimating the potential market for a product which has not yet been designed, that is, one for which there can be no demand as yet, for example, a window cleaner which is simply sprayed onto a window and needs no polishing. If the potential demand at a particular price is high enough then the next task is to set about designing the product!

Different as all these situations are, they are dealt with in the same way – through planned marketing research programmes coupled with the informed manipulation of the elements which make up the marketing mix.

The Marketing Mix

Marketing planners need to be able to design the broad strategies required to enable the organization to achieve its objectives. They must also be able to originate detailed strategies and tactical programmes for individual products, some of which might actually be competing with each other. This is very much the case in washing powder/liquid markets where the majority of the available products are concentrated in the hands of two large international manufacturers.

Additionally, budgets have to be agreed and allocated between the various elements of the marketing mix, which is one of the core theories of modern marketing practice. This concept is used to describe the set of marketing tools available for marketing managers in enabling their organization to achieve its objectives in its chosen market.

These are actually the controllable variables that enable the organization to compete successfully in its marketing environment which, of course, it cannot control. Also known as the '**four Ps**' these cover the broad areas of which **product** (or service); what **price**; what **promotion** strategy and which **place** for selling it. **Promotion** and **place** of sale are concerned with reaching sufficient potential customers to make the product or service viable for the organization, while **products** and **prices** will enable the organization to give convincing answers when a potential customer asks why the product is good. The effective management of these four **controllable variables** welds them into a single profitable entity which satisfies customers.

Most markets consist of several sub-markets, each with different customer wants and needs, and organizations must create a different, and appropriate, marketing mix for each. For example, the airline market consists of both freight and passenger transport. The general passenger market itself can be sub-divided according to the specific needs of the traveller – those visiting friends and relatives, high-rated business travellers, charter passengers and so on. All groups of airline customers have their own individual needs and the airline must deliver a separate and appropriate marketing mix for each – a mix which provides the desired services at an acceptable price (see figure 1.2).

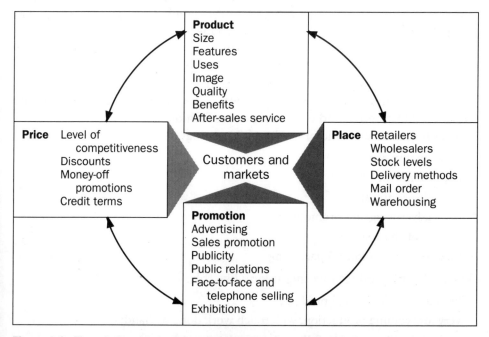

Figure 1.2 The relationship between the different elements of the marketing mix.

Each of the four Ps presents an ongoing opportunity to the professional marketer. Each P must be considered separately *and* in relation to the other three Ps in the marketing mix. A satisfactory mix for one period may well need to be revised because:

- Products or services will be improved as they begin to approach the end of their lifecycle or made obsolete as new ones are introduced.
- Prices may be undercut by the opposition or margins eroded as wholesalers and retailers demand a larger share.
- Promotions can be 'lost' due to more creative ideas produced by the opposition or swamped through the heavy weight of competitive promotional activity.
- The place at which products or services are offered to consumers can become less appropriate as business increases, for example, a small business might grow too much to be run from the proprietor's home, or a new out-of-town shopping centre might make a high street position obsolete.

Consider, for example, the problems concerned with marketing a product like machine tools. To what extent can a higher price, coupled with more effective promotion, improve the overall marketing impact and thus help to produce higher profit levels? Is it possible for faster delivery times not only to cover the cost of the more expensive system it has been necessary to install but also to lead to still higher profits, through producing extra sales?

The answers to these and other similar questions are vital to the success of any marketing operation as they will affect the balance between the various elements of the marketing mix. Unfortunately, these questions are not easy to answer – they need to be the focus of well-organized research and forecasting projects, and even the most detailed research activities can never eliminate risk entirely – they can only lessen it.

The different elements of the marketing mix all overlap and interact and they need to be developed with the same level of care as that given to developing the overall strategy of which they are the physical expression. Take, for example, two marketing mixes – one for a mass market product like a breakfast cereal and one for designer fashions.

This might be a profile of the breakfast cereal mix:

basic quality product;

high volume production;

mass distribution;

mass advertising and promotion;

middle-of-the-road price;

functional but colourful packaging.

The exclusive product mix might look like this:

high quality, individual product;

very low volume production, with much work done by hand;

limited distribution, carefully chosen outlets;

restricted promotion;

high price level;

personal selling important.

In recent years, the steady increase in the importance of being competitive, the enormous growth in the service sector and the rapid adoption of marketing techniques by organizations in the non-profit sector has begun to suggest that the number of Ps should not be four but seven.

Please refer to Box MKT1.9 which develops this 'service mix' idea. We have examined the nature of marketing and turn now to its management. This internal organizational co-ordination will take us to the end of this unit before we go 'outside' the firm in Unit Two to examine the external environment.

BOX MKT1.9

Additional Ps

A traditional definition of marketing usually revolves around the four Ps: price, product, place (distribution) and promotion.

Booms and Bitner suggest that this approach is not adequate for marketing in the service sector. The **product** from the quality to warranty exists; the **price** from level to terms is relevant; the **place** from location to channels must be important; and **promotion** from personal selling to channels gets the message over.

They advocate **people, physical evidence** and **process**. Services tend to involve much interaction between personnel within the firm and the customer, from staff training to client attitudes, and this is seen as another 'P'.

The physical evidence gives weight to an often intangible service, it adds tangibility through colour, layout, brochures etc. The process is the flow of activities between the customer and the organization. It involves customer discretion and employer's procedures etc.

It would seem that the process aspect is inherent in any concept of the basic 4 Ps. The people dimension may be there as well in the basic formula but it is writ large in services. The physical evidence is product-linked but very relevant to service marketing.

Source: Booms and Bitner, 'Marketing strategies and organization: structures for service firms'

What Does It Mean to Be a Manager of the Marketing Effort?

In many ways, the task of being a marketing manager differs little from that of managing any functional speciality in any type of organization – all managers share common tasks. They are responsible, within their own departments and outside them, for *getting things done through other people*, this being one of the simple definitions of management. Please refer to Activity MKT1.3.

ACTIVITY MKT1.3

THE WORK OF A MARKETEER

Activity code
- ✓ Self-development
- ✓ Teamwork
- ✓ Communications
- ✓ Numeracy/IT
- ✓ Decisions

Kotler has examined marketing and used the following themes to represent its concept and application. From the checklist below, derive the duties of a marketeer and then weigh the tasks in importance to the organization. Assume a fast-moving consumer goods environment (FMCG) in a medium-sized organization.

The themes are:
- a concept of marketing management;
- analysing opportunities;
- planning programmes;
- product strategies;
- the marketing mix;
- administering the programme;
- broadening marketing, for example, international.

Using the themes of marketing as noted by Kotler, your (group) role is to determine which of these themes are more important than others. Please rank importance from 1 (the most) to 7 (the least).

1

2

3

4

5

6

7

Source: Kotler, *Marketing Management*

Like all managers, marketing managers have to be prepared to make decisions and, again like all managers, they are responsible for *analysing, planning, organizing and controlling*. In the case of the marketing manager, this would mean in practice:

- *Analysing* markets and the marketing environment to discover new marketing opportunities, then *researching* products and markets in order to select promising target markets.
- *Planning* marketing programmes after having first *designed* appropriate marketing strategies.
- *Organizing* the marketing effort in order to *implement* the chosen marketing plan.
- *Controlling* budgets and the efforts of the marketing department, *receiving feedback* on the results of the implementation of marketing plans and programmes, then *analysing* this and working to adjust plans and programmes accordingly.

In the first part of this unit, we examined the fact that successful companies need to be marketing orientated and, if so, then someone has to ensure this is what happens by making sure the philosophy continues to permeate the whole organization. That someone is most likely to be the marketing manager or marketing director. Unless the managing director has a marketing background it is unlikely that he or she will have the skills to ensure all departments work to pursue the company's marketing aims. Even if the skill is there, it is most unlikely that the time will be available. It is also very common for functional departments to work to achieve their own aims, that is, for the benefit of the company as they see it. It makes sense, therefore, for the marketing director to take on the role of marketing co-ordinator to the company. It may be the marketing manager who actually carries out most of this task but, to ensure success, it really needs the weight of a board-level individual behind it, although in smaller companies the weight at board level may come from the managing director.

If the necessary level of marketing co-ordination between the various departments is to be achieved then there needs to be a plan to work to. It makes sense if this plan is produced by a marketing specialist as part of the planning role referred to above. Therefore, we can see that the actual *process* of marketing also needs to be managed by a marketing specialist. In addition, it is worth looking individually at the various process areas which need to be managed by the marketing manager.

The task of analysing

The basic tasks of analysing and investigating markets, competitors and customers come under the headings of **gathering marketing information** and **doing marketing research**. These areas are covered in detail in Unit Three.

The first stage in the **marketing planning process** is also one of analysis through the **marketing audit** followed by the analysis of the organization's own internal **strengths and weaknesses** plus that of the environmental **opportunities and threats** with which it is faced. The analysis of opportunities and threats is dealt with in Unit Six, as is the marketing audit.

The marketing audit is the 'where are we now?' of the company's marketing plan and, as the annual financial audit is a snapshot of where the company is in financial terms on the last day of the financial year, then is the marketing audit a similar picture of where the company is, in marketing terms, at the time the audit is carried out.

The next stage in the process which leads to the production of a marketing plan is the development of the information gleaned in the course of the audit into an analysis of the company's strengths and weaknesses in marketing terms (see figure 1.3).

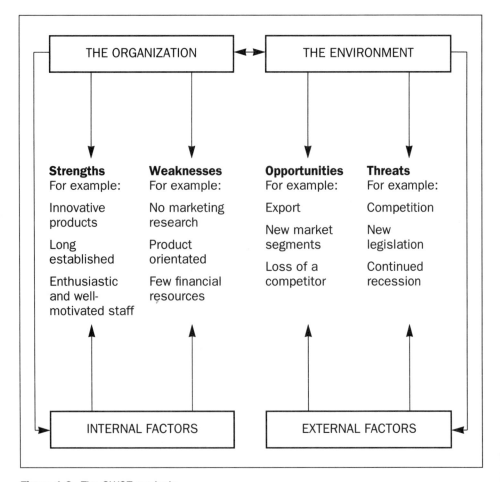

Figure 1.3 The SWOT analysis.

The carrying out of a marketing audit and audit of internal strengths and weaknesses is an example of how the influence of the marketing department flows out through the whole organization as both of these activities cover it as a whole, not just the marketing operation. These areas, plus that of the analysis of environmental opportunities and threats, need to be considered together because the task in hand is to find the best possible fit between the abilities and strengths of the company and the demands and threats of the markets which it serves.

The task of planning

The completion of the necessary analysis as described above begins to put the organization in the position of being able to develop a marketing plan which will begin to move it in the direction indicated by the corporate mission statement. However, before there can be a plan, there have to be **objectives.** This means that, if the marketing audit coupled with the SWOT analysis, provides the answer to the question of 'where are we now?' it is objective setting that answers the next question, which is, of course, 'where do we want to go?' (See Box MKT1.10.)

BOX MKT1.10

Objective setting

Companies need objectives in order to be able to measure their progress towards their corporate aims and the marketing department needs to set the company's marketing objectives in order to be able to produce a viable marketing plan. However, objectives also have other functions:

- They give the company *something to work towards* and without this it will be unable to focus its efforts on a company-wide basis.
- They provide a means of ensuring that there is *consistency* between the activities of the different functional departments.
- They provide a *motivating force*.
- They give managers the ability to *control* the activities for which they are responsible because, unless there is something to aim at, it is impossible to know whether or not there has been real improvement.

Source: Adapted from Lancaster and Massingham, *The Essentials of Marketing*

Once appropriate objectives have been set, we are in the position of being able to set about the production of the plan proper, that is, of formulating **marketing strategies** and **marketing programmes** which will answer the penultimate question of 'how are we going to get to where we want to go?' During this process of strategy development we can call on planning tools like the Ansoff Matrix and the Boston Matrix which are explained later. Additionally, the whole subject of planning is covered in detail in *Effective Business Policy*, another book in the *Effective Management* series.

The task of organizing

This task would cover both the way the company's marketing effort is organized as a whole and the fact that different parts of the overall marketing programme need to be organized to make sure that they are carried out efficiently and effectively. This latter part of the task would involve the allocation of the tasks, activities and resources.

The twin tasks of organizing, as outlined above, mirror the responsibilities and activities of the marketing manager. On the one hand, there is the set of pure management tasks which are needed to ensure that the way the company's marketing effort is organized is appropriate to the meeting of its marketing objectives in the same way that the production manager is responsible for ensuring that the organization of that department is appropriate to the meeting of its targets. On the other, we have the pure marketing-based- responsibilities involved in developing appropriate marketing strategies, marketing mixes and marketing programmes. Box MKT1.11 illustrates decision-making areas for the marketeer.

BOX MKT1.11

Areas in which marketing managers must make decisions

- The allocation of tasks within their department according to the specialisms of the available staff and the requirements of the marketing plan.
- Methods and frequency of communication both within and without the marketing department. This would include the establishment of appropriate information systems, liaison with other functional and staff departments and also with outside agencies such as market research companies and the company's advertising agency.
- The grouping of work within the marketing department into appropriate units, for example, research, advertising and sales promotion, marketing services.
- The use of outside specialists such as public relations companies or advertising agencies, that is, where the line is to be drawn between in-house activity and that bought in from outside.
- The method of organizing the marketing effort, for example, geographically by functions or by product and brand as discussed later in this unit.

Source: Adapted from Lancaster and Massingham, *The Essentials of Marketing*

So far as the actual organization of the overall marketing department is concerned, Kotler[7] gives us an appropriate breakdown, while saying that all marketing organizations must be able to accommodate four different areas of marketing activity: **functions, geographical areas, products and brands, customers and markets**:

- *Organizing in a functional manner* is the most common way for companies to structure their marketing effort. It provides for the employment of a number of functional specialists all of whom then report to a marketing director or marketing manager. The list of specialists would vary according to the size and nature of the company involved, but might include: a sales manager; a marketing services manager; an advertising and promotions manager; a marketing research manager.

  This is a simple structure which fits in well with any company organization chart and may function very well in a medium-sized company where the width and depth of the whole product range is not large. The disadvantages of this form of organization begin to show as the variety of products and markets grows larger, because there is no one with specific responsibility for any particular product or market area. This means that some may get less attention than others or, specifically, not enough attention at the most important times. Additionally, co-ordination (the responsibility of the head of marketing) between the different functions can be difficult and there may also be a good deal of competitiveness between them.

- *Organizing geographically* can make sense for companies which operate in national and international markets. This form of organization is more likely to apply to the personal selling effort than to other areas of marketing. In a UK-wide selling operation there may be, for example, a national sales manager (who reports to the head of marketing) with, in turn, four regional managers each of whom is in charge of a number of area sales people. This form of organization has the advantage of offering a short span of control and also of allowing area sales staff to become very familiar with the people and the situation in their area of operation.

- *Organizing for products and brands* is a method often used by large companies with a wide variety of products operating in a variety of markets. This system does not do away with the functional managers listed above – it adds another layer of management – and the arrangement makes sense where the company produces products which are very different, for example, toothpaste and washing powder, or if there are so many products that it requires many people to look after them.

  Product managers were first introduced by Procter & Gamble well before the Second World War and the system has been in use in marketing ever since. Product managers concentrate on one product, or one group of products, so that close attention is given to the development of appropriate promotional strategies and there is room for close monitoring of results with a corresponding opportunity for fast corrective action when necessary. On the negative side is the fact that product managers are usually young and ambitious so that they quickly move on, leaving the product with less chance of a coherent long-term strategy.

■ *Organizing for markets and customers* makes sense when a company's products are sold into clearly defined markets or market segments, for example, in industrial markets, the field sales force might be organized into groups which concentrate on different industries, or hotel chains may have a travel trade market manager and a courses and conferences market manager.

There are many similarities between the jobs of product managers and market managers. However, the latter system has the distinct advantage of being focused on markets and customers rather than on products something which makes sense in a marketing orientated company.

■ *The matrix organization* has both product managers and market managers, a system which helps to solve the problem of a wide variety of products aimed at a wide variety of markets when neither the product management system nor that of market management will suffice on its own. The biggest disadvantage of this system (apart from the obvious area of conflict between the two different types of manager with different sets of priorities) is cost, because it adds a whole extra level of management.

The task of controlling

The final task of managers is to control – their departments and their resources, both financial and human because no department can play its part in reaching company objectives if it is not run efficiently and effectively. This means that there must be both **evaluation** and **control** and the question of evaluation is dealt with in detail in Unit Six.

However, we can look briefly here at the essentials of a system of control which would involve the following:

■ setting standards;

■ measuring performance against these standards;

■ taking corrective action where actual performance does not meet the required standards.

The measurement of activities against the standards set for them is an activity which is common to all managers at all organizational levels, but where these tasks become specific to the marketing manager is in the evaluation and control of the company's marketing plan and of its declared marketing strategy.

Relationships with Other Functional Departments

We have already seen that the marketing department often adopts a co-ordinating role in order to ensure that the marketing philosophy is accepted throughout the organization and because it is the marketing department which is usually closest to the company's markets and customers. Yet the marketing manager certainly has no authority over other departments and, at board level, it is unlikely that the marketing director has any direct authority over the production director or the financial director. This means, in practice, that relationships with other departments are often strained and that the marketing department needs to persuade rather than require.

Perhaps the greatest potential for conflict is between the marketing department and the production department, with the accounts department close behind. The production department is concerned with ease of manufacture, stock levels and economies of scale, and with the relationship between management and the people on the shop floor. Conflict occurs when the marketing department wants a variety of different models with special features so that costs are bound to rise (as well as overtime levels) or when they promise special delivery dates to important customers.

The accounts department, in turn, frequently comes into conflict with marketing, which is often seen as woolly headed and inexact when it comes to dealing with costs and budgets. Nobody is able to predict with any certainty the level of extra sales which will result from an expensive advertising campaign.

All departments have their own special areas of expertise and their own particular axes to grind. However, it is obvious that what is best for the company is the creation of balance and understanding between the different departments. In reality, the only sure way for this to happen is firm leadership and a high level of commitment to a marketing-based approach. This starts at the very top with the chief executive.

Now turn to Activity MKT1.4 and respond to the tasks from the perspective of an independent marketing adviser.

ACTIVITY MKT1.4

THE ALBION HOLIDAY CENTRE OR THE CAMBRIDGE BLUE

Activity code
- ✓ Self-development
- ☐ Teamwork
- ✓ Communications
- ☐ Numeracy/IT
- ✓ Decisions

Tomson and Smythe had started working in the hotel sector some twenty years ago. Tomson's family wealth and Smythe's industry had allowed the two friends to buy a medium-sized three-star hotel near Duxford in Cambridgeshire. Their initial motive had been to provide a stopover facility on the A505 for passing trade and to act as an overspill hotel for the tourist-infested city of Cambridge, a pleasant fifteen to twenty minutes' drive from the hotel. The Albion, as it was called (George Tomson and Phil Smythe being quite patriotic), had prospered over the last few years. It had a further shot in the arm with the opening of the north-bound London motorway, the M11. More passing trade came off at the Duxford exit for a comfortable night's rest, a reasonably priced meal and a soothing drink. Duxford is fairly close to the expanding third London airport at Stanstead.

Both men were ambitious – not only for themselves but for the hotel. There was a division of opinion over where the hotel business was going and both partners had fairly fixed ideas on the matter.

George: Look Phil, for goodness' sake, here we are doing quite nicely. But if we stand still we're dead – competition will come in and take everything. All we need is some big company to come around here, build a motel and there goes our pension.

Phil: I understand that – I don't want to sit about all day, either. You appointed the manager, Des Reeves ... you pushed for him ... I would have been happy keeping my hand in on the operations.

George: We're partners, we are the entrepreneurs here, not managers. Let someone else get on and manage the detail. We need to look at the big picture. You must agree.

Phil: Yes, yes, I can see that, but we must agree on the picture.

George: Absolutely. So what do you think of the plan, eh? We're three-star at the moment. It's okay for the middle-of-the-road traveller.

Phil: The A505 is bad enough for safety without travelling in the middle of the road!

George: Quite. Anyway, I've made an inventory (with the manager's help of course) of where we're at now. Once we know that, it's easier to plan.

Phil: I should have been involved in this stock taking ...

George: Yes, you are – of course you are. Stop being so sensitive about everything. There is no *fait accompli*. I'm just taking a snapshot of the present to help us deal with the future. Come on Phil, give it a shot ... we'll need to look at what we've got even if you have something else up your sleeve.

Phil: Well, as a matter of fact, I've been doing a lot of thinking as well. [George interjects: 'Oh yeah!' Phil ignores him and keeps going as George does this to him all the time.] Well, it's like this. We've got acres and acres of space out at the back there. We could expand and I know old Farmer Wells has some land up for sale as well – he's never away from the pub anyway – and I'm sure that we can get a deal.

George: We don't need more land, surely. We must upgrade what we've got – go for a better marketplace.

Phil: We would need more land. Look, for years and years Mary and I used to get in the car, hitch up the caravan and go. It was great

	away from the city doing your own thing – and plenty of different scenery – every day if you wanted, you could be somewhere else.
George:	Memories, memories.
Phil:	No – you miss the point. Caravan holidays are expanding. I'm still a member of the club. Once a quarter I get the booklet. I know what caravan people want. I know the prices they'll pay and the amenities they look for. Look, what we do is to screen the Albion off with pine trees two or three thick – the trees will grow in no time, so the holiday park will be separated from the hotel. A path will lead down to the lounge and restaurant, of course. We'll have a captive audience in the summer. We could have some 60 pitches (that's 60 separate pieces of land for each caravan or trailer tent).
George:	Tents! For goodness' sake, what is this all about? This is crazy. We need to go upmarket – not become some refugee camp for the displaced.
Phil:	They are not displaced. Most of these people are wealthy 'townies' who want to escape in their Volvos and their BMWs. These cars and caravans together can cost up to £30,000, if not more. The potential is immense. Cambridge is not far. Thetford and Thetford Park are within travelling distance, there is only one site and a couple of CLs around there.
George:	CLs – what's that, then?
Phil:	A CL is a small stopover place for a couple of vans (as we call them), usually without electricity and often linked to a farm or a pub.
George:	We're in a different market.
Phil:	All the more reason for diversifying, then.
George:	Yes and no. Let me have my say now. [He passes Phil the inventory.] We're half way there already. At the moment we're really a three-and-a-half star, although we have a three-star category. We must go for a four-star and later a five-star rating to attract a wealthy clientele. A health farm, a country retreat, a bit of old England – the foreigners will love it – so will the executives from London and those passing through the airport.
Phil:	Let's focus on this inventory thing, but it has an equal application for my idea as well.
George:	Sure, sure. The reception has to be manned at all times by uniformed staff. No change. We've got old Harry, the night porter, and we can give him a uniform. The lift system is fine. We have a limited laundry service but that can be expanded and we'll need shoe cleaning equipment. The general decor and the public lounge is more than adequate. There is no problem with the lights or the telephones. The rooms have TVs, en suite facilities, and tea and coffee can be upgraded and advertised as such. We'll need to put in some more showers. Hairdryers are a nominal expense, as are the writing materials. Private suites will be added on in the new extension.
Phil:	Extension?

George: Yes, the extension. We can attach a new restaurant as well, a cock-tail lounge and separate office facilities for busy executives. There are no problems with the bathrooms, and the public lounges are fine. We'll need more table service though – but there are plenty of students who will take this work. The food will be upgraded to inter-national standards and we'll get rid of Mario and get a French chef instead. ['Charming', Phil interjects.] We'll need to extend the dinner hours and provide afternoon tea. The range and depth of the cuisine will change. We already have the swimming pool, and the gym/fit-ness centre can be upgraded with a sauna and jacuzzi.

Phil: This will cost a fortune.

George: Ah, at least you're talking money. So that means that you are not unhappy with the principle.

Phil: No, no, no. We need to take a view on both proposals. But I'm no accountant and we can't manage to do both things. Let's prepare more detailed plans and we'll take it from there. I can study the inventory at the same time.

George: Fine. By the way, we should rename the Albion, The Cambridge Blue.

Phil knew that he could well lose the argument and that the hotel would be moving upmarket sooner or later. He said that he would reflect. He did. A friend of a friend was involved in service marketing and he would call upon an external specialist to kill off this whole idea. If it did not kill it at least there would be a tighter logic to the process.

Michael Hay duly arrived on the scene to give some advice. After listening to both views he suggested that they take stock of their existing situation and that he could conduct an environmental analysis on their behalf. The fees looked reasonable and it was only advice after all; George could always reject it. Anyway, George was convinced that he was right.

Weeks later the interim report landed on their desks. The gist was as follows:

1   We work in the service sector. Unlike IBM, for example, with physical products which can be packaged accordingly, we are unable to do this.

2   We are in the land of physical imagery: manipulating the psychological environment for our own ends.

3   The core argument is as follows, and I quote a specialist in the field: 'Elements of a firm's environment can be used to establish or reinforce an image, reposition the firm in customers' perceptions, or influence customer satisfaction or dissatisfaction with the service they receive.'[1]

4   Before we look to creating new images, the analysis of your existing image is important, as you said at our last meeting that you wished to hold on to your core clientele. I concur with this viewpoint as radical departures may alienate this core.

5   We must start with the four Ps. The traditional mix is inadequate for our purposes. We need to reflect the service vision to include 'participants', or the people involved, from customers to employees who take part in your transaction. The 'physical evidence' where buyer and seller interact gives another dimension. The 'process' or flow of activities at the hotel consolidates this picture. The traditional

mix plays a role, of course. This includes the place that you are established, the well-heeled targets of your promotion, the not-inexpensive pricing structure and the 'product' of this hotel. This all adds up to a middling-to-upper level of supply catering for a middle-to-upper population.

6 To return to the other three Ps. The customers seek a good level of service and they receive it from an efficient and courteous staff. The hotel itself is set in a charming part of the country near Cambridge, England. The facilities, whilst quite good, could be improved. The relationships through the process which I have observed consolidate the view of a middling-to-upper level type of hotel.

7 I will not say that you should go down- or upmarket, for that is an executive decision. The logic of my enquiry is self-explanatory and I am sure will lead you to the proper decision.

1 Analyse the adviser's view of marketing.
2 Where should the partners go and why?

Source:
1 Booms, 'Marketing services by managing the environment'

Notes
1 Ryan and Hermanson, *Programmed Learning Aid for Principles of Marketing*.
2 Drucker, 'Managing for business effectiveness'.
3 Kotler, *Marketing Management*.
4 Ibid.
5 Peters and Waterman Jr, *In Search of Excellence*.
6 Kotler, *Marketing Management*.
7 Ibid.

Unit Two

The Competitive Environment

Learning Objectives

After completing this unit you should be able to:

- conduct an environmental scan through examination of both the near and far environment;

- carry out an analysis of competitive activity;

- decide on appropriate ways of segmenting example markets;

- apply the principles involved in dealing with patterns of buyer behaviour;

- apply the generic skills.

Contents

Overview

Why Look at the Environment?

The Far (Macro) Environment

The Near (Micro) Environment

Environmental Constraints

What is Consumerism and How does it Work?

Legislation and Codes of Practice

The Opportunity Environment

Coping with Competition

▶ Industry competition

▶ Market competition

Understanding Your Customers

How Buying Decisions are Made

The Buying Process in Industrial Markets

The Need to Segment Markets

Types of Segmentation

▶ Segmentation by level of usage

▶ Benefit segmentation

Positioning Products and Services in Their Markets

Unit Two

❝ In the external appraisal the team looks for those features of its *environment*, both present and future, which also must shape its strategic future – features outside the company, in its external environment, but not always, outside its control!❞

J. Argenti, Practical Corporate Planning[1]

Overview

An attempt to dictate to the environment may indeed be difficult, as the world outside the organization is very fickle. Yet this external environment and the attempt to 'manage it' is crucial to the long-term success of the organization. We now focus on this environmental analysis and turbulence. Constant competitive analysis and monitoring is advocated as a means to understand and 'manage' this environment. The buying motives and the needs and wants of customers, both in industrial and consumer markets, form much of the substance of this unit. Dividing up, classifying and segmenting these buying units conclude this section. (See figure 2.1.)

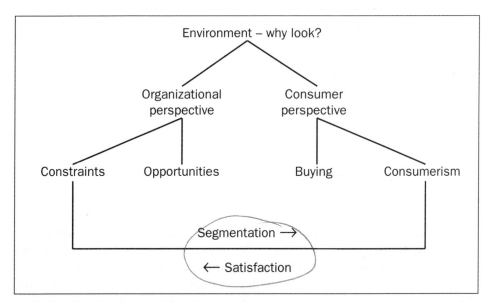

Figure 2.1 Outline diagram of Unit Two.

Why Look at the Environment?

In Unit One, we examined the fact that truly marketing orientated organizations are those which are constantly looking outside themselves into the environment in which they operate because, without an awareness and understanding of what is going on around them, they are unlikely to be able to succeed in the long term.

This need for environmental scanning can be dealt with in large part by a company's marketing information system (described in detail in Unit Three) so long as it is set up in advance to cover the requisite areas. Additional, specialized information can be gathered through desk and/or field research surveys (also dealt with in Unit Three).

For scanning purposes, the environment can be divided into two main areas: the **far environment** and the **near environment**. The former covers areas which are distant from the organization itself, for example, government policies, but which may well have an effect on the way it operates and its level of profit. The latter deals with areas which are much closer to home, for example, this might be literally close to home if the environmental policies of local authorities affect a company's mode of operation, or it may be close to home in the marketing sense if it has to do with customers and competition.

Analysing markets in this way is the start of the marketing process. Peters and Waterman[2] emphasize very strongly the fact that successful companies understand, and are close to, their customers. To do this, they must first understand the overall environment in which they are operating (the far environment). Secondly, they must have a detailed knowledge of the particular market (or markets) in which they are involved plus the fullest possible understanding of their customers, their needs and wants and their buying behaviour (the near environment).

This process of marketing analysis has been described by Hill[3] as: 'The gathering and analysis of information concerning all the forces and institutions outside the firm which may be relevant to its present and future activities'. This clearly indicates that the environment which affects a company's operation exists *outside* it, which means that what happens there is naturally beyond its control. However, there is a school of thought which views the matter differently (as described by Kotler[4]): 'A company's marketing environment consists of the actors and forces external to the marketing management function of the firm that impinge on the marketing management's ability to develop and maintain successful transactions with its target customers.' This places departments other than marketing into the situation of being part of the near environment in which the company operates in marketing terms. If the company is fully marketing and quality orientated then the marketing philosophy would have permeated the whole organization. However, the marketing department still has to find a way of operating within the particular internal environment of a company and, additionally, it has to compete for resources with the rest of the operational departments. This means that, although the marketing department is heavily involved in the interface between the company and its markets, the way that it deals with those markets is influenced by what happens *inside* the company as well as what happens *outside*.

The Far (Macro) Environment

This deals with the wider or far external environment. It can also be termed the macro environment. Please refer to figure 2.2, showing the organization in its environment.

The necessary examination of a company's wider, or far, environment is often categorized in a way which is useful to students faced with case study analysis – it is known as a STEP (or PEST) analysis and covers the **social, technological, economic** and **political** aspects evident in that environment.

■ *The social environment* in which an organization operates can be divided into two sections – **demographic** and **behavioural** – which cover two very

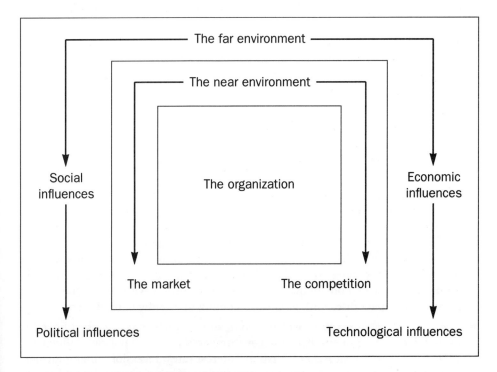

Figure 2.2 The organization in its environment.

different elements of that environment. Demographic trends use quantitative and factual information to plot the future composition of markets and, a useful fact for marketing people, this information is collected regularly by government departments for their own uses which means that it is readily available and does not need to be gathered separately. Useful information includes:

◆ Population size and growth rates – useful measures for marketing people involved with basic, mass appeal products as they can help with forecasting sales and give information about whether the market is growing or static.

◆ The geographic distribution of population is important in relation to targeting efforts; for example, it might make sense to launch a new product into high-population areas but it certainly would not make sense to do this in some of the more sparsely populated areas of northern Scotland. This is information which is also vitally important in export marketing.

◆ The breakdown of populations by age is something which has become of great interest to marketing people during the recent past. The youth market has been in decline since the birth rate began to fall in the 1960s, the children of the post-war 'bulge' have become middle-aged and are seeking very different types of products from those they wanted when they were twenty years younger, and finally, the continuing increase in the number of elderly people in the population has produced a large market for products like health care, winter holidays and sheltered housing.

So far as the behavioural aspects of present day society are concerned, much of the information gathered is likely to be qualitative rather than quantitative and it will cover areas such as:

◆ Social trends which may include factors such as the increasing social pressures against smoking in public places, the rising number of working mothers and the continued emancipation of women in general. Other useful trends are the growing interest in health and fitness and in health foods and environmental issues.

◆ Tastes and fashions evolve and change continually. The stark furnishings and styles of the 1960s have given way to softer styles, hemlines move up and down and it has become acceptable to buy and serve many varieties of ready-made foods, particularly those which are frozen or chilled.

■ *The technological environment* in which organizations operate is changing at an ever faster rate. This is important both for companies which produce technical products either for industrial, or for consumer, markets and also for the companies which use technological equipment in their offices and factories, since being left behind can affect long-term survival. Cash dispensers are becoming rapidly more sophisticated, for example, and, where one bank leads, all the others will soon follow. Long-playing records have been abandoned in favour of compact discs with laser discs coming up rapidly behind them.

■ *The economic environment* in which a company operates is very closely linked to its political environment because government styles and policies influence a country's economic situation. Inflation, interest rates, recession, unemployment levels and growth rates all play their part in determining a company's economic operating environment.

■ *The political environment* is ultimately determined by the political system in every country in which it operates. For example, in the UK the spate of privatizations in the 1980s and 1990s altered the country's business environment in a way which even a change of government is unlikely to be able to reverse. Additionally, a government's attitude to imports can make export marketing difficult in some parts of the world such as Japan. Political stability, particularly in overseas markets is another important factor and here, a useful example is the situation in Hong Kong as it nears reunion with China.

Additionally, the political environment may be linked to legislation in the form of statutory material such as the Trades Descriptions Act or clean air and environmental regulations. Please tackle Activity MKT2.1.

ACTIVITY MKT2.1

THE RANDY BROTHERS

Activity code
- ✓ Self-development
- ✓ Teamwork
- ✓ Communications
- ☐ Numeracy/IT
- ✓ Decisions

The Randy brothers were Greek Cypriots. The invasion of Northern Cyprus by the Turks had obliged the young brothers to move south with their successful restaurant business.

Interests spread through the years into Spain, Italy and the Balearic Islands. The formula was similar: good quality food at reasonable prices.

An opportunity arose to acquire an English country house hotel near Bath. One of their compatriots, a business studies student at a London college, agreed to conduct an environmental analysis for the brothers. The specific competitive analysis would follow and he hoped to get a vacation job so that his 'intelligence' system could relate back to Cyprus concerning the internal environment of the firm.

'Geographically, the house is based in southern England, which provides a stable political environment. Terrorists are active in some parts of the country but there has been no crusade against the rich, other than the occasional flurry against business leaders in Northern Ireland and by Welsh nationalist extremists setting fire to property owned by absentee landlords. Our potential clientele is rich but should not be affected by these forces.

'It is a Grade II listed Georgian building with 30 rooms, swimming pool, leisure centre and 29 acres of parkland. Planning permission to amend the Grade II building may be difficult.

'The government does not really interfere with the hotel and restaurant sector, believing in a climate of free enterprise, so labour is particularly cheap. Furthermore the rural area means that wages are already depressed. Legislation does exist in health and safety and there are very strict hygiene requirements.

'Within a 35-mile radius there are 11 other hotels and, with the inclusion of this country house, some 300 rooms are provided by these hotels. Prices are in line with the competitor at about £130 per night and an average dinner costs approximately £30 per head. There are no real high quality restaurants in this 35-mile area. A good report in the wine and food guides is critical for business.

'Some conferences and seminars for senior managers are occasionally held here. The locals in the area do not frequent the hotel, although some 'A/B' socio-economic categories do frequent the restaurant. It certainly has 'snob' value.

'The technological aspect of the external environment does not really apply. The house is served by a good transport and distribution network, it has old-world charm, there is some modern technology in the leisure areas, but this industry, and indeed the hotel, is not at the forefront of the technology, and no 'threat' is expected from this quarter. Some would argue that a kitchen revolution has occurred in terms of food preparation and the speed of cooking, but this has not affected the house.'

Assume that you are an independent marketing adviser to the Randy brothers.

1 What do you make of this external environment? How 'turbulent' do you feel this environment actually is and how much control is possible over it?
2 What marketing advice would you give to the brothers concerning this scenario?

The Near (Micro) Environment

Environmental influences close to a company might include both internal and external forces. The internal influences will determine how the marketing department is able to operate in its efforts to reach organizational objectives. These influences will determine the company's overall attitude to marketing and will also determine the budgets allocated to the marketing function.

Outside the company, the near environment can be divided into four broad areas: **customers, competitors, suppliers** and **channels (of**

distribution). The question of customers and buyer behaviour is dealt with in detail later in this unit.

■ *The competitive environment* in which companies operate is often extremely hostile, for example if there is a variety of closely competing products with not a lot of real difference between them such as soap powders. The extent of direct competition in mass market consumer products can be understood very readily after a quick stroll around the shelves of any local supermarket. The opportunity for choice is enormous and it is often areas like branding, sales promotion and advertising (dealt with in Unit Four) which determine the ultimate choice rather than the composition of the product itself.

Additionally, there is indirect competition to be faced – particularly in the case of non-essential products. Once their immediate needs for shelter and security have been met, individuals can choose how to spend their disposable income. Therefore, competition becomes fierce in these areas as holiday firms cut their prices to attract satisfactory levels of business while consumers are choosing whether to forgo a holiday this year in favour of a new car or the addition of a conservatory. This can also be known as **need competition** as consumers whose incomes are not enormous choose which need to satisfy first, for example, the need for a holiday may be balanced against the need for roof repairs before winter sets in.

■ *The supplier environment* is one which is closely linked to the more recently introduced theories of **quality management** and **relationship marketing** in which a partnership is forged with suppliers in the same way as that with customers. Suppliers are essential to any organization because it is they who supply the raw materials, components or other resources needed to produce goods and/or services. Please refer to Box MKT2.1. A box has been used here to emphasize the much neglected relationship between customers, organizations and suppliers.

BOX MKT2.1

Customers, organizations and suppliers

Elsewhere we note the potential relationship between these three groups in a form of 'stakeholding' within the organization and an ethical-cum-social responsibility dimension between the three groups is seen in another text.[1]

Here we will focus on this relationship on an example in the context of marketing.

The recession is hitting the EC's car industry. Japanese competition is compounding its current difficulties. The pressure is on to cut costs and, as we know, labour is being shed.

There is a knock-on effect to the core components' suppliers. This industry, worth some £70 billion per annum, is being caught in the middle between customer demand slackening (17 per cent drop) and the manufacturer's need to cut costs.

The components can make up to 60 per cent of the total cost of the vehicle, so the suppliers are coming under increasing pressure. The 3,000 or so component makers/suppliers to the carmaking sector look to be on a loser. Cost cutting and rationalization (amalgamation?) would seem to be inevitable at the time of writing.

Source:
1 See Anderson and Barker, *Effective Business Policy,* and Anderson, *Effective General Management*

Sounder partnerships of this nature are those forged between companies like Marks & Spencer and their suppliers. However, from the supplier's point of view, this type of relationship may be dangerous if they become linked to a single large customer on whom they are totally dependent.

In many manufacturing companies, purchasing is looked upon as a vital management function and it is quite possible that *all* purchasing (including even the printed material used by the marketing department) is done by a single person, or a single department if the company is a large one.

However, the idea of the formation of a close link between manufacturer or service provider and their suppliers is an attractive one as each is dependent upon the other for economic survival – something which is particularly true in industrial markets. Suppliers can be changed, but this often involves a good deal of upheaval for all concerned. Another example of this close form of business relationship can be identified in the relationship which often exists between a company and its advertising agency.

■ *The channel environment* very often concerns consumer products and consumer markets more than industrial ones as industrial products are frequently delivered by the supplier straight into the customer's warehouse or factory. However, as examined in detail in Unit Five, consumer products frequently pass through a number of hands before they reach the final consumer.

Companies need constantly to be aware of changing trends in shopping habits, for example. The future in retailing is moving rapidly towards shopping malls and away from small shops whether in towns or in the country and it is important to keep up with developments of this nature.

Environmental Constraints

As well as having to be aware of, and understand, the environment in which it is operating, a company has to recognize the constraints in that environment. As seen above, political and economic situations influence the ways in which a company's marketing activities can be carried out but, in fact, the constraints do not stop there.

Ultimately, the environment in which we operate is made up of individual consumers (or individual companies in the case of industrial marketing) and our interface with those consumers and customers is vitally important for long-term survival and growth. There are two main areas in which this producer–consumer interface is influenced by outside, or environmental, forces. These are **consumerism** where the influences come from consumers themselves to question the activities of companies and **codes of practice/legislation** (the first being voluntary and the latter being statutory) which act on behalf of consumers to ensure that they are treated correctly. However, it is true to say that, in some cases, it is consumerism which has influenced the other areas.

What is Consumerism and How does it Work?

Over the last two decades or so, there has been increasing disquiet in some circles about the activities of business – particularly big business, and it was this which brought about the birth of consumerism, first of all in America, initially through the activities of Ralph Nader. The important thing here was that Nader, particularly through taking on the American motor car industry, gave individuals the belief that it was possible for them to challenge big business and win – at least some of the time. In the UK, the rise of consumerism has been closely linked with the development of *Which?* and the Consumers' Association. One of the most important facets of the consumer movement has been its insistence that both buyers and sellers have rights.

Perhaps the fact that we have witnessed the growth in consumerism means that 'pure' marketing is not being implemented, for if it were, the need for consumerism would not really exist. Anyway, it does exist and consumer rights are enshrined in legislation and in codes of practice. Please refer to Box MKT2.2.

BOX MKT2.2

The rights of buyers and sellers

Consumerism has been defined as *a social movement which sets out to extend the power and rights of buyers in relation to sellers.* However, it is also held that both sellers and buyers have rights in the process of exchange that goes on between them.

Traditional rights of sellers

- To sell any product they choose so long as it is not inherently dangerous. Even dangerous items like guns, poisons and explosives can be sold so long as appropriate warnings are given and suitable controls are in place.
- To sell their products and services at any price they choose so long as they do not discriminate against certain classes of purchaser, such as ethnic minorities.
- To promote their products or services in any way they choose and with any words they choose so long as the message is not misleading or untruthful and it does not contravene any of the legal or voluntary codes which are in force.
- To spend any amount they choose on promotional activities and buying incentive schemes.

Traditional rights of buyers

- That whether to buy or not to buy is a matter of free choice.
- To be able to expect that products should not be harmful or dangerous in any way.
- To expect not to be misled over the purchase, that products should perform as it is claimed they will.

A product of consumerism

One of the products of consumerism has been extra expectations on the part of consumers and the claiming of additional rights for buyers:

- To be fully informed about all product ingredients and additives, particularly in food.
- To be protected against doubtful products, service and marketing activities.
- To expect products not to be actively harmful to the environment, for example, the current feeling against the use of CFCs and tropical hardwoods.

Source: Adapted from N. Hill, *Marketing for BTEC*

The demands of consumerism have to a great extent been met by legislation. For example, in America Ralph Nader's efforts were very closely connected with the National Traffic and Motor Safety Act of 1962 and the Wholesome Meat Act of 1967. However, perhaps there are new areas of operation beginning to develop through the activities of environmentalists linked to consumerism as the voice of the individual consumer. Animal testing and cruelty in farming are just two of the issues under debate today, others being the introduction of recycled and recyclable products. The ultimate point to remember is that consumers do have rights. Please refer to Box MKT2.3, derived from the radical work of JFK's presidency.

BOX MKT2.3

What rights should consumers have?

In 1962 United States President John F. Kennedy declared four basic rights for consumers:

■ *The right to safety.* Products should not include hidden dangers. This had been the cause of Ralph Nader's first campaign against the automobile industry in America. The first campaign of this nature in the UK was that which occurred after the revelations of the birth problems caused by thalidomide. Present-day campaigns have often focused on food additives and tranquillizers.

■ *The right to be fully informed.* There should be protection against misleading product claims and information and against deceit in advertising and product labelling. Government health warnings on cigarettes and the Trades Descriptions Act operate in this area.

■ *The right to choose.* There should be no pricing cartels but instead there should be real competition among producers and always the right not to buy at all.

■ *The right to be heard.* Consumerists hold that this right should best be exercised through bodies set up to speak on behalf of consumers, e.g. the Consumers' Association. However, this should not inhibit individual consumers from expressing their dissatisfactions in an appropriate manner.

Source: Adapted from Lancaster and Massingham, *The Essentials of Marketing*

Legislation and Codes of Practice

In the UK there are a number of official bodies which have been set up to look after the interests of consumers, for example:

■ The Office of Fair Trading, including bodies like OFTEL and OFGAS.

■ The Advertising Standards Authority which frequently mounts advertising campaigns encouraging members of the public to write to them about advertisements which they consider are not 'legal, decent and truthful'.

■ The British Standards Institute which gives a 'kite mark' to products which reach the appropriate safety standards, these being set by the BSI. In recent years, these BSI set standards are being increasingly sought after by service companies, even educational establishments and old people's homes through the award of the British Standard 5750.

■ The Monopolies and Mergers Commission has been given the role of investigating mergers or acquisitions where the creation of a large bloc within a certain industry might be considered to be against the interests of the public. Newspapers are one area where investigations of this nature have taken place.

Box MKT2.4 on 'Legal aspects of consumer protection' should now be examined to give an illustrative context in the UK/EC environment.

BOX MKT2.4

Legal aspects of consumer protection

Since the early 1960s, a variety of statutory instruments have been introduced which strengthen voluntary codes of practice. Naturally, these instruments all act to alter the balance of the relationships forged between buyers and sellers:

Consumer Protection Act	1987
Sale of Goods Act	1979
Babies Dummies (Safety) Regulations	1978
Cosmetic Products Regulations	1978
Unfair Contract Terms Act	1977
Aerosol Dispensers (EEC Requirements) Regulations	1977
Business Advertisements (Disclosure) Order	1977
Mail Order Transactions (Information) Order	1976
Consumer Credit Act	1974
Cooking Utensils (Safety) Regulations	1972
Electric Blankets (Safety) Regulations	1971
Nightdresses (Safety) Regulations	1967

Source: Adapted from Lancaster and Massingham, *The Essentials of Marketing*

Many industries now have their own voluntary codes of practice and regularity bodies – for example the Association of British Travel Agents (ABTA) – to which their members must adhere. Within this, there is a school of thought which says that if an industry can be seen to be regulating itself voluntarily then it is much less likely that there will be legislation introduced which might cause it much extra difficulty.

In general, the marketing and advertising industries in the UK pride themselves on being self-regulating through instruments like the Code of Advertising Practice. These voluntary codes can also be seen as vital elements in the marketing mix as they contribute to the quality of the company image through helping to assure customers that they are dealing with an organization with a high level of integrity. Please refer to Box MKT2.5 which gives in-depth examples.

The Opportunity Environment

Much of the discussion about environmental constraints may have a negative atmosphere and may be concerned with threats; however, we must never allow ourselves to forget that the environment in which a company operates is also the place in which it will find its opportunities. The issue of whether we find them or seek them out is more debatable.

BOX MKT2.5

Marketing Codes of Practice

In the UK, all members of the Chartered Institute of Marketing are expected to abide by the organization's Code of Practice which covers many areas of professional conduct, including:

- honesty;
- conflict of interest;
- confidentiality;
- misuse of the Code;
- adherence to other relevant codes;
- professional competence;
- securing and developing business;
- procedures for handling complaints.

Similar Codes of Practice have been established by:

- the Advertising Association;
- the Institute of Sales Promotion;
- the Market Research Society;
- the Institute of Public Relations.

Kotler[5] defines a marketing opportunity as: 'an attractive arena for company marketing action in which the company would enjoy a competitive advantage'. He defines an environmental threat as: 'a challenge posed by an unfavourable trend or development in the environment that would lead, in the absence of purposeful marketing action, to the erosion of the company's position'.

Threats need to be met with contingency plans and action to minimize them as much as possible as they are outside the company's direct control. Opportunities are there to be taken advantage of and, in order to be able to do this, the company must calculate the probability of success for each opportunity which presents itself. At this point please refer to Box MKT2.6.

Coping with Competition

As we have already seen in the first part of this unit, the whole question of competition, whether direct or indirect, comprises an important part of the environment in which companies operate. Competitors form part of the atmosphere in most market areas and government action has, in recent years, forced organizations which previously operated in monopolistic conditions into competitive situations, for example, British Telecom and British Gas.

BOX MKT2.6

Dealing with opportunities and threats

Simple matrices can be used to help analyse the probability of success or failure when dealing respectively with opportunities and threats.

The opportunity matrix looks like this:

Success probability

	High	Low
High	1	2
Low	3	4

Attractiveness

- *Segment 1:* The company develops a better product or service.
- *Segment 2:* The company develops a lower-cost product or service.
- *Segment 3:* The company develops a spin-off product which research has shown to have a limited appeal.
- *Segment 4:* The company has an idea for a product which might complement that in segment 3.

Obviously segment 1 is the most attractive area for future development.

The threat matrix follows the same pattern:

Probability of occurrence

	High	Low
High	1	2
Low	3	4

Seriousness

- *Segment 1:* A close competitor develops a superior product.
- *Segment 2:* The market is in depression.
- *Segment 3:* Costs escalate.
- *Segment 4:* New legislation affects the design of the existing product/service range.

Here the threats are classified according to their seriousness and probability of occurrence. Contingency plans need to be prepared to meet the threats in segment 1 but those in the corner diagonally opposite are very unlikely to develop so they can be ignored at the present time.

Source: Adapted from Kotler, *Marketing Management*, and from Argenti, *Practical Corporate Planning*

Marketing thought always emphasizes the fact that companies need to understand their customers if they are to survive and succeed in the marketplace. However, in today's fast-moving marketing environment, understanding and analysing the competition is at least as important. When markets are in a growth stage, there may be room enough for all organizations which choose to enter them. But when markets are static or even in decline, as they have been throughout the recession of the 1990s, then the only way to continue to grow, or even to survive at all, will be to take market share away from the competition.

Effective marketing planning can only be carried out in the light of the competitive situation in which the company is operating, but, before this can happen, we need to decide how to view the competitive environment and what we need to know about our competitors. As stated earlier in this unit, we need to think about:

- *Direct competition:* those companies which produce the same products or services and sell them to the same customer groups at the same price levels.

- *Industry competition:* those companies which operate in the same broad product areas but not necessarily in the same market segments.

- *Method competition:* all suppliers of transport might be said to be in competition with each other, whether they are run by agencies like British Rail or whether the need is filled by bicycles or privately owned motor cars.

- *Indirect competition:* all forms of entertainment might be said to be in competition with each other as they all compete for disposable income.

Once areas of competition have been recognized then we need to think about what it is that we need to know about each of the companies involved. For example, we need to know:

- *Who they are:* which companies, where they are located, what products or services they offer, who they offer these to and how they make them available.

- *What strategies they adopt:* which market segments they aim for, what kind of communications mix they use and whether they are market leaders or followers.

- *What their aims appear to be:* do they want to increase market share or move into other markets or market segments?

- *Where their strengths and weaknesses lie:* for example, whether or not they are strongly market orientated or whether they have an innovative R&D function.

- *How they operate in the market:* for example, whether or not they are likely to involve themselves in a price war or whether they deliberately set out to take business away from certain companies.

Industry competition

The issues set out above need to be looked at against the background of the particular industry in which the company is involved. In this case, the term refers to a group of *companies or organizations whose products/services are close substitutes for each other.* For example, there is little real difference between the petrol sold by one company or another, and the petrol industry is one where there is a high level of competition, although it is an area dominated by a few large companies. This is another point to note – that the atmosphere of the competitive environment depends to a large extent on the structure of the industry concerned through the operation of a variety of factors, such as:

- the size of the market;
- whether that market is growing, static or declining;
- the production capacity of the companies already operating in the market;
- the barriers to entry, that is, whether they are high or low, the latter case meaning that there might be new entrants on a frequent basis;
- the state of the market, that is, whether it is steady or volatile;
- the geographical spread of the market, that is, whether it is concentrated or fragmented;
- the level of product differentiation that exists or might be introduced;
- whether or not economies of scale are an attractive proposition;
- whether or not the purchasers of the industry's products are a few large customers.

Market competition

Industry competition, as described above, involves regarding companies which make the same product as yours as your main competitors. However, it is possible to consider the situation from another point of view – that of the market. This approach takes a much wider view of competition through looking at companies which satisfy the same customer need or look after the same customer segments. For example, it is possible to satisfy a desire for foreign holidays either by booking holidays through travel companies, or by buying a house in France, or even by buying a boat which could provide accommodation in a variety of different countries.

Understanding Your Customers

Perhaps the most important environment in which firms operate is their **customer environment** because this is the most basic belief of the marketing orientated company – that the customer is the hub around which the business revolves. Therefore, understanding what makes people in general buy and what makes your customers in particular buy is a vital part of business success. You need to know the following.

- *Who buys (or is likely to buy)?* This information will cover age; sex; occupation; education level; income; leisure interests and activities; type of property lived in and family position – with or without children, newly married or with children who have grown up and left home. In fact, as much information as possible about the lifestyles and potential of customers needs to be amassed and analysed.

It is only through the acquisition of such detailed knowledge that the best matching process between the needs of customers and the ability of the firm to supply suitable products can be attained. In fact, in order to be able to do this sufficiently accurately, markets frequently divide the total market into smaller portions or segments. (The question of market segmentation is dealt with in detail later in this unit.)

- *What do they buy and why do they choose one particular product rather than another?* This is a question which is usually answered through the use of marketing research as part of a process which might include desk research, surveys and focus groups. Why people buy Ariel rather than Bold or Radion is a question of vital importance to the manufacturers of all three products because if they are to produce a successful matching process then they need to know what people buy now and why.

- *Where do they buy?* Many household goods are bought at supermarkets, cameras are likely to be bought from specialist shops and items like bread and milk might be bought from the corner shop.

- *When do they buy?* So far as toys are concerned, over 90 per cent of annual sales are made in the three-month run up to Christmas. Holidays might be booked early to take advantage of special early booking discounts and to get the best choice of hotels and resorts. However, many people choose to book at the last minute, hoping for bargains or simply because they do not like to plan a long way in advance. Garden furniture is likely to be bought early in the summer and bulbs are bought in autumn.

  Many purchases follow this once-a-year pattern, but milk and vegetables may be bought little and often for the sake of freshness, and supermarket shoppers often like to shop on Friday evening so as to leave the weekend free for leisure activities.

  The main pattern here is that the less frequently bought items like holidays or suites of furniture are likely to be significant purchase decisions for most people; therefore, they are likely to spend a long time deciding and shopping around. Purchases of this nature are looked upon as **high-involvement decisions** while purchases of basic items like newspapers, which are usually made almost automatically, are **low-involvement decisions**.

- *Do they always buy the same thing?* Brand loyalty is important in consumer markets and manufacturers put a great deal of effort into creating it.

Models of consumer buying behaviour can be found in Box MKT2.7. These models crystallize the concept of buyer behaviour.

How Buying Decisions are Made   Related.

Marketing people need to understand the processes that their customers go through when making buying decisions. In some cases, as noted above, the decision is an important one because the customer will have to live with

---

BOX MKT2.7

Models of consumer buying behaviour

Mercer's[1] discussion of the behavioural aspects of marketing looks in some detail at a variety of models of consumer behaviour.

- *The Sheth model of family decision making* sets down different psychological preferences of various family members – father, mother and children – and looks at how these come together to produce 'family' decisions. The model also shows seven family and product factors which determine whether a particular purchase will be the result of a joint decision or whether the decision will be made by one person only. The seven factors are: (1) social class; (2) lifestyle; (3) role orientation; (4) stage reached in family lifecycle; (5) the perceived risk involved in the purchase; (6) the importance of the product; (7) the time available for making the decision.

- *The Howard and Sheth model* examines responses to a variety of stimuli as a way of explaining long-term brand choices. These stimuli actually come from the environment and are broken down into three areas: (1) the elements of the brand, such as price; (2) the message delivered by the manufacturer's advertising and promotion; (3) stimuli provided by social groups. Responses to these stimuli are categorized as: attention, comprehension, attitude, intention, purchase behaviour. These stimuli and responses are then linked to a series of hypothetical constructs and variables in an effort to categorize purchase behaviour.

Source:
1 Adapted from Mercer, *Marketing*

---

the consequences of his or her decision for a long time, for example, in the case of a new car, an expensive holiday or a new house. However, whatever the purchase, and whether or not it is one which needs a high-involvement decision, the basic steps are always the same.

The question of need is an interesting one as it is an area which often comes under attack from individuals who are anti-marketing because they believe it encourages and manipulates the public into buying things it neither needs nor wants. The answer lies in Maslow's 'hierarchy of needs'[6] which states that once an individual's basic needs have been met, that is, for food, shelter and security, then he or she is free to develop higher-level needs such as job satisfaction or social success. It is these needs and others like them which are met through the marketing process (see figure 2.3).

Needs can be stimulated either internally or externally. For example, a feeling of hunger can arise simply because it is a long time since the last meal but can also be aroused by the sight of someone standing outside McDonald's eating a hamburger. Once this need is aroused for whatever reason, it becomes a *drive* because the individual concerned feels driven to satisfy that need.

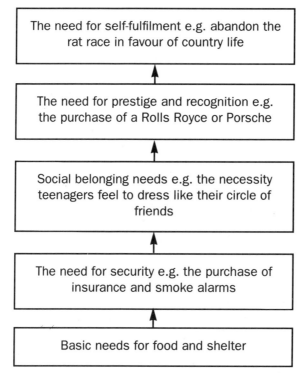

Figure 2.3 The hierarchy of personal needs.

Source: Adapted from Maslow, *Motivation and Personality*.

Marketing people need to understand these drives and which of them it is which leads to the purchase of what product or service. For example, fish and chips might satisfy an immediate physical, or even emotional, hunger but a gourmet meal will be needed to satisfy other drives such as a feeling of 'having arrived' on the social scene or the need to impress a new girl or boy friend.

In the marketing sense, it is often advertising which stimulates the need, and the level of need being approached will influence the contents and the media deemed suitable. For example, the advertising produced by insurance companies and the manufacturers of smoke alarms is homing in on the second-level need for security.

At the other end of the purchase process is the outcome, that is, the result of the search, the weighing of options and the final decision. If the outcome is total satisfaction then the purchase is likely to be repeated although it is likely that some purchasers will be more satisfied than others. However, if the product or service does not live up to expectations by fully satisfying the need then purchase will not be repeated. Indeed, the concept of cognitive dissonance which we develop in the organizational behaviour book in this series will come into effect. Please refer to Box MKT2.8.

BOX MKT2.8

Cognitive dissonance

Buyers need to be satisfied with their purchases, particularly if the purchase represents a high level of expense and involvement, such as a new car. After making purchase decisions of this nature, individuals often start to worry about whether or not they have done the right thing and they begin to look for reassurance.

Leon Festinger[1] coined the phrase 'cognitive dissonance' to describe this state of mind, although he applies it also to decisions other than purchases, for example, the acceptance of a new job. However, so far as marketing people are concerned, the importance of this state of mind lies in the fact that, even after actual purchase has been made, individuals are still receptive to promotional messages.

Buyers are really trying to convince themselves that they made the right purchase decision, so they use advertising for reassurance. They look at advertising for competing products hoping to be convinced that they were right to reject them and they look at advertising for the chosen product in the subconscious hope that it will prove that they made the right decision.

With this in mind some advertising for products like cars is very much aimed at recent purchasers through emphasizing the vehicle's good points and, often, through showing individuals who are delighted with their purchase.

This type of post-purchase activity, which might take the form of advertising or perhaps direct mail, is also important because purchasers who are not convinced of the rightness of their purchase might pass on those feelings to other possible purchasers who are still at the decision-making stage.

Source:
1 Festinger, *A Theory of Cognitive Dissonance*

The Buying Process in Industrial Markets

The obvious difference between industrial or institutional markets and consumer markets is that, instead of purchases being made for individual consumption, they are made from businesses on behalf of other businesses which will use their purchases either directly or indirectly in the production of goods and services for sale to other organizations or individuals. The research findings on industrial buying make intriguing reading, so please turn to Activity MKT2.2 and complete the set task.

The need to understand customers and why they buy is just as important as in consumer markets. Whatever the industry or whether the organization is a manufacturer or a government department, it is still people that we have to sell to and people who make the ultimate buying

ACTIVITY MKT2.2

INDUSTRIAL BUYING

Activity code
✓ Self-development
✓ Teamwork
✓ Communications
✓ Numeracy/IT
✓ Decisions

First read the research findings and then complete the task in around 200 words, in memo format.

The traditional picture of buying is that of consumer purchases having an emotional dimension and industrial (company to company) purchases being based more on rationality.

Pettigrew's[1] study of industrial buying does not live up to this rational and reasoned perspective by the actors. His text illustrates the power dynamics of buying. A classical example is shown by his later empirical study of a competitive bidding scenario concerning the purchase of expensive (£3.5 million) computer equipment which emphasizes two themes:

- the political aspects within the purchasing firm influences the decision to buy or not to buy;
- the 'gatekeeper' interacting between the firm's buying unit and the outside external environment can make the political dimension writ large in the final decision to buy or not to buy.

A form of editing and filtering of information is seen to exist in the activities of the 'gatekeeper'. In turn, these gatekeepers are seen to play key roles not only in evaluating a range of alternatives but in selecting the final supplier.

The relationship between buyer and suppliers cannot only be seen in the frequency and reciprocity of communications; the senior levels of contact prior to and during the decision may be very important. The acceptance of invitations by the buyer to social occasions of the seller may also be indicative of a 'special relationship'.

The positive transmission of information about suppliers between the gatekeeper and his or her own senior management seemed to give a bias to the information supplied.

In spite of technical competence, good products and competitive pricing, other suppliers seemed to be in a different league of the tendering process.

Now that you have studied the main argument of Pettigrew's findings, assume that you are selling into such organizations. What sort of strategies would you adopt in order to be in the running for tenders?

Source:
1 Adapted from Pettigrew, *The Politics of Organisational Decision Making*

decisions. In large organizations there is likely to be a purchasing department or unit where the decisions are made, although, in the case of technical purchases and purchase decisions, specialists are likely to be involved as well. Additionally, in the case of high-involvement decisions like those pertaining to the installation of a new company-wide computer system, board members may also be involved.

At the stage which involves the evaluation of potential suppliers, extensive discussion may take place followed by invitations to certain of them to submit quotations for consideration. The negotiation stage may also be protracted and, in marketing terms, the relationship between seller and purchaser is extremely important. The higher up the decision-making chain it can be established, the better.

We will now move to the process of segmenting markets – industrial or consumer – for most markets need to be classified and broken down in order to be manageable.

The Need to Segment Markets

We have already established that marketing is about understanding customers and working to satisfy their needs. These needs are not satisfied simply by the products or services themselves. The products are a mix of tangible and intangible attributes, much of the latter conveyed by the image of the company so that buying decisions are actually extremely complex.

However, customers are not all alike – they have different tastes and preferences, are at different ages and have different types of lifestyle. This means that they do not all want the same products and services, hence the development of systems for segmenting markets. There are many different methods of segmenting markets and it is important that the right one is chosen. But even before decisions regarding methods of segmentation can be made the question of targeting has to be considered. The chief need of companies is to find a group of potential customers whose needs will be satisfied by offerings which the company is capable of making, whether these are in the form of products or of services.

In marketing terms, this process is known as **targeting** and there are three broad strategies from which to choose:

- *Mass marketing* which involves producing one product for the whole market is also sometimes known as *undifferentiated marketing*. This was the strategy initially adopted by the Coca Cola Company and by Ford in the days of its Model T. This approach to the market involves looking at the similarities between customers rather than the differences, for example, a need for an affordable automobile. However, both companies do now produce different versions of their original product aimed at different customer groups.

- *Selective, or differentiated, marketing* involves aiming at a number of specific market segments through producing a different marketing mix for each one. Most car manufacturers produce a range of models which are aimed at different market segments, for example, from the Ford Fiesta up through the Escort and the Orion to the Mondeo.

- *Niche marketing* means that the company's efforts are all concentrated on one or two small market segments or niches. This is a strategy often adopted by small companies that can operate very successfully on segments which are too small for large companies to bother about.

After having decided which targeting strategy to adopt, companies which have opted for segmentation need to examine the marketing environment, including the competitive environment, as described earlier in this unit, in order to come up with an appropriate form of segmentation. However, as well as the actual type of segmentation to be employed, the chosen segment must be:

- of sufficient size to enable enough products to be sold to allow an acceptable level of profit;

- identifiable, in that its characteristics have to be capable of being differentiated from those of other segments;

- accessible, in that, particularly if the chosen segment is a small one which might be well scattered among the population at large, it must be possible to reach potential customers both through appropriate promotional media and a suitable distribution network.

Types of Segmentation

The first forms of segmentation looked at the tangible attributes of the market while those most recently developed have used more intangible and psychological attributes as a basis for dividing up markets.

- *Geography* covers areas of concentration by region of the country, for example, north or south-east and whether customers are in urban or rural areas.

- *Demographic factors* apply to age, sex, marital status, ethnic group.

- *Socio-economic factors* cover income, social class, level of education, occupation.

- *Psychographic factors* deal with culture, lifestyles, attitudes, personality types.

- *Geo-demographics* deals with a combination of demographic and geographic factors of segmentation. The most often used of these is ACORN (A Classification Of Residential Neighbourhoods) which classifies households according to the type of residential neighbourhood in which they are located.

From this we can see that segmentation is both a *strategy* for approaching markets and a collection of *techniques* for dividing up those markets in such a way as to benefit both the firm and its customers. One set of such techniques is outlined above and the approach used is to divide up customers according to what they are likely to buy. However, there are other ways of approaching the task of producing meaningful market divisions.

Segmentation by level of usage

Here, the emphasis is on the rate of consumption; for example, where beer is concerned, there might be heavy drinkers of beer who always choose it over any other type of alcoholic drink, medium users and occasional drinkers. This approach can also be applied to other markets, such as cars, where some individuals drive thousands of miles every month and might therefore look for different product characteristics than those sought by Sunday drivers. Petrol can also be linked to level of usage.

Benefit segmentation

Here the assumption is that different groups of customers look for different benefits from the products they buy, so that it makes sense to offer products aimed at the benefits so sought.

However, although the system is an attractive one, it is not as clear cut as it might seem. A good deal of in-depth research might actually be needed to ascertain the exact set of benefits looked for by purchasers because it is unlikely that there will be one clear and obvious benefit – it is much more likely to be a bundle of benefits which provides the motivating factor.

In the car market, for example, some purchasers might look primarily for the benefits of fuel economy combined with ease of parking in town, or reliability, while others might be more interested in comfort and speed on the motorway. We believe that benefit segmentation is a useful approach. The two boxes, 'Benefit segmentation' (Box MKT2.9) and 'Lifestyles segmentation: demographics plus' (Box MKT2.10) should be consulted as they contain details of such a 'benefit approach'.

BOX MKT2.9

Benefit segmentation

The rationale behind benefit segmentation is that the individual has specific reasons to buy a product or service and these reasons are tied up with the potential benefits of the purchase.

Haley[1] sees benefit segmentation as a decision-making tool. He argues that the traditional methods of segmentation – geographic, demographic and 'heavy half' based on the assumption that one half of consumers account for 80 per cent of the consumption – are all inadequate as they are *descriptive* in nature and do not seek out causal relationships.

The benefits approach to dividing up the marketplace is seen as *causal*. Segments are based on what people are seeking from the product or service. Thereafter, demography, geography and brand perceptions can be superimposed upon these core segments to build up a fuller, more detailed picture.

It is the total configuration of the benefits that make up a segment as opposed to one benefit differentiating one segment from another. A toothpaste market can be cited:

Benefit characteristic required	Core segments
Flavour/appearance	The sensory types
Brightness of teeth	The sociable types
Decay prevention	The worrying types

and so on.

A basic typology of segments is then forwarded by Haley:

'The status seeker'	Prestige oriented
'The swinger'	Modern/up to date
'The conservative'	Popular/established orientation
'Rational'	Benefits sought, such as durability
'Inner directed'	Self-concept/awareness to the fore
'Hedonist'	Sensory benefits sought

This benefit approach is an embryonic type of lifestyle classification.

Source:
1   Haley, 'Benefit segmentation: a decision-oriented research tool'

BOX MKT2.10

Lifestyles segmentation: demographics plus

Atlas[1] makes use of the 'VALS' concept of segmentation developed at the Stanford Research Institute (SRI International). 'VALS' identifies different segments of the market by *values* and *lifestyles.* The segments are classified by a combination of the aspirations of the group, the products they use and their self-image/self-concept. It is aimed at giving the marketeers an in-depth analysis of how people live, what they buy and the reasons for buying it. As such it combines a demographic base with a psychological type of profile of buyers and can be seen as 'pyschographics'.

The classification scheme is as follows:

Category	Segment
Need-driven	Survivors and sustainers
Inner-directed	'I am me', socially conscious, aware and experimental
Outer-directed	Belongers, emulators and achievers

The *survivors* are a marginal class who may live in dignified squalor. The *sustainers* are a more seedy group with a similar poverty but without the dignity.

The *inner-directed* groups have a greater self-sustaining power than the need-driven groups. The *'I am me'* types are often young and psychologically separated from older generations, still in some stage of rebellion, perhaps, against society. The *socially conscious* group would not adhere to Margaret Thatcher's dictum that there is no such thing as society as they are into social issues and politics. The *experimentals* are perhaps more mature than the 'I am me's' but they still like fun, adventure and excitement.

The *belongers* tend to be more conservative in their approach, identifying with the 'best of America or the best of Britain'. We can see them in middle America or in places like Norfolk, in England. The *emulators* aspire to wealth, greatness and so on and are almost there with one more push, or so they think, while the *achievers* have made it and they are the richest sector of the population.

Hence we have a demographic base, a social class differentiation and 'value' systems coming together to give us a wider vision of 'lifestyles'.

Source:

1   Adapted from Atlas, 'How Madison Avenue knows who you are and what you want – beyond demographics'

Positioning Products and Services in Their Markets

Once the overall approach to the market has been decided and certain market segments selected for targeting, firms still have to decide where to **position** their product in those segments – whether to aim for the centre of the segment, the top or the bottom. Positioning refers to the way that a product is seen by customers and potential customers in relation to other competing products and has a good deal to do with the image created for the product and the company itself.

In the development of a new product, it may be obvious that there is a gap at a particular level in the market and so efforts can be directed towards filling this. This can be done with a 'me too' product which is very similar to the strongest product in that area but significantly cheaper, or, it can be filled with a very different product which will then attract attention because of this. Activity MKT2.3 should now be tackled as this consolidates buyer behaviour in a fluid environment with a product line which can be subject to the fickle whims of consumers.

ACTIVITY MKT2.3

KD DESIGNS

Activity code
- ✓ Self-development
- ☐ Teamwork
- ☐ Communications
- ☐ Numeracy/IT
- ✓ Decisions

KD stands for Kerry Designs. The firm started in Malaysia in 1985. It is a fashion company dealing mainly in smartly designed casual wear, T-shirts and jumpers, with some fashion accessories such as scarves and jewellery. The clothes were designed and sold by Kerry and manufactured to her specifications by a local textile company, ABC textiles. The designs created the uniqueness while the cotton fabric T-shirts and the heavier sweaters were manufactured to a high standard. The only outlet was a market, although it was a 'classy' market on a par with London's Covent Garden.

Kerry, an ex art school student and a designer, at first had difficulty making a living and paying off her initial bankloan of £3,500. Thankfully, ABC textiles were not too pushy and a regular spot on the market was paying dividends. The designs were catching on and rich Western tourists soon began to invade her pitch. The T-shirts had an apparent uniqueness which flattered the wealthy Westerners. The T-shirts were not really unique, but careful merchandising helped to create a feeling of uniqueness, with no two T-shirts of the same type on display at any one time. Spares were kept in the van and could be used to replenish the stock on a half-daily basis. Soon the loan was paid off. Kerry, a tidy-minded artist, was very shrewd and lived quite frugally, preferring to reinvest the profits on building up more varied lines and new products such as belts, jewellery, bangles and earrings – all with her unique artistic eye. Her reputation was going before her.

A mutual friend introduced her to Jo Meade, an experienced marketeer and former financial manager with a multinational firm. The relationship blossomed, and soon they became the best of friends. A partnership was formed and the firm changed its name to KMD. If Kerry had the artistic prowess, Jo complemented her skills with his business acumen and his commitment to the main chance. The firm looked destined for success: the market was there, the skills were there, and both could tap the growing market for smart casual wear. The issues were really: where next, and at what pace should they develop?

The partners were taking stock. There was no doubt that their goods were serving the wants (rather than needs) of their young (under 30s) market. Their whole plan of campaign had been centred on the leisure/smart casual dress of this young affluent group with plenty of purchasing power.

This market was compatible with what the organization's image was all about: 'the young affluent trendy'. It was not quite a mass market, as the designer clothes with the KD label did separate their clothes from others. Increasingly, though, as in the case of trainers and boots, the young looked to labels as a mark of esteem (if not quality) so the label was in effect reaching more of a mass market than the partners would have liked to believe.

Both were ambitious. Both looked for growth. Their total market had clear common denominators. In fact it was a clear segment of the total market-place. Both felt that possible expansion could come from greater segmentation or through a policy of multiple segmentation.

The age-cum-lifecycle of the target audience seemed to be an important factor in the past to the partners in their marketing strategy, so they decided to go down this route and examined other segments based on buying patterns by family lifecycle stage.

A matrix was developed and a commentary was added by the partners to each stage.

Stage 1: 'bachelors' (working)

■ With few financial difficulties and money to burn on playing the mating game and preening themselves, this group had been their target to date.

■ Their lead was often followed by an 'older' group into their 30s if not 40s, striving to keep young.

■ *Plan:* they would continue to target this group.

Stage 2: married/no children

■ Quite well off, enjoying leisure and vacations but spending a lot of money on consumer durables in setting up home.

■ *Plan:* Target this group as their leisure interests and age along with money make them quite close to the first stage.

Stage 3: married/young children under school age

■ Although money is tight, some wives do work and both adults seem to be hooked on advertising.

■ *Plan:* to make a foray into this market; besides, the advertising will help their name. This group may want designer labels for going out to escape domestic drudgery.

Stage 4: married/children at school age

■ This group is better off, as many wives work.

■ *Plan:* perhaps less influenced by advertising but still worth a shot on the same basis as stage 3.

Stage 5: older, married with children

■ Financially stronger with many wives working and spending money on tasteful clothes.

■ *Plan:* Target this section with tasteful advertising in the quality press.

Stage 6: older, married with no children as dependants
- Financially well off. May give gifts to younger adults. Like vacations for themselves.
- *Plan:* 'his' and 'her' designer clothes for the leisure market.

Stage 7: older or retired or solitary survivor
- Little disposable income and should be avoided at all costs.

From this new segmentation strategy the partners began to examine the implications of each strategy in the marketing mix.

1 Assume that KD Designs were to proceed with these plans. Outline the possible effect on these target segments upon the specific marketing mix.
2 Comment critically on their whole policy of segmentation.

Notes
1 Argenti, *Practical Corporate Planning.*
2 Peters and Waterman Jr, *In Search of Excellence.*
3 Hill, *Marketing for BTEC.*
4 Kotler, *Marketing Management.*
5 Ibid.
6 Maslow, *Motivation and Personality.*

Unit Three

Research and Intelligence

Learning Objectives

After completing this unit you should be able to:

- apply the techniques of strategic marketing planning;
- forecast sales over a given period;
- design, and put into operation, a marketing information system;
- understand the design of marketing research programmes;
- apply the generic skills.

Contents

Overview

Why Do We Need Marketing Information?

What is a Marketing Information System?

Why Do We Need a Marketing Information System?

How Do We Work Out What Information We Need?

How Do We Set About Collecting Our Information?

▶ Internal sources of information

▶ External sources of information

Marketing Research

Forecasting

Types of Forecasting Technique

▶ Qualitative techniques

▶ Quantitative techniques (1): time series analysis

▶ Quantitative techniques (2): causal

Marketing Planning

Where Do We Start?

Where Do We Go Next?

Developing Communication Plans

Feedback and Control

Unit Three

❝ 'research' has almost become a dirty word. To many people it smacks of intellectual aloofness; to others it appears the play-thing of arrogant academics; whilst by some it is regarded as a luxury which can seldom be enjoyed just to let boffins pursue fallacious flights of fancy. Some people say that research has no real role therefore, and at worst must be tolerated: it is not the practical way of life.❞

R. Bennett, 'Using Research in Training'[1]

Overview

If marketing is to be successful it must reflect the needs and wants of actual and potential customers. Research is writ large in this process and underpins the whole intelligence and planning systems of marketing. This unit examines the need for marketing information and provides an overview of the available methods of information gathering and forecasting. The tools of research, intelligence and forecasting are then developed which leads us to the concept and practice of marketing planning. (See figure 3.1.)

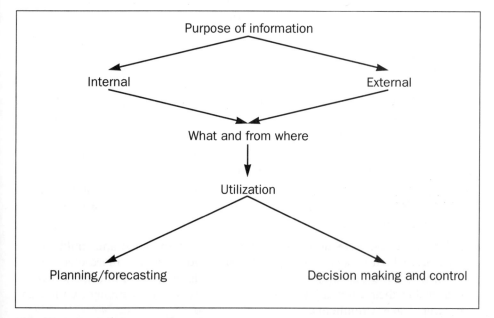

Figure 3.1 Outline diagram of Unit Three.

Why Do We Need Marketing Information?

In the introductory unit of this book, we looked at the fact that marketing orientated organizations are constantly looking outwards into the environments in which they operate, that they need to monitor the activities of their competitors in an ongoing fashion and that they should seek to listen to their customers to make sure that the products or services supplied are still satisfactory and whether, or where, improvements can be made. It is for the satisfaction of these requirements (plus quite a portfolio of others) that we look towards **marketing information systems** and **marketing research**, and it is also here that we begin to cross over from the more traditional marketing approach into the newer disciplines involving the **maintenance of competitive edge** and the development of **total quality management.**

This is also the place where we once again recognize that the adoption of the marketing concept, together with the ongoing goal of providing complete customer satisfaction, is not (or should not) be the province of the marketing department alone but the shared responsibility of every director, manager and employee in the organization. For example, all organizations have, filed away in their accounts departments, a mine of useful information about past and present customers. Invoices give us order quantities and order patterns as well as the geographical spread of our customers and this is information which is not necessarily available from the sales department (if there is one). It makes sense, therefore, for accounts people to be made aware of the value of the information they hold, and, within the confines of their departmental work, to become more proactive in collecting it and making it available.

The gathering of marketing information *should* be an ongoing activity but, even with computerized information banks and networking systems, this philosophy has not been adopted wholeheartedly by many companies. Yet these very developments make it imperative for firms to have up-to-date marketing information available when they make their operating decisions.

The environments in which we live and work are changing faster every year and the markets in which many of us operate are growing geographically larger at the same time. Since the marketing approach to business really began to develop after the Second World War we have moved an astonishingly long way:

■ We have moved from domestic operations to international and multinational activities, which means that our managers need more and more quantities of information and that they also need the specialized types of information which will enable their companies to operate successfully in unfamiliar cultural and geographical environments.

■ Whether we are at home or abroad, we are also operating in marketplaces which are growing increasingly sophisticated. Buyers have many choices to make when they are considering how to spend their disposable income. They have learned to be selective in their decision making and, without good information and research, it becomes increasingly difficult to predict which new products will actually achieve sales of an acceptable level.

■ Markets are also becoming more and more competitive and, as well as competition from the actual products and services, we have to face competition from their advertising, branding and sales promotion activities. We do not only have to supply better products at more acceptable prices, we have to use more effective advertising and give potential customers compelling reasons why they should buy *our* product or use *our* service rather than that of some other company.

What is a Marketing Information System?

As we have already accepted, being marketing orientated means that we look at, and monitor, our operating environment from an outsider's point of view, that is, that of customers and other publics. Having decided that we require information about the changing needs and wants of customers, about new competitive initiatives, about new modes of distribution and so on – how then do we go about collecting and using this information?

We start by installing a marketing information system (MkIS). As defined by Lancaster and Massingham,[2] an MkIS is: 'A system designed to generate and disseminate an orderly flow of pertinent information to marketing managers'. This means that the successful MkIS:

■ stores and integrates information on marketing issues from many sources;

■ disseminates this information to its users;

■ supports marketing decision making in planning and in control;

■ is almost certain to be computerized;

■ is much broader in function and context than marketing research.

In other words, *marketing research* is concerned with the task of gathering information (although it is by no means the only source from which organizations get their information) and the *marketing information system* is concerned with the overall management of the ways in which the flow of information is made available to marketing decision makers. That is, its task is to collect, analyse and evaluate *all* the information that will be of interest to the company when decisions are being made about its strategic and operational activities. This is an important point because information, however much there might be of it, achieves nothing on its own – it must be both relevant and effectively communicated to the people whose job it is to make use of it, that is, the marketing decision makers. In fact, although it is possible to carry out research without having an MkIS, it is *not* possible to have an MkIS without research and it is also vital to remember that the marketing information system is (or should be) just a sub-system of a company's overall management information system.

In its turn, the MkIS has four sub-systems:

(1) *The internal information system.* This is for gathering a variety of data from inside the firm. These data would include:

- orders, plus information about which are the most frequently ordered products and which lines are the most profitable;
- sales, including the most profitable individual customers and the most profitable customer groupings, for example, by geography or by market segment;
- stock levels
- payments received;
- payments outstanding;
- geographical locations of customers.

Much of this internal information is automatically gathered by the accountants who need, for their own purposes, information about both sales and profits, production levels and costs and stock levels. Marketing departments also need this information although their purpose is different. The marketing department needs to know the geographical locations of customers, what delivery patterns have developed or are developing and which product lines are ordered most frequently. They can then highlight ways of improving the marketing effort; for example, knowing the geographical locations of existing customers may show the way towards pinpointing additional potential customers and may also improve the department's targeting procedures. It is also important for the marketing department to discover whether the 'Pareto principle' (or 80/20 rule) applies, that is, whether 20 per cent of the firm's customers actually do provide 80 per cent of its turnover. If this proves to be so then, again, targeting procedures may need to be improved or new market segments investigated.

Computerized record-keeping systems make it reasonably simple for marketing decision makers to receive regular information on sales and profits by customer, by product and by geographical area. This information is then fed into the marketing decision-making system to help with the targeting of advertising and promotion, the planning of the sales effort and the installation of the most economic and advantageous distribution and service systems.

One problem which often surfaces is the fact that marketing and accounts departments need the same information but for different reasons and in different forms. Therefore, when management information systems are installed it should be ensured that the methods used in generating information for accounting purposes also produce the information in a form which is useful to the marketing department. There is no point in introducing a system which needs to generate information twice over – this would be, to say the least, an inefficient use of available resources. An excellent example of this type of immediately available information is that produced by the new generation of electronic tills used in department stores and at supermarket checkouts.

(2) *The marketing intelligence system.* This is another sub-system. It is a set of procedures and sources used by marketing managers to gather everyday information about relevant developments in their marketing environment, for example, a subscription to a press-cuttings service will provide information about competitive activity. Marketing intelligence comes from outside the organization rather than inside it.

Many larger companies operate a library system with full-time staff engaged in monitoring the organization's wider environment – both far and near. Much of this information comes from published sources such as:

- stock market reports;
- national press;
- financial press;
- bank reports;
- reports published by trade associations;
- government publications;
- academic research;
- annual company reports;
- appropriate trade magazines;
- competitors' publicity material;
- retailers and wholesalers who stock and sell competitive products.

All this information, when gathered regularly over a long period, should show up trends in the company's environment, for example, a move from eating red meat to chicken, or a change in the pattern of outlets selling car accessories from specialist shops to supermarkets. Although the information gathered through this process is not specific to the company which is collecting it, it is a vital part of the decision-making process because it provides the background against which company-specific strategic and operational plans are made.

In this area of marketing intelligence, it is also vital for the marketing department to be in close touch with the field sales force (when there is one) as their reports can be a very useful source of information about competitive activity. It is, for example, possible that sales people may hear directly from customers some criticism of the company, its products or its delivery schedule. This information would probably not reach the marketing department in any other way.

(3) *The marketing research system.* This is a sub-system which involves:

- the design of marketing research projects and surveys;
- the collection of data;
- the analysis of data;
- the reporting of findings relevant to a specific marketing situation which is being faced by the company.

The information gathered through both internal systems and the external marketing intelligence system should provide the basis for all of the company's marketing research (MR) activities. It should be possible to complete much of the desk research which will be the first stage of any MR project in the MkIS library. The word 'library' sounds very grand and, in large multinational corporations, it might actually be so; however, it is still possible for small organizations to have a similar system through the use of box files and a book, or books, with press cuttings pasted into them.

Marketing research (which is dealt with fully in the coming section) covers the following areas:

- new product, or service, investigation;
- levels of satisfaction produced by existing products or services;
- research into the effectiveness of past advertising campaigns and on the likely effectiveness of new ones;
- packaging research;
- pricing research;
- branding research;
- research into competitive activity.

(4) *The analytical marketing system.* This is the last of the four sub-systems. It is a system for analysing marketing data using statistical procedures and mathematical models. Again, in large organizations, this system is likely to be computerized. However, it is still possible for small organizations which do not have the use of sophisticated technology to perform this task. For example, sales forecasting can be tackled through the use of some of the techniques explained in later sections of this unit.

With these four units organized and in place and their efforts assimilated, the activities involved in a company's marketing information system should fit together as shown in figure 3.2.

Why Do We Need a Marketing Information System?

The purpose of a marketing information system is to collect, analyse and evaluate *all* the information that is likely to be of value when making

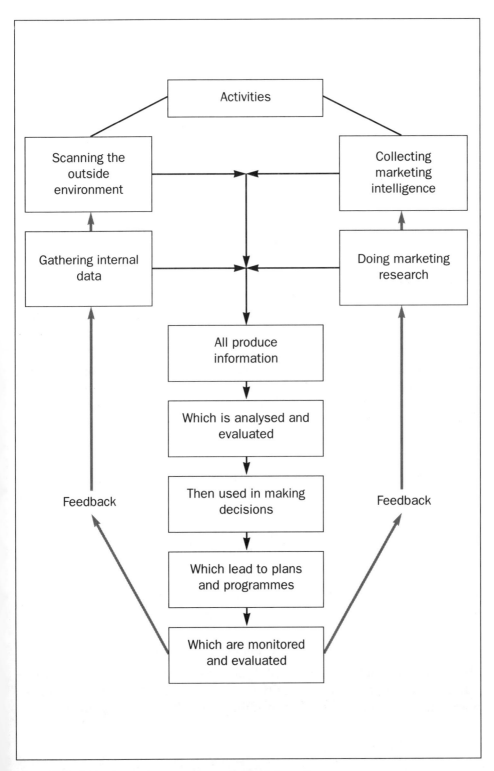

Figure 3.2 Gathering and processing marketing information.

decisions about *all* of a company's activities, in both the short and the long term. Its overall role then, is to integrate the diverse sources of information which are used and to give the decision makers more information, faster. This means that the information system stands between company decision makers and the environment in which they operate. It is not just the marketing department which needs information from the marketing environment, it is also the R&D department, the production department and the main board. This is because, in order to plan successfully for its future, the company must find the best available opportunities and must then continually monitor its progress in taking advantage of them. Additionally, the MkIS helps the company to anticipate changes rather than simply to react to them and, in the long term, the company which has the greatest understanding of its particular market sector(s) is likely to have the greatest competitive advantage.

Some companies do not have a formal system, although the larger the company, the more complex the system is likely to be. Even the proprietor of a small firm makes decisions based on the things going on in the world around his or her company. There may, however, be no conscious awareness of that fact and no formal attempt either to maintain an MkIS or to operate the company in a marketing-based fashion. It has to be accepted that, as companies grow larger and markets grow more dynamic, there is a positive need for a formal, proactive, system to be implemented so that management is kept constantly informed about what is going on in areas likely to affect its operational and decision-making processes.

Accurate marketing information will enable companies to do the following:

- Recognize developing trends more quickly than their competitors.
- Evaluate marketing action and planning more thoroughly, that is, it will help them to check the results of their decisions and activities.
- Integrate information for central planning purposes. This type of planning is an activity which is essential for successful strategy development.

Within the firm, the big issues are likely to be as follows:

- Who is going to decide what information we collect (and what we do not)?
- How do we know which pieces of the information gathered we actually need to take notice of?
- How can we make sure the information we receive is objective?

However, one thing that it is vital to remember is that the marketing-information system cannot actually make the decisions for us – ultimately, marketing decisions are the responsibility of marketing management.

How Do We Work Out What Information We Need?

What we want is to make sure that we are building a successful organization (however we choose to define success, and how we do this will ultimately depend on what type of organization we are involved with, for example, whether it is profit making or non-profit making). Therefore, the information we need is that which will help us to achieve this objective. It must help us to identify market opportunities, to find gaps both in the market and in the product/service portfolios of our competitors which we are then able to exploit and it must also help us to check up on the progress we are making in our efforts to take advantage of those opportunities.

The precise details of the information needed will vary according to the type of organization, the type of product/service and the type of market(s) we are operating in. However, whatever the exact details turn out to be, what we are trying to gain is a better and more effective understanding of our particular market sector than that achieved by our competitors – and we want to gain it faster!

According to West,[3] the most vital issues within the marketing information context are what he terms the 'six Os of marketing':

- **Occupants**. Who are the potential customers?
- **Objects**. What do they currently buy?
- **Objectives**. Why do they currently buy what they buy?
- **Organization**. Do consumers influence each other in the purchase decision and, if so, how?
- **Occasions**. When do they buy?
- **Operations**. Where do they buy?

If we look at every information-gathering problem under each of these six headings then we will find ourselves well on the way to knowing what kind of information we need. Each of these headings is a very wide one, so what we need to do is to consider each of them in turn, then, using the broad heading as a guide, begin to define our information needs in a very specific way. For example, under 'Where do they buy?' we might need to ask:

- Do they buy through retailers?
- If so, where are these retailers situated?
- How many of these outlets are there?
- Do all manufacturers of the same product sell in the same way?

When defining our specific information needs it may be necessary to involve other departments within our organization, for example, production, distribution, R&D, accounts.

According to Kotler: 'The company's marketing information system should represent a cross between what managers **think** they need, what

---

ACTIVITY MKT3.1

MARKETING INFORMATION NEEDS

Activity code
- ✓ Self-development
- ✓ Teamwork
- ☐ Communications
- ☐ Numeracy/IT
- ✓ Decisions

Your role is to construct a questionnaire (by individual effort or through a team) to determine marketing information needs for a medium-sized firm. Bear in mind that we gather information not for its own sake but to help us make informed decisions.

---

managers **really** need and what is **economically feasible**.'[4] Please now tackle the Activity MKT 3.1.

Once decisions have been made about what information is actually required, it will then be gathered on a regular basis, so that it can form the nucleus of the organization's ongoing information-gathering activities. But other additional information will have to be gathered from time to time in order to help with the solving of specific problems, for example, with the development and launch of a new product where specific research will need to be carried out.

Whatever information we eventually decide needs to be gathered, we must make sure that:

- We are able to develop sources from which to obtain the information, both internal and external.

- We create a system which will allow us to produce comparative analyses so that these can be fed into the decision-making process (see figure 3.3).

We may, therefore, have a basic MkIS which feeds in information on an ongoing basis according to long-term decisions made internally. On the other hand, it will be necessary from time to time to generate specific information to solve a specific problem, for example, to discover the reasons for the disappointing performance of a new product or a sudden dive in the sales of an established one.

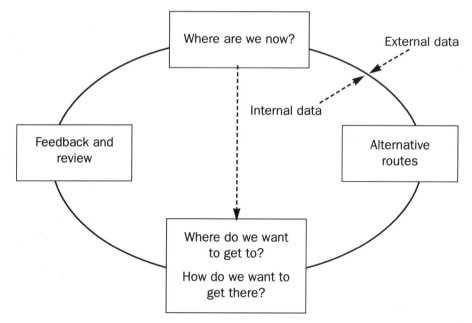

Figure 3.3 Information gathering and decision making as an iterative process.

Source: Adapted from West, *Understanding Marketing*.

How Do We Set About Collecting Our Information?

As we have already seen (pp. 74–6), there are two broad sources of marketing information:

■ that which we can find inside the organization and which is often already available;

■ that which comes from outside.

It is under the second heading that we find the actual activities which are known as marketing research and which are dealt with in the next section of this text.

Again, as seen previously (p. 74) the internal data are usually gathered for purposes other than those of the marketing department, for example, product development costs/delivery schedules/stock levels. What is needed in this case is the development of an internal system which will generate information which can be used for marketing purposes. This will have to be done in a co-operative fashion and will have to involve heads of department other than marketing. However, computer-based systems can make this task comparatively easy these days, once the basic computer system is available.

Internal sources of information

When properly organized, these can provide information which is vital to the marketing department. For example, order processing and invoicing data should be the basis for the provision of accurate sales data broken down by product, type of customer (for example, by size, industry and profile) and by geographical spread. This information is likely to be computerized anyway so that it should often be easily available at any time from an organizational computer network.

Reports from members of a company's field sales force (or, in the case of a voluntary organization or charity, these may come from fund raisers) can feed valuable information into the marketing system. They may well produce numerical information, such as a customer's ordering intentions for the coming year but they also produce qualitative details. The sales person will have actually *spoken* to the customer and most likely visited his or her office or factory, and the information gained may cover product satisfaction levels/how busy the customer's premises seemed to be/the fact that a competitor's van was seen in the car park. However, if members of the sales force are to bring back the right kind of information then it may be necessary to provide appropriate training.

External sources of information

These begin to move further towards the realms of marketing research, desk research in particular. However, the ongoing information fed into the MkIS may come from an ongoing **environmental scan**. Sources of such environmental information are listed on p. 75, where, for example, subscribing to appropriate press-cuttings services is suggested. Other sources of environmental data are trade or professional magazines as well as the business sections of daily and Sunday newspapers. Annual reports are an additional source of useful information.

If one works for a large international corporation then it may be possible to have the advantage of an internal library system with skilled librarians who gather and file useful information; if one is not in this enviable position then it may be that all the staff in the marketing department look out for, and pool, relevant information.

In addition to this ongoing gathering of data and marketing intelligence, it will be necessary to make specific searches when special projects are under way, for example, when new products are being developed. This is where we come to desk research and move firmly into the overall area of marketing research.

Marketing Research

As we have already seen, marketing research is part of our overall marketing information system. Some information like that from retail audits, may be gathered on an ongoing basis, other information is gathered as part of a specific project. This section of the present text takes a broad overview of marketing research and its uses in the information-gathering, forecasting and planning tasks of marketing management. The detailed aspects of

ACTIVITY MKT3.2

MARKETING RESEARCH

Activity code
- [ ] Self-development
- [ ] Teamwork
- [ ] Communications
- [ ] Numeracy/IT
- [ ] Decisions

The work of D. Warren Twedt has been adapted below. The study, although some years old, gives us a feel for American organizations and their activities in marketing research. The importance by the firms of the respective research activity can be seen in the percentage engaged in a given activity. Your role is to give a ranking from 10 (low) to 100 (high) on each of these selected items. So if you think that less than 10 per cent would be involved in a given activity, enter 10, and so on. Your answers can be compared to the actual results in the handbook.

Category	Activity	Approximate % involved
Corporate research	Forecasting (up to 1 year)	
	Business trends (study of)	
	Pricing issues	
	Acquisition studies	
Products	New products (potential etc.)	
	Competitive products	
	Packaging (e.g. design)	
Advertising etc.	Motivation research	
	Media	
	Advertising effectiveness	
Sales and market	Potential features of sales	
	Test marketing	
	Consumer panels	
	Share of	

Source: Adapted from Warren Twedt, *Survey of Marketing Research*

BOX MKT3.1

Research: decision type and research design

Luck et al.[1] distinguish three main types of research: opportunity, alternatives and decisions. That is, the opportunity research looks to a tentative decision after searching through the problems and constraints. The alternative-seeking research looks for options while the decision-oriented approach looks to a more conclusive evaluation.

The authors' criteria for the selection of a design method, albeit descriptive, as in a longitudinal study, or experimental, as in a pre-test/post-test scenario, are based on the following:

- **Time**. Time pressures mitigating against over-elaborate research.
- **Cost**. Cost dimensions to be balanced with research rigour and the use of the outcomes.
- **Secrecy**. The competition must not know about the new product or service.
- **Validity and reliability**. The 'experiment' must meet the hypothesis and be capable of being duplicated elsewhere.

Source:
1   Adapted from Luck et al., Marketing Research

---

research planning and the techniques involved in carrying it out are the subject of a separate text in this series (*Effective Market Research*).[5] The Activity MKT 3.2 should now be tackled as it gives an overview of the value of market intelligence to the whole process of marketing.

Research can be classified into the traditional divisions of 'desk' and 'field'. This is a useful device to understand the research process. However, the *type* of research itself must first be examined before we embark on this desk/field categorization. Please refer to Box MKT 3.1.

Marketing research is often something which is not tackled by companies themselves; rather it is carried out on their behalf by specialist research agencies, particularly where primary research is concerned (see figure 3.4). Traditionally, the two broad areas of marketing research are:

1 *Desk research*. This gathers data from secondary sources.

2 *Field research*. This gathers data from primary sources.

Desk research has usually been sub-divided into internal sources (information available inside the organization) and external sources (information gathered from outside the organization). With the introduction and increasing popularity (and sophistication) of the MkIS, more and more useful data should be moving towards the marketing department on an ongoing basis. This means that, hopefully, it should less often be necessary, for example, for someone to have to sit down in the accounts department and go through their records. However, it may well

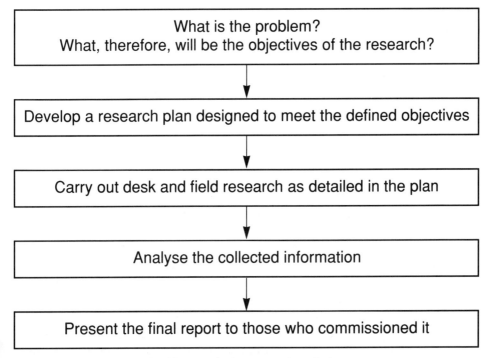

Figure 3.4 The steps involved in a marketing research project.

Source: Adapted from Kotler, *Marketing Management.*

be necessary to search for internal information in this way if the MkIS is still in embryo stage or if a special project is under way.

The details of gathering information from internal sources have been dealt with in the previous section on marketing information systems. West[6] tells us that surveys of the research carried out by companies show that those using research most frequently are the ones that rely most on internal data. For example the amount of information produced by the new generations of electronic tills in the retail trade provide continuous up-to-date information on what is selling and what is not. He further says that one survey of company research in the United States put the reasons for carrying out research into a series of categories which, in descending order of frequency of use, are reproduced below:

1 Determining the nature of the company's customers.
2 Monitoring the level of profitability on a product-by-product basis.
3 Evaluating and directing the sales force.
4 Evaluating distribution and other potential cost savings in the level of stocks.
5 Providing forecasting information. (Methods of forecasting are dealt with in detail in the next section of this text.)
6 Estimating the competitive position of the company's products.
7 Analysing the size of the market.

8 Economic research.

9 Measuring the acceptability of new products.

10 Comparing competitive products.

In a marketing text it is reassuring to find that the most frequently used area of research is that which is looking at the nature of customers. However, we are not told if the level of customer satisfaction is also investigated.

Desk research is based on published data, in whatever form the information is available, the limiting factor being that this has been gathered by some other organization for some other purpose and is second-hand. This also means that we may not know exactly what the purpose of the original data-collection exercise was, nor may we know under exactly what conditions it was gathered. The amount of information available from secondary sources is increasing – governments are gathering a great deal of information every year which is of interest to marketing people. In addition, the number of commercial databases is rising.

Although there is a vast amount of information available, the most difficult part of desk research is actually finding *relevant* information. Often when we start off on one of these projects (no matter how tightly the research plan has been drawn) we do not know what we are likely to come up with, or where we are likely to find it. Doing desk research is certainly one of the least glamorous activities associated with marketing. However, it is sensible to make the best possible use of information available already, even for no other reason than that it saves the time and expense involved in collecting it again!

Desk research is a valuable first step in any research project and it is the gaps left in the company's knowledge of the situation being investigated after it has been completed which determine the level and scope of field research projects. Research is carried out in all areas of the marketing mix: that is, research is carried out on products, on pricing, on distribution and on the effectiveness or otherwise of promotional campaigns. In addition, the level and success of competitive activity is investigated together with analyses of market size and composition.

Field research itself can be divided into three areas of activity:

1 *Observation.* This is often carried out by hidden cameras in supermarkets.

2 *Quantitative research.* This involves estimates of market size, turnover of merchandise in supermarkets, and is often carried out through syndicated systems like retail audits and consumer panels.

3 *Qualitative research.* This kind uses open-ended methods like depth interviews and group discussions to tease out attitudes towards products, services and shopping in general.

Box MKT3.2 gives an overview of a range of techniques open to the marketeer while an intriguing method of research is contained in Box MKT3.3.

BOX MKT3.2

Research methods

Secondary data have been collected by others and may not meet your purpose. Such research provides a context, though, and 'internal' records/information systems can be used – from accounting data and sales analysis to the reports of your sales teams. External records and published research from government records to journals to specialist trade reports can also be tapped. However, primary data will be required if you wish to study a particular question. A comment is made on some of the methods below, all of which are based on some survey format so the survey has to be statistically valid.

Type	Plus	Minus
Observation e.g. in a retail outlet	■ Useful for studying consumers 'at work' ■ May help future design/packaging ■ 'Objective' if formal record is maintained and observer is trained	■ Expensive ■ Is the information representative? ■ No personal rapport ■ Current behaviour (not past or proposed) is stated
Personal interview e.g. usually a structured format	■ Rapport established ■ Any 'resistance' can be overcome by skilled interviewer ■ Sample limits can be controlled, e.g. age/sex etc. can be monitored ■ Useful for small(ish) sample ■ Good for 'fact' gathering	■ Expensive and time-consuming ■ Subjectivity of interviewer ■ Time pressures ■ Questions must be limited owing to time pressures ■ Geographical limits of interview
Telephone interview	■ Cheap, although dearer than mailing ■ Good response rate in time available ■ Difficult issues can be probed ■ Anonymous ■ Less inhibiting than fact-to-face methods, so good for attitudes/views	■ Phone can be put down ■ Limited information re timescale ■ No observation possible

Type	Plus	Minus
Postal questionnaire Design is important, e.g. pre-coded or free response	■ Cheap ■ Good potential coverage ■ Anonymous (if not pre-coded beforehand) ■ Some thought into the questions is possible ■ Speedy response (see rate of return, though) ■ No interview bias so, if properly constructed, should be objective ■ Good for industrial markets where potential sample may be too busy to interview (but see response rate)	■ Response rate is low ■ Long questionnaires tend to be ignored ■ No control over the respondents ■ No observation possible ■ Updated mailing lists can be problematic ■ Information (e.g. scales used) may be limited ■ Is the willing respondent typical? ■ Omissions
Panels Permanent 'standing' group used, particularly in consumer research, perhaps under-utilized in industrial research	■ Highlights trends, e.g. attitudes ■ Continuous/ongoing awareness of the market and any changes ■ Members learn procedure so cuts down time (but see 'sophistication' opposite)	■ Panel becomes too 'sophisticated' so expectations are not typical ■ Panel members may be difficult to replace with a similarly representative person

---

BOX MKT3.3

Groups and research

Perhaps discussions with groups can be used as a tool of market research. A wide range of ideas, a creative synergy, spontaneity and a free flow of information may result.

Yet standardization, group awareness of being observed, smallish samples which may not be representative and 'group think' amongst the team of respondents may lead to a biased result.

Perhaps with strong planning, statistical sampling and good chairing and observing skills, some of the negative factors may be reduced or minimized.

Yet the followers accepting the lead of the formal or informal leader can cause difficulties in a potentially constructive marketing tool.

Forecasting

In order to plan for the successful development of our company in the future, we need to be able to predict sales as accurately as possible and also determine which new products or services will be actively accepted by the market in the first place. Most of the available detailed forecasting techniques concentrate on company sales forecasts, several of which include marketing research activities. However, the company's system of forecasting really needs to start much further back than this.

Philip Kotler[7] recommends a three-stage forecasting process and, looking at this, we can see that it links in very satisfactorily with much of the data which will have been produced by our marketing information system. Kotler's process covers:

1 *An environmental forecast* including, for example:

  (a) projections of inflation;

  (b) unemployment levels;

  (c) interest rates;

  (d) trends in consumer spending and saving;

  (e) government expenditure;

  (f) net exports.

  This should already form part of the data gathered in by the company's marketing intelligence system through its ongoing scan of the far environment.

2 *An industry forecast* covering, for example:

  (a) competitive activity;

  (b) general sales patterns;

  (c) general trends in spending in the market area being examined;

  (d) companies entering or leaving the market.

  Again, this can be linked with the ongoing scan of the near environment which should form part of the marketing intelligence system already in operation.

3 *A company sales forecast* using a selection of the available techniques which will be reviewed in the next part of this unit and might well include a test marketing operation.

From projected industry sales produced in the second phase of the forecasting process outlined above, it should be possible to develop a **sales potential forecast** for the company. By *potential* sales, we mean the absolute upper limit which is likely. It is then necessary to develop sales forecasts for individual products or markets by attempting to determine what share of its market each is likely to be able to take. Projected levels of advertising and promotion will also be taken into account during this calculation, including such information about competitive activity as it has been possible to obtain.

As well as involving ourselves in this three-level process of forecasting, we need to be looking additionally at three different timescales:

1 *Short-term:* for up to approximately three to twelve months ahead. These short-term forecasts concern themselves mainly with tactical planning, for example, dealing with the problems of seasonality or for production planning purposes.

2 *Medium-term:* a period which might cover from one up to three years depending on the products and the industry in which the company operates. One-year forecasts are made mainly for financial budgeting reasons and are the start of the company's planning process. This medium-term forecast might also be used for projecting the likely staffing and production levels which will be necessary if enough goods are to be made to meet the anticipated level of sales. Plant and machinery requirements would also be included.

3 *Long-term:* which might be five, ten or even twenty years ahead. These longer-term forecasts are intended to help the company make major strategic decisions. The definition of 'long-term' is again decided by the type of market in which the company operates. For example, for companies involved in high-tech markets, long-term is likely to be less than five years because of the speed of technological change in that area, while fine malt whisky, which takes ten years to produce, would hardly look on even twenty years as long-term.

Whatever the period involved, forecasting is, or should be, the start of the company's planning process. One of the problems often encountered at this stage is the fact that, historically, planning has often been seen as an accounting function, and so it might be – so far as budgeting is concerned. Budgets are usually prepared for the financial year ahead, which is seen as a short- to medium-term forecast, and it often does make sense for the accountants to produce these.

However, if the company is to get the largest possible slice of its potential market, then it should be the marketing department which forecasts the likely level of sales. In practice, once the company reaches a situation where it is looking at new markets and/or new products then the marketing department *has* to be involved.

If forecasting is the first stage in a company's planning process then it follows that, before it is able to plan, it must first forecast. Ideally, the forecast will reduce uncertainty, and thus the planning will be more accurate. However, even with the use of all the mathematical techniques available, forecasting is not an exact science and forecasts have been known to be wrong. Therefore, we need to make sure that our forecasting is as accurate as possible and this is where the specialized techniques of forecasting come in.

Types of Forecasting Technique

Sales forecasting techniques may be either **qualitative** or **quantitative** in type and, as the name suggests, the first is made up of more subjective methods which often rely heavily on the opinion of the person or persons making the forecast. However, these techniques do assume that the opinions expressed are based upon the accumulated experience of the individual expressing them so that they still should be very much worth taking notice of. Quantitative or mathematical techniques are becoming more popular as it becomes increasingly easy to purchase computer software to handle this type of work. The actual mathematical techniques are again divided – into what are known as **causal** techniques and as **time series analysis**.

Qualitative techniques

In many cases the use of these techniques is the first stage in the forecasting process, in the same way that desk research is performed as the first part of the overall marketing research process. They may be in the process of losing out to sophisticated computer-aided techniques, but they still produce valuable information to be used as part of the overall forecasting process and they are exceptionally valuable to smaller firms which may not be making use of the most up-to-date technology.

1 *Market research.* This involves using field research surveys to ask existing and potential customers about their purchasing intentions for the period for which the forecast is desired. One of the main disadvantages of this method is the fact that what customers say they are going to do and what they actually do may be two very different things! In the case of industrial products, these surveys are often carried out by the field sales force, with mixed results. Customers may be willing to tell a sales rep what their likely levels of purchasing will be during the coming year but it is unlikely that they will actually say how these purchases are to be divided up among the list of their suppliers. Additionally, the estimates of the purchasing officers themselves may well be on the subjective side.

   Naturally, in the case of consumer products, it is not possible to use the company's own sales force unless they call on retailers and find out something of these retailers' intentions for the coming year, although this is probably unlikely. In this case, the questions must be put directly to the consumers themselves. Purchase intentions, rates of consumption and strength of brand loyalty are some of the types of information which can be obtained from consumer surveys and panels.

   On the basis of replies to questions about buying intentions, a quantitative picture of likely demand can be formed. So long as the sample has been drawn effectively through the use of the correct sampling techniques, then the resulting forecast may be quite accurate.

2 *The Delphi technique.* This technique, developed by the Rand Corporation in America, attempts to channel expert opinion into objectivity through the use of questionnaires. Members of the chosen panel have no contact with each other and are, in fact, even unaware of the composition of the panel which may contain twenty or so members and is usually made up of people from outside the organization doing the forecasting. The group convenor analyses the

questionnaires and then asks panel members whose opinions differ substantially from those of the others to justify their opinions.

There may actually be several rounds of questionnaires. After each round, the panel leader circulates its results together with another questionnaire which is structured so as to refine the focus more sharply. These rounds of questionnaires continue until sufficient information is elicited to enable the company to make production and marketing decisions.

This structure eliminates the chance of stronger or more authoritative panel members influencing the others but it is more useful when making long-term strategic decisions than for short-term operational forecasting and planning. This is because it is not sufficiently exact to be useful in short-term decision making.

3 *Jury of executive opinion.* This method uses a committee of experts from both inside and outside the company, but who are all experts on the particular industry being examined. As a committee they are asked to deal with topics such as estimates of market size and sales for several years into the future. They then try to reach a consensus. This method combines historical data with experienced judgement in an effort to reach informed decisions, but it makes no real allowance for environmental changes.

One of the most basic precepts in this method of forecasting is that, before the committee meets, each member must have prepared a personal forecast and must come along to the meeting prepared to support that opinion through the production of hard evidence. It is hoped that, through discussion, a consensus will be reached.

This is a 'top-down' method of forecasting in that projections are first made for the industry as a whole, then an estimate is made of how sales will be broken down among the companies active in that industry. It has the drawback that sales are not estimated from hard market data but from opinions about the industry as a whole. This method of forecasting is sometimes known as the 'market breakdown' technique.

4 *Market build-up technique.* This method uses an approach which is opposite to that of the jury method. In this case, the firm gathers information on a few specific market segments and then builds up this information to form a picture of the market as a whole. The segments used may be built upon geographical areas, age, sex or other demographic features. For instance, a firm which makes a soft drink may know that its main sales come from young people who look on it as a refreshment and from people over thirty who use it as a mixer with alcoholic drinks. The firm may therefore first estimate potential sales for each of these segments and then add them together.

5 *Market share analysis.* This starts with the assumption that market share will remain constant. Then, if the assumption is made that the whole market will grow by, say 5 per cent over the next three years then it is assumed that sales will grow by 5 per cent over the same period. The main drawback of this method is that it does not allow for environmental changes, nor does it allow for changing levels (and effectiveness) of advertising and promotion by both the firm and its competitors.

6 *Basic trend analysis.* In this case, managers within the firm examine historical data, primarily sales figures, and use this to project future sales. Again, one of the problems with this technique is that it ignores the possibility of environmental changes such as economic conditions, competitive strategies and the development of new consumer tastes.

7 *Barometric techniques.* Again, this involves the examination of past trends as a means of predicting the future. This method was developed by an American, John Naisbitt, who identified ten 'megatrends' which could be used for forecasting. His company receives six thousand newspapers each month then, from these, cuttings are taken and classified under subject headings. These categories are then analysed according to frequency of appearance and future trends are predicted according to the data thus gained. In this way, trends are used as a barometer of what is to come.

8 *Scenario analysis.* In this case researchers try to produce a subjective picture of several differing possible futures. For instance, what often happens is that attempts are made to produce three different pictures of the future – one which is neutral, one which is pessimistic and one which is optimistic. In this method, the internal aspects of the firm remain constant. Its main use is in the development of contingency plans as part of the strategic planning process.

9 *Estimates produced by the sales force.* This has many points of similarity with the jury of expert opinion method outlined above except that it adopts a 'bottom-up' approach. Sales people are asked to make informed estimates of sales in their own territories during the coming year. These forecasts are then agreed with the sales manager and/or sales director and all estimates are aggregated in order to produce a total estimate for the coming sales period.

It is assumed that, as sales people have regular contact with customers, they will be aware of their wants and needs. They may also have some idea of what effect competitive activity is likely to have on sales. As with all other methods, this one has its limitations. For example, the sales people may not be aware of coming changes in competitive activity or fully aware of changes in the wider environment. However, this is a very inexpensive method to use and it can provide some valuable information which may not surface elsewhere.

An additional problem which may be encountered when using this method is that these estimates are often used when setting sales targets for the coming year. Therefore, for financial reasons, sales people may be tempted to set their estimates too low, a fact which could have implications when production levels are set.

10 *Bayesian decision theory.* This technique, first developed in the eighteenth century by an English clergyman, combines both subjective and objective material. Complicated to apply, it involves the use of a network diagram similar to those used in critical path analysis but here the forecaster estimates a probability for each event in the network. The levels of probability given to each event depend on the strength of the forecaster's opinion about them, which is where the subjectiveness of the technique comes in. This method is often ignored by forecasting experts because of the levels of subjectivity involved in plotting probabilities but it does have its uses however as, very often in forecasting, the actual probabilities may not be known.

11 *Test marketing and product testing.* Sometimes there may be no historical data on which to base forecasts and projections. This is obviously the case where a new product is involved. In these situations test marketing programmes are often carried out as they involve putting the product on sale in a series of carefully selected outlets. In the UK this usually takes place in a specific TV area. Test marketing is often the very last stage in the research process before the product actually goes fully on sale. Sales during the test are carefully recorded then they are grossed up to give a forecast for the whole of the intended market area.

New Product

This method of forecasting can, of course, only be used in the case of either completely new products or those which have been substantially modified. It is also possible that the product's largest attraction is that of novelty which means that early sales may not actually be maintained in the longer term.

Quantitative techniques (1): time series analysis

1 *Moving averages.* This is a mathematical method which allows the forecaster to even out some of the fluctuations caused, for example, where sales have a high level of seasonality. The method used is to combine sales for a year or two years, adding current months and removing sales which occur outside the chosen time period. This system, which appears complicated at first glance, is actually easy to apply and it is also quite accurate over short periods of time (see figure 3.5).

2 *Exponential smoothing.* Where there might be rapid changes in the levels of sales, recent events will be much more important in explaining the near future than sales of one or two years ago. This is one of the drawbacks of the moving averages technique which can be overcome through the introduction of a smoothing constant which gives greater importance to the more recent sales figures. The skill involved lies in the forecaster's ability to judge which parts of the time series are most typical of what is likely to happen in the future. For true success, this technique needs the use of a computer.

3 *Time series analysis.* The sales figures over a particular period will fluctuate, but underneath this there is a trend which the forecaster is attempting to find. Time series analysis examines the seasonal ebb and flow of sales in terms of the amount by which they deviate from the average trend and then adds them back into the forecast once the trend has been established.

These methods really need computer assistance, particularly if a variety of figures is to be examined. Lotus 1–2–3 is an ideal tool for work of this nature.

Month	1	2	3	4	5	6	7	8	9	10	11	12
Sales ('000)	10	12	9	11	10	8	11	10	12	14	18	18
3 months' moving average				10	11	10	10	10	11	12	15	17
6 months' moving average							10	10	10	10	11	12

Figure 3.5 An example of moving averages; figures are rounded to the nearest whole number.

Quantitative techniques (2): causal

1 *Leading indicators.* Here, we use the technique of linear regression to establish a relationship between an established measurable observation and what has to be forecasted. For example, there may well be a relationship between rising levels of unemployment and the UK demand for holidays both at home and abroad.

This technique really needs a computer if it is to be applied successfully, but it is not difficult to illustrate how it might work. For example, the level of sales of children's clothes will depend upon the size of the child population and, ultimately, on the birth rate. Therefore a manufacturer of children's clothes would use birth statistics as a leading indicator.

2 *Simulation.* This technique depends heavily on computer modelling for its application, instead of using leading indicators in an effort to produce a useful forecast it uses trial and error (or iteration) in order to arrive at the forecasting relationship.

Please now refer to Activity MKT3.3.

The sales forecast is thus the stage before the planning process can begin and, as competition continues to increase, companies have to fight harder to maintain their level of competitive edge which, in turn, means that their forecasting methods have to be as accurate as possible. In general, it is extremely unwise for a company to rely only on one method of forecasting when attempting to predict future sales levels. All forecasting techniques have their strengths and weaknesses. Many firms therefore use several techniques simultaneously. If they do this and all the results produced are similar then greater confidence can be placed in these forecasts. However, if the use of several different techniques produces an inconsistent forecast then the company needs to check both the assumptions it has made and the accuracy of its data.

ACTIVITY MKT3.3

FORECASTING

Activity code
- ✓ Self-development
- ☐ Teamwork
- ✓ Communications
- ✓ Numeracy/IT
- ✓ Decisions

Assume that your managing director has asked you to complete a note on forecasting methods for your firm. Building on the information so far, prepare a critique of the various methods in the context of a two-year planning cycle for fast-moving consumer goods (max. 200 words).

Marketing Planning

The gathering of information through marketing information and intelligence systems and through both desk- and field-based marketing research is very closely linked to the first stage of marketing planning – deciding where to go (objective setting). Forecasting is also linked because planning of any kind is about the future. It is very important to grasp the critical function of **planning in management**. Before we examine planning from a marketeer's perspective we will broaden out the discussion by referring to Box MKT3.4.

BOX MKT3.4

Planning: a checklist on its concept and principles

Management needs to have some vision of where it is going. The concepts of managerial planning and the derived principles can help the marketeer.

In a sense planning is a form of futuristic forecasting based on decisions of today and extrapolated trends.

Concept
- Determine and define objectives.
- Outline the guiding principles and context in which these objectives exist.
- Procure and mobilize resources.

Principles

- Have a policy which includes specific aims and the means of how to get there.
- Make use of available intelligence systems within and outside of the organization. Indeed, you may have to develop this intelligence system from scratch.
- Be flexible in your approach.
- Co-ordination of the activities may be delegated but there should be no abdication of responsibility.
- Targets with the appropriate stages/phases must be established, worked towards and monitored for variance.
- Control methods, from budgets to costing techniques, can act as 'monitors'.
- People are not robots so account must be in-built for 'slippage'.

To return to marketing planning, we find that it is a key component of the marketing initiative for utilizing our information. The gathering of marketing information and the use of that information in forecasting what is likely to happen, for example in the case of a new product launch or a move into new and untried markets, lead to the development of a strategy for exploiting the market and the production of a plan for putting that strategy into effect.

We have to remember that companies do not operate in a vacuum, they operate in an increasingly volatile environment, and if they are to survive in that environment in the long term then they must learn to cope with it. One stage in this process is the gathering of information, but sooner or later organizations have to take the risk of moving on to new areas of operation and it is the function of planning (based on the best information available) to make that move as risk free as possible. Please refer to figure 3.6 on the process of marketing planning.

Where Do We Start?

In an ideal situation, the marketing plan is always based upon the corporate plan and is geared towards the successful implementation of corporate strategy. The corporate plan covers all future activities of the company during the period for which the plan is drawn. At this level, the company might be looking five years or more into the future. However, the marketing plan (strategic and operational) may well be looking only one to two years ahead. The concepts of strategy and planning alongside 'sub-strategies' are covered in a different way from the mainstream approach in Box MKT3.5.

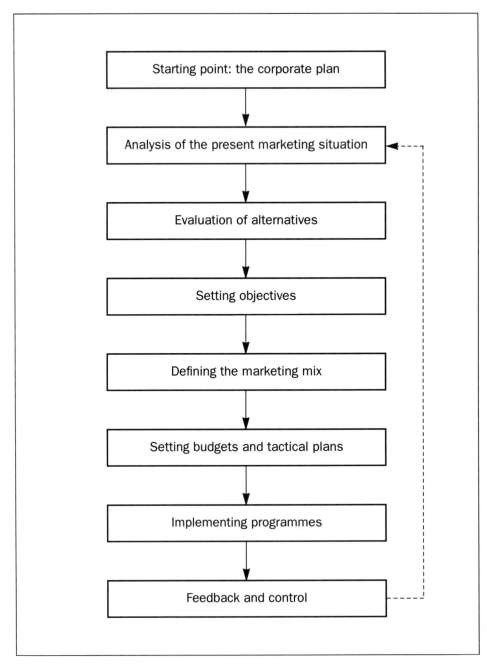

Figure 3.6 The steps involved in marketing planning.

Source: Adapted from McDonald, *Marketing Plans.*

BOX MKT3.5

Marketing strategies or sub-strategies?

Leven[1] argues that a strategy is essentially an action to achieve a desired end as it is the road map to results. The team strategy is open to wide interpretation. In business terms, it tends to deal with the organization's interface with the external environment, has a longer timespan than normal plans, involves senior personnel and gives the business its overall guiding principles. Leven tends to use the term 'strategy' to delineate a plan at the tactical or sub-strategy level. Apart from terminology which we can debate, his concept is useful.

We need to start off with a *living plan* which is dynamic and accountable. Again, too many plans may inhibit real action. The so-called *mission statement* gives an overview of what the organization is about. To Leven it is more: it documents the description, location and position of the establishment and it outlines what is required in terms of finance, operations and marketing (people?). *Objectives* follow on from this overview. In the case of the hospitality sector which Leven is involved in, these aims include:

■ positioning the unit;
■ room revenue;
■ food and beverage revenue;
■ other income.

The specific *strategy* follows thereafter and may cover sales promotion to advertising. These 'strategies' are quite specific and usually quantified for a given timescale.

The more traditional approach to marketing has a strategy/operations division. The strategic viewpoint concerns the longer-term future of the organization. It should have the following dimensions:

■ decisions tend to be held by top management;
■ the timescale may run into years;
■ it involves an ongoing interaction with the external environment;
■ it gives an overview of where the organization is directing its effort(s);
■ it gives a plan of campaign;
■ objectives may be set.

Operational marketing is about putting the strategy into practice. It may mean making the best of the resources available, and it may (depending on the firm) mean that resource allocation is involved in the various tasks to meet the guiding strategy(ies).

Specifically it tends to mean:

■ decisions are often more 'constrained`' and made by less senior marketeers;
■ the timescale can be day to day (hour by hour in some firms);
■ some interaction with the external environment may be involved owing to the nature of marketing but it is more organization-bound than the strategic perspective;

- it tends to be more of an implementation phase in line with the plan of campaign;
- targets may be used to meet objectives.

Leven's work is interesting, and not only is his terminology different but his view of strategy (or sub-strategy) is particularly useful in what we would term operational marketing. Indeed, this attempt to 'operationalize' policy is an ongoing issue in business[2] and Leven does contribute meaningfully to the debate.

Sources:
1 Adapted from Leven, 'How to develop marketing strategies'
2 See Anderson and Barker, *Effective Business Policy,* which operationalizes the concept of strategy in a wider sense than 'pure' marketing

As a way forward we can start from where we are now – that is, from where the organization is in marketing terms *today*. As a financial audit is a snapshot of where a company is in financial terms at a particular time, usually the last day of the financial year, then the marketing audit is a picture of where it is in marketing terms at a particular time, that is, when the audit is carried out.

As marketing managers involved in carrying out an audit, we need to stand back and look at our operation in as objective a way as possible. This is not always easy! Some companies call in an outside consultant to conduct the audit for them. In carrying out this audit (which should be done regularly, perhaps annually) we need to look at the marketing environment both inside and outside the company:

Internally we need to look at:

- the product/service mix;
- the present customer base;
- the potential customer base;
- customer profiles: size, type, ordering patterns, geographical spread, satisfaction levels – all information which should be available through the internal information system;
- existing budget levels and the reasons for setting them so;
- present marketing activities and capabilities;
- sales and promotional efforts;
- image.

Externally we need to look at:

- the political, social, economic and technological environment the company is operating in;
- the market;
- competitive activity.

Again, the information needed for this examination should be available through the marketing information system. The next step is to examine the organization's strengths and weaknesses in relation to the picture produced by the audit.

Where Do We Go Next?

The next step is the examination of market opportunities. The activities on 'The vegetarian market' (Activity MKT3.4 and Activity MKT3.5) should now be used to consolidate the use of intelligence and market opportunities. This pulls together macro research of other external bodies and specific micro research of the firm within the case study.

ACTIVITY MKT3.4

THE VEGETARIAN MARKET (MACRO)

Activity code
✓ Self-development
✓ Teamwork
✓ Communications
✓ Numeracy/IT
✓ Decisions

Critically comment on the trends in the survey below. In particular gauge the macro response to eating habits.

UK findings

- Some 2 million people are total vegetarians.
- Some 3.5 million people are part-vegetarian.
- Some 24 million people are cutting down on their red meat intake.
- The reasons for this reduction in meat include health (c. 20 per cent) finance (c. 11 per cent), taste (c. 8 per cent) and moral/ethical reasons (c. 6 per cent).
- Women tend to be non-meat-eaters (c. 13 per cent).
- Some 7 per cent of men are non-meat-eaters.
- Younger women (16–24) make up some 22 per cent of the non-meat-eating/vegetarian population.
- On social class, 'pure' vegetarians tend to be found amongst the upper and middle classes.
- Those avoiding meat in their diet are found in the skilled working classes (c. 12 per cent).
- The lower classes tend not to avoid meat or be vegetarian.

- Those cutting out red meat and/or becoming vegetarian tend to be found in the south of England.
- Single people seem more inclined to drop meat or become vegetarian than married people (14 per cent compared to 9 per cent).
- Widowed, separated and divorced people tend to be more likely to be non-meat-eaters/vegetarians than married people.

ACTIVITY MKT3.5

THE VEGETARIAN MARKET (MICRO)

Activity code
- ✓ Self-development
- ✓ Teamwork
- ✓ Communications
- ✓ Numeracy/IT
- ✓ Decisions

Analyse the figures below and tabulate them after collation for a market research report to a company which is contemplating opening a vegetarian restaurant. The research is particularly interested in the profile of existing non-meat-eaters/vegetarians.

1 Do you shop locally?
   500 people approached – 450 shopped locally.

2 *Age banding*

Age banding	Total
Under 21	90
22 under 30	65
30 under 45	105
45 under 65	100
65+	90
	450

3 Sex
   53 per cent female; 47 per cent male

4 Social class (occupation)

Class	Numbers (self-reported)
A	50
B	82
C	181
D	100
E	37

5 *Children*   *Number*
    (Dependants)

None	92
One	106
Two	162
Three+	90

6 Are you a meat-eater/non-vegetarian?
    66 said they preferred non-meat diets.

7 Of the remainder, 100 said that they had or would consider being a non-meat-eater/vegetarian.

8 The 66 non-meat-eaters were:

Class	*Number*
A	20
B	20
C	32
D	3
E	1

9 The 66 non-meat-eaters were:
    c. 60 per cent female; *c.* 40 per cent male

10 The 66 non-meat-eaters were aged as follows:

Under 21	10
22 under 30	33
30 under 45	17
45 under 65	4
65+	2

11 The 66 non-meat-eaters had the following dependants:

None	45
One	20
Two or over	1

12 How often do you purchase vegetarian food? ($n = 500$)

Never	324
Occasionally	160
Quite often	100
All the time	66

Using Ansoff's Matrix[8] as a guide, it is possible to see that marketing objectives are about two things only:

■ products;
■ markets.

The four options offered by Ansoff are:

1 selling more of the existing products to existing markets;
2 extending existing product ranges into new markets, either geographically (perhaps through exporting) or into new market segments;

3 developing new products for existing markets;

4 diversifying by developing new products of new markets.

Developing Communication Plans

Here we come to tactics in deciding how to publicize/promote the activities decided upon and these must be drawn up so as to ensure that the organization is presented to its market(s) in a consistent fashion. The details of the communication methods available are dealt with in a separate section of this text and are also the subject of an additional book in the *Effective Management* series.

Feedback and Control

Control procedures need to be built in from the start to monitor the actual performance of activities against the plan. For example, the sales force might be asked to gather opinions from customers about the new advertising campaign or the performance of the product. Again, the effectiveness of an advertising campaign can be judged against sales and ad hoc research can be carried out to ascertain recall levels. Whatever feedback is instituted, it is vital that use is made of the information gained. For example, it may be necessary to modify an advertising approach – even the product itself. We now turn first to the product and then to the promotion of the product.

Notes

1 Bennett, 'Using research in training'.
2 Lancaster and Massingham, *The Marketing Primer*.
3 West, *Understanding Marketing*.
4 Kotler, *Marketing Management*.
5 Anderson and Chansarkar, *Effective Market Research*.
6 West, *Understanding Marketing*.
7 Kotler, *Marketing Management*.
8 Ansoff, 'Strategies for Diversification'.

Unit Four

Product and Pricing

Learning Objectives

After completing this unit you should be able to:

● distinguish between innovative, imitative and 'me too' products;

● understand, and deal with, a variety of practical marketing concepts;

● apply the concepts covered in a range of practical exercises;

● establish a pricing policy for a new product;

● apply the generic skills.

Contents

Unit Four

> ❝ Calvin Klein or Jordache blue jeans are not blue jeans. They are a sex symbol and a fashion status symbol. ❞
>
> Adapted from *R.H. Bloom,*
> 'Product redefinition begins with the consumer'[1]

Overview

This unit has a dual focus: (1) finding the right products which are the means to meeting benefits; and (2) deciding how much to charge for them. Consequently we examine various methods of generating ideas for both new and improved products. The value can be estimated through such tools as the product lifecycle (PLC) and the Boston Matrix. The costly process of new product development with its screening and testing as well as its successes or failures must be one of the core processes in the study of products.

The customer takes account of price and quality in most purchases, while the pricing policy adopted by the firm is crucial in hitting the right marketing 'pitch', so we conclude this unit by examining pricing policies. (See figure 4.1.)

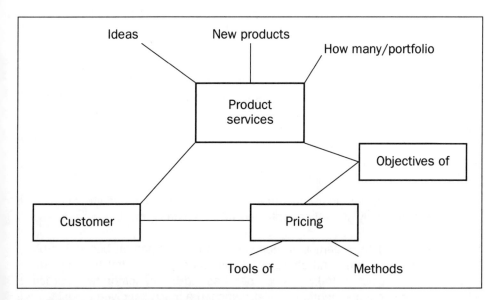

Figure 4.1 Outline diagram of Unit Four.

What is a Product?

As already explained in Unit One, taking a marketing approach to business involves listening to customers and potential customers to find out what it is they want in the way of products and services and then organizing the company so that this is what they get. However, no company can be all things to all customers so choices have to be made. Markets, and customers, have to be segmented (see Unit Two), and a balance has to be struck between the needs and wants of those markets and the abilities of the company. This exercise leads us back to the exchange process which is also described in Unit One.

Once the right balance between the supplying organization and the potential customer has been identified through the use of marketing information systems and marketing research, this is developed into the production of the right **marketing mix**. Again, this involves a balancing act, this time between the four elements that go to make up that mix: product, price, promotion and place. But, whatever the weightings eventually given to the individual elements, it is always the product (or the service) that comes first and it is upon this that everything else rests. Brilliant advertising might sell a product once but, if it fails to live up to the expectations of the buyer, if the latest miracle cleaner fails to clean, then repeat purchase is unlikely to take place and sales will fail to rise to the level necessary to support continued production.

BOX MKT4.1

Defining the product

If your organization is going to be market orientated instead of sales orientated or product orientated, then you should look on a product not simply as an object which you sell, but rather as a solution to your customer's problem; so, it is possible to define a *product* as:

- a definite set of solutions
- to a definite set of problems
- for a definite set of people
- at a particular moment in time.

Here, the emphasis is on the fact that the solution must be 'definite' because customers are likely to be most satisfied with a solution that they see as specific to them.

The last point 'at a particular moment in time' is important because problems change with time and changing circumstances, and what is welcomed as the perfect solution today may be seen as old hat by tomorrow – particularly if your closest competitor has just launched a much improved product.

So, just what exactly is this product upon which so much depends? The production manager no doubt knows that he makes products and the sales manager knows that her department is responsible for selling them, but are they both talking about the same thing? Is what the production department *makes* exactly the same as what the sales department *sells*?

The marketing department will tell you that it is not, because the company makes products and the customer buys **benefits**, that is, the company makes drills while what the customer actually wants is a picture on the living room wall. The drill is merely the means of getting it there – because the wall has to be drilled in order to insert a plug to take the weight of an elaborate frame. Please now refer to Box MKT4.1.

Nor does the argument stop there. The business consultancy produces nothing remotely resembling a drill, in fact it produces nothing physical at all (other than, perhaps, a report) but its 'product' may still be very much in demand. The ultimate result of its activities may be *higher profits* or even something as vital as *survival* for the client companies seeking its aid, both of these being products in which it is obviously very worthwhile to invest.

The whole question of the marketing of services (of designing, producing and selling intangibles) is one which is receiving an increasing amount of attention from marketing writers at all levels. That this should be so is hardly surprising at a time when manufacturing as a whole is still very much on the decline, at least in western countries, while the service sector becomes more and more vibrant through offerings that range from pension plans to personal fitness training to tourism and to concerts of classical music. Indeed, service marketing is not the only area where the

---

BOX MKT4.2

Services

The marketing of services is not the same as the marketing of products. Some characteristics of services include:

- *Perishability.* They tend to be short-lived and storage or hoarding is difficult.
- *Intangibility.* They do not have a physical form and they tend to be 'soft' rather than 'hard' on a scale of abstraction. It is useful to harden the softness with, say, promotional literature, for example in insurance.
- *Buyer needs.* A variety of needs may have to be met and standardization of the 'product' may be difficult.
- *Service value.* This may be difficult to gauge, particularly before the purchase.
- *Production/consumption.* Many services are made and consumed at the same time. The example of a bank loan can be cited.
- *Lack of ownership.* Rental, short-term use is the norm: the hotel room is normally hired for a short time.

Sources: Adapted from Bain and Kurtz, *Contemporary Marketing,* and Foster, *Planning for Products and Markets*

idea of marketing is on the increase. Non-profit organizations of all types from charities to hospital trusts and schools in charge of their own budgets are embracing the idea of marketing with great enthusiasm. Box MKT4.2 gives some of the main characteristics of services which differentiate them from a manufactured product.

So, in effect, what a customer is buying when he or she purchases a product is a whole bundle of attributes both tangible and intangible which, when bunched together, combine to make up a solution to a particular problem or are perceived as offering a particular set of satisfactions. This means that when products are evolved they must be seen not only as pieces of well-engineered metal or plastic (as the production manager might see them) or even as an improvement on what the competition has to offer (as the sales manager might see them) but as combinations of state-of-the-art design and technology, methods of presentation, packaging, brand image, cost of purchase and desire satisfiers (as the marketing manager should see them). This means that what is really being bought is an overall product package that, in many cases, might include the whole of the marketing mix.

BOX MKT4.3

Five levels of a product

Marketing managers need to think their way around five different levels of product when working through the essentials of the offer which is going to be made to customers.

- *The core benefit.* The basic service or benefit which is what the customer really wants when deciding on a particular product. For example, a visit to the dentist might mean 'freedom from pain' or the purchase of face cream might mean 'youth' or the booking of a holiday 'rest and freedom from stress'.
- *The generic product.* This is the basic version of the actual physical product, for example, a stainless steel saucepan or an electric toaster.
- *The expected product.* A set of attributes and conditions that buyers normally agree to when they purchase a product. For example, an umbrella is expected to be large enough to keep off a reasonable level of rain and strong enough to stand up to normal wear and tear for a reasonable length of time.
- *The augmented product.* At this level, the product includes additional services and benefits which help to distinguish it from competitive offerings, for example, a manufacturer of typewriters might extend the normal guarantee period from one to two years or the hotelier might place complimentary flowers and fruit in all bedrooms.
- *The potential product.* At the final level stands the product of the future, namely all the transformations and augmentations that a particular product might undergo in the future. This is where companies search for new ways to satisfy their customers and differentiate their products. The emergence of the all-suite hotel is still a fairly recent innovation and development of the traditional hotel product.

Source: Adapted from Kotler, *Marketing Management*

For example, when buying perfume it is the image conveyed by the advertising and the packaging which attracts as much as does the sensation which reaches the nostrils – sophisticated as in the case of 'Chanel N°5' or sporty as in the case of Revlon's 'Charlie'.

This is certainly the view taken by Kotler who said, as far back as 1977, that a product is *'a bundle of physical, service and symbolic particulars expected to yield satisfaction to the buyer'.*[2] In 1991, he went even further to say *'products consist broadly of anything that can be marketed, including physical objects, services, persons, places, organisations and ideas.'*[3] Please refer to Box MKT4.3.

Where Do New Products Come From?

Before thinking about how and where we are actually going to be able to find new products, it is useful first to consider why they are needed. If our products are of high quality or our services are in great demand, why, then, do we need to consider either replacing them entirely or adding extras to the list of those we already have on offer? The basic answer is that, in many ways, products and services are like people – they gestate, they are born, they advance towards maturity, then, eventually, they grow old and die. Also like people, they can be revitalized through the addition of new features or the improvement of old ones which might be looked upon as the marketing equivalent of a hip replacement or, in some cases, as vital as a heart transplant!

The theory and practical application of the product lifecycle is dealt with later in this unit but the basis of this approach, which is one of the most universally accepted in marketing, is that products or services which are never changed or adapted to fit in with new market conditions will eventually stagnate and die. They must be the beneficiaries of the hip replacement or the heart transplant if they are to survive in today's ever-changing marketplace. But (and here the analogy must end), unlike the human being, products can survive long beyond the normal human lifespan if they are regularly improved and relaunched. For example, Bovril was first produced as a food supplement for soldiers during the First World War and it has survived to flourish in consumer markets as a warming winter drink sold through advertisements which feature happy, contented and stylish young people. The product is substantially the same but the image has changed. Please now refer to Box MKT4.4 for an elaboration of these points concerning change.

Additionally, new and improved products and services need to be introduced if a company is going to be able to continue to be competitive. The level of intense competition visible in most markets today means that any company which fails to develop new and/or improved products is taking the risk of losing out, perhaps permanently, to its competitors.

BOX MKT4.4

Why have our customers' needs changed?

- *Customers have more money and higher expectations in life.* During the post-war period, the developed western world has experienced a time of affluence never previously known. The fridge, once regarded as a luxury item, is now seen as one of the essentials in any modern kitchen where it has been joined by the washing machine, the freezer and, increasingly, by the dishwasher.

- *Customers are better educated and more sophisticated.* Access to higher education, holidays abroad and, thanks to universal television, an appreciation of many different lifestyles and exotic cultures, has resulted in a great readiness to try new things – from Mexican food to bungee jumping.

- *Customers' social habits have changed.* Social habits have become much freer and more fluid – new unstructured approaches to fashion and lifestyles have evolved, it no longer matters whether skirts are short or long or (usually) whether a tie is worn. Nor does it matter whether the mince pies at Christmas come from Marks & Spencer rather than their own kitchen.

- *Customers appreciate technological development.* Technology is moving ahead increasingly rapidly to make available more and more sophisticated products, most notably in the realms of home entertainment, where computers have taken over from wooden toys and camcorders coupled with laser discs have turned basic holiday snaps almost into a thing of the past.

Source: Adapted from Wilmshurst, *The Fundamentals and Practice of Marketing*

New products, and ideas for new products, come from a variety of sources; these can vary from the flash of brilliance which led Henry Ford to develop the first production line, to the deliberate decision to develop a 'me too' product because every other company in the same market already has one. For example, when Vidal Sassoon developed the first 'wash and go' shampoo, a product which contains conditioner as well as a washing agent, it was genuinely something new in the home hair-care market and was extremely successful, to the extent that other manufacturers followed until there were a dozen or more similar products to choose from.

Ideas for new or improved products can come either from inside a company or from outside, they can be logically developed or they can be the result of 'eureka'-style thunderbolts. Useful techniques for idea generation are:

- *Portfolio analysis* linked with the *ongoing collection of marketing information* (through the marketing information system described in Unit Three) and also with planned *marketing research projects* (also described in Unit Three) can throw light on new trends in the needs and wants of customers, for example a desire for colour television as an improvement over watching programmes in black and white once the first novelty of having TV at all has worn off. At this stage, there is a gap between the company's present offerings and the requirements of the market which will need to be filled (preferably with something better than what is already available from the competition) if the organization is going to be able to survive and grow.

■ *Market analysis* can show up market segments which are not being covered by the present product range. This may originally have been a deliberate choice but the company may now be in a better position to develop products suitable for new market segments, for example, a successful fashion designer may, once well established, choose to introduce a range of ready-to-wear garments and Honda once developed a moped aimed at teenage girls.

■ A company's own planned *research and development activities* can result in products designed to fit a specific brief, such as a sleeping pill with no side effects, or they might result in something much more innovative, for example the glue used on 'Post-it notes'.

■ *Independent* organizations can be used for the development of new products or they can be *acquired* through *buying patents or taking out licences*.

■ *Brainstorming*, the encouragement of ideas from staff in all parts of the company, and *searches in overseas markets* can also be a useful source of ideas for investigation in the never-ending search for new product ideas.

■ *Customers*, particularly in industrial markets, are often a source of stimulus in the development of new products. For example, a customer might ask for a machine to do a particular type of drilling job or for a new kind of fastening device.

However, truly innovative 'land mark' new products like digital watches or 'Post-it notes' are far more rare than are new products which are produced through the development of existing ones, although 'wash and go' shampoos and biological washing powders may still be described as

---

BOX MKT4.5

Five innovative ways of improving penetration into existing markets

1 Introducing new products or services in order to ensure that marketing objectives can be achieved.
2 Developing new products before technological change can make existing products obsolete.
3 Making improvements to existing products to take advantage of changing technology and so that they can continue to increase their share of the market.
4 Improving processes like those of manufacturing and delivery so that pricing objectives can be achieved.
5 Making innovations and introducing improvements into areas of necessary activity, for example, computers into accounting and stock control activities, or introducing quality management techniques in order to keep up with developments in knowledge and in the techniques and skills of product and people management.

Source: Adapted from Drucker, *The Practice of Management*

major innovations in their time. Even more common, however, are what we might call the 'new and improved' varieties of product where 'miracle ingredient X' is guaranteed to wash whiter than ever before, or oat bran added to a breakfast cereal is said to help avoid heart disease. These are the weapons of increased market penetration, that is, of selling more of your existing products to more people in your existing markets. This is the first variant in the four offered to marketeers by the Ansoff Matrix (see pp. 103–4).[4] Please now refer to Box MKT4.5.

With regard to the further development and improvement of existing products there are four overall methods:

1 *Modifying the existing features of the product or service.* For example, an estate agent might introduce a commercial sales service alongside the existing one of house sales or an automobile manufacturer might introduce drivers' airbags as a standard on all models, thus offering increased safety to drivers.

2 *Increasing product/service quality* through the use of new technology. For example, the standard of photocopying obtainable from normal office machines has increased enormously in recent years.

3 *Updating the style of the product.* For example, the styling of the Ford Cortina was updated and modernized many times during its lifetime and long-standing products such as Pond's cold cream have their packaging redesigned to give a more modern appearance.

4 *Modifying the product's image* through redesigning the logo or the advertising approach. For example, Johnson's baby products are now offered to 'babies' of any age or gender.

How are Ideas Developed into Products?

New products, particularly in consumer markets, have a high failure rate in spite of the high levels of marketing expertise inside the companies that develop them and in spite of an enormous amount of testing and screening. How long, for example, is anybody going to remember 'New Coke' – one of the most spectacular new-product failures of the 1980s? Please refer to Box MKT4.6.

In fact, every opportunity for product innovation means a corresponding opportunity for the taking of an organizational risk. Overall, it has long been estimated that between 50 and 90 per cent of new products introduced into consumer markets fail. However, a more recent study (in 1981) by Booz, Allen and Hamilton[5] suggests that the number of new product ideas actually needed in order to get a successful new product to market has fallen from around fifty-eight (in 1968) to seven (1981). These figures suggest that product screening and testing methods have improved considerably in the twenty-odd years between the surveys. The complexity of new product development in the pharmaceutical sector can be seen in the case of AZT in Box MKT 4.7.

BOX MKT4.6

Problems encountered in the development of new products

- *The difficulty of actually finding new products.* Basic products like soap or sheet steel are difficult to develop in new ways.
- *Increasing fragmentation of markets.* Competition is increasing and this can lead to over-segmentation of markets as competing companies fight for market share.
- *Social and ecological restraints.* New safety and environmental constraints can inhibit the introduction of new products in some areas, e.g. fire safety regulations for fabrics and furniture and safety rules in the pharmaceutical industry.
- *Increasing development costs.* New products are expensive to develop and a company may need to develop several for every one which actually makes it to the market. Research both into new products and into markets is also increasing in cost.
- *Time constraints.* For a variety of reasons companies sometimes fail to get a new product to market before the competition.
- *Shortening product lifecycles.* New products can now be copied very quickly so that a lead in the marketplace can no longer be guaranteed to allow sufficient time for the full recovery of development costs before the advent of a competing product starts to bring prices down.

Source: Adapted from Kotler, *Marketing Management*

BOX MKT4.7

AZT: as difficult as ABC

The need for a wonder drug to combat the late twentieth-century plague Aids is self-evident, with around two million people with full-blown Aids and with approximately five times that number of people with the HIV virus without its symptoms.[1]

AZT, made by Wellcome, with its trade name Retrovir, was developed to meet this obvious need. With its overall margins around the 30 per cent mark anyway, Wellcome seemed to be on a commercial and humanitarian winner with this new product.

Unfortunately for Wellcome and for Aids sufferers at large, a major research study, the so-called Concorde study, concluded in March 1993 that the drug did little to prevent those with the HIV virus from developing full-blown Aids.

The Wellcome share price went into a fall (it had already dropped owing to the prospect of Clinton's health care reforms in the USA). Hitherto, the company had noted that its drug worked better in conjunction with other drugs such as ddl made by Bristol–Myers–Squibb. Equally, earlier tests on the product with smaller samples had proved far more encouraging.

The importance of new product development seems to be writ large in this case. More fully researched work with larger samples and longitudinal studies may have prevented this occurrence. In the interim, studies presumably go on but the product looks a little dented, although ongoing research may pull it back.

Source:
1   Adapted from Parker-Jarvis, 'AZT: Wellcome's bitter pill'

In many cases, the failure seems to be the result either of a product change, or the introduction of an entirely new product which does not appear to offer very much to the consumer, that is, it can be the result of a product/company orientation (perhaps the desire to fill a gap in the product range) rather than market/consumer orientation. In this area, the introduction of 'New Coke' came as a result of Coca-Cola's (very understandable) desire to reverse the inroads that Pepsi-Cola was making into Coke's position as market leader rather than as a result of newly identified consumer preferences.

The reason for the generation of a wide variety of ideas for new and improved products is to allow for the detailed screening and testing process which will result in most of them being discarded (see figure 4.2). The purpose of this screening process is to make sure that poor, or unmarketable, ideas are discarded very early in the process so that the cost of examining them is kept as low as possible. The closer to the market a new product is allowed to get, the greater is the amount of money and time which has been invested in it and the more pressure there may be (particularly from non-marketing departments) to go ahead and launch it anyway, in order to get at least some of the investment back. This is a *bad* idea and the ideal is to make sure that the screening process which a company puts into place is as rigorous as possible!

The first-level filter

How well does the proposed new product fit with the company's declared corporate and marketing strategies? New products are easier to deal with if they are complementary to existing product ranges. The market is more likely to accept, say, a new style of breakfast cereal from Kelloggs than it is a new soap powder which carries that same brand name. This need for a 'match' with existing products also carries over into issues of quality, price and distribution methods. At this stage, it is also appropriate to subject the proposed new or improved product to a strict financial analysis. Is it likely to make a profit and, if so, how long is it likely to be before that profit is

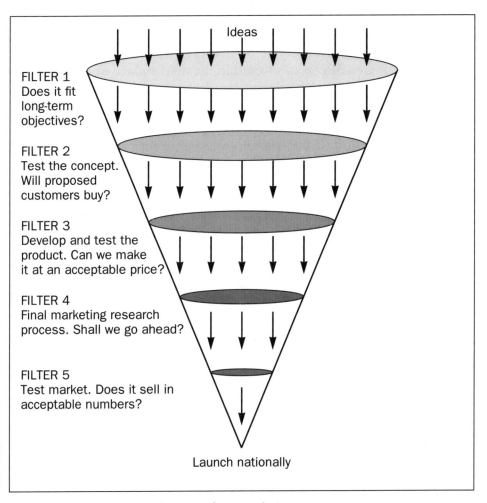

Figure 4.2 Steps in the development of new products.

actually shown? The introduction of computer-based spreadsheets with their 'what if' capacity makes this a relatively easy task once the initial costs have been estimated as closely as possible and a break-even analysis carried out.

The second-level filter

Is the consumer likely to accept the new product? If this is not likely to be the case then the sooner this is established the better, before too much finance has been committed. At this stage, standard marketing research techniques are used to ascertain likely attitudes and purchase levels. However, this is a difficult task to carry out accurately, particularly where really innovative products are concerned – 'Post-it notes' for example, or even Sellotape, where it is difficult for respondents to imagine what it might be like to use the item if they have never seen it. For this reason, dummy products may be produced or a mock-up of the packaging that might be used can be shown as part of the research carried out. These techniques are not perfect, but they can still be a vital part of any exercise aimed at weeding out products which are unlikely to succeed in the marketplace while they are at the earliest possible stage in their development.

The third-level filter

Testing the product itself. If the concept tests are positive then the next stage (which might take years in the case of pharmaceutical products or cosmetics) is the development of the product itself. This task should be approached in the light of the results obtained from the concept tests.

This third weeding-out stage tests the product itself on potential customers. In the case of food or beverage products, these tests might take the form of tastings, while, in the case of products like ironing boards of a new shape, they might take the form of usage tests actually in the homes of respondents. At this stage it is important to try to find out if the subjects of the research would be willing to buy the product (as opposed to being willing to use it for a time free of charge or to taste it if it is put in front of them).

Filters four and five

Will the public buy? The last research followed by the test market. This is the final, and most expensive, form of marketing research. However, even having gone this far, it is still cheaper to withdraw a consumer product which performs badly in a test market than it is to launch it on a national scale and stand even bigger financial losses. Even here, decisions regarding the extent of the test are not easy to make because there are different levels of test market available. The nearest thing to a national launch is to use a complete TV area as the test market and to replicate everything – advertising, sales promotion and distribution outlets – as well as having the product itself on sale. From here, the possible areas of testing can be scaled down to a single town, a single neighbourhood or even to a single supermarket. In the latter cases, it will not be possible to test TV advertising campaigns nor those scheduled to appear in the national press. However, they can be very useful in testing out whether or not the product will actually sell.

What Happens to Products after They are Launched?

As already stated, we all live and work in an increasingly dynamic environment. This means that companies and their managers must accept that all products have a limited life, although the actual length of that life

---

BOX MKT4.8

Leaders and followers

- *Innovative products* are the first on the market with a new idea.
- *Imitative products* are those that follow. They may never be the market leaders but they avoid the risks involved in being the first on the market. By the time they are launched, the market has accepted the original product and may be ready for an alternative, particularly if it is cheaper than the original.
  The imitative product is not necessarily inferior in any way to the original – it might even be better! In some cases, companies take apart the new product and see where they can exceed its standards before they make their own – the Japanese have long been masters of this approach and one of its results has been the demise of the British-built motor cycle.
- *'Me too'* products are those that are put onto the market simply because all similar companies already have one. They may be launched at a low price in order to attempt to get a toehold in the market.

---

will depend on factors like fashion, technological development, changes in consumer needs and competitive activity and whether the company concerned adopts a strategy of 'leading' or 'following' in the marketplace. In the area of marketing, this concept is usually expressed in terms of the product lifecycle (PLC). Please refer to Box MKT4.8 which gives some context to innovation.

The curve illustrated in figure 4.3 shows the product lifecycle and is a generalization; in reality, the curve may drive very rapidly up and then

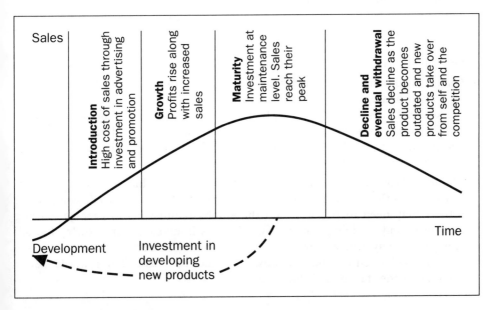

Figure 4.3 The product lifecycle.

down (as in the case of skateboards or hulahoops) or seemingly be ready to go on forever (as in the case of Bovril, Guinness or baked beans). The concept does need to be applied carefully and, as in the case of most management and marketing concepts, organizations must be prepared to modify the theory in order to be able to apply it to their own situation. Additionally, looking again at skateboards as an example, it is necessary to be clear about whether we are in fact talking about a *product* lifecycle or whether it is actually a *market* lifecycle.

Although it is safe to accept that a product's life does follow a predictable course, it is important to remember that all products are by no means alike and that the markets themselves are different and subject to ongoing change. Timescale is also an important factor which differentiates the curves of different types of product; so too is the way in which they are managed by the company responsible for launching them. For example, it is vital that product managers or marketing managers should be able to identify the stage at which their products move from one section of the curve to another in order to make sure that the right strategies are adopted at the right times.

- *Development.* The development process for new and modified products has already been described in detail; however, it is worth remembering that this phase may begin a very long time before the product reaches the marketplace, a fact which has implications for the whole of the lifecycle and the way it is managed. It should also be noted that modified products can usually be brought to the market faster than completely new ones.

- *Introduction.* At this stage, the budget needed for a successful launch is usually larger than the revenue received in terms of profit and sometimes also in terms of sales revenue. At this stage, the prime necessity is to create awareness and, after that, the required level of acceptability throughout the target market in the knowledge that, if this is done effectively, then the required levels of profit will be achieved at a later date. Promotional budgets allocated at this stage ought to be regarded as investments in the same way that R&D costs are so regarded.

- *Growth.* If the first-stage activity has been carried out successfully then, during its growth phase, the product should achieve general acceptance in the chosen market, and sales should rise steeply. In this phase it should be possible to cover development costs as profits increase, and, as sales continue to increase, additional profit will be made as unit costs will decrease with the greater volume of production.

- *Maturity.* Normally, this is the longest stage in the lifecycle of a product. Market growth will be low, investment levels will have reduced, competitive activity may need to be faced and the emphasis must be on keeping existing customers and retaining market share. Sales will increase more slowly, if at all, and profits may suffer – perhaps even beginning to decline. This is also the stage at which effort and investment should be channelled towards newer products at the start of their lifecycle.

■ *Saturation and decline.* At this stage, sales (having reached their peak) will begin to fall off and decline and profits will continue to decline. Additionally, it will become more and more difficult (and costly) to maintain sales at an acceptable level, so that the eventual answer will be to withdraw the product from the market in favour of its successors.

A critique of the 'global' application of the PLC can be seen in Box MKT4.9. Thereafter, you should tackle Activity MKT4.1.

BOX MKT4.9

The product lifecycle and its contribution to strategic marketing

Most products certainly pass through phases of: *introduction, growth, maturity,* and *decline.* There is more of a debate about the product lifecycle's value in strategy within marketing. Doyle examines the concept in a useful piece of work.[1]

First of all the value of the PLC should be noted:

■ most product sales go through these phases;

■ profits tend to peak in the rapid-growth phase;

■ competition becomes tougher as things go on;

■ the average length of the PLC is tending to shorten owing to socio-economic and technological change;

■ the cycle is product-dependent and the maturity stage can be extended through innovative advertising, for example;

■ greater promotion at the end of the cycle can also extend the last breaths of the decline stage.

However, Doyle argues, these trends apart, the PLC is not an accurate or stable enough 'given' to make key decisions. A time-dependent relationship does not account for managerial decisions which impact on the longer-term pattern of sales. Innovation and costing variables can also skew the cycle. The competition is never a 'given' and can impact on market share and so on.

Consequently, the product lifespan may go through key 'critical incidents' within its phases. These could include the degree of saturation in the market; the nature of the competitive environment; and the possibility of substitution by alternative products and technologies.[2]

These 'turning points' in the cycle, level of saturation, nature of competition and the presence of substitutes or alternatives can thus shorten or lengthen the cycle and change the focus of the PLC accordingly.

Sources:

1 Adapted from Doyle, 'The realities of the product life cycle'

2 Porter, *Competitive Strategy.* Indeed Porter's variables of the competitive environment could be added to these factors. See Anderson and Barker, *Effective Business Policy,* for a wider discussion of these variables

ACTIVITY MKT4.1

MARKETING AND THE PRODUCT LIFECYCLE

Activity code
✓ Self-development
✓ Teamwork
✓ Communications
✓ Numeracy/IT
✓ Decisions

The five phases of the product lifecycle – introduction, growth, maturity, saturation and decline – may have distinct implications for the work of the marketeer. Here we will outline the phase and its immediate plan of campaign with a note on competitor activity. Your role is to establish the corresponding key tasks of the marketeer by each phase.

1 *Introduction phase.* The aim is to gain acceptance from the marketplace. There is a genuine product differential in this case and the advantage is not easily copied by competitors. Hence the competition exists as always but we have a considerable edge over them.

   Action =

2 *Growth phase 1: establishing the market.* At this stage we are building on our foothold (toehold) to establish a greater share of the market. The competition is more evident now and are known, for they are taking a higher profile.

   Action =

   Growth phase 2: expansion. The aim here is to go for growth. Volume sales are important. Segments may have to be extended and new products are in the development process. The competition is far more alert now, and it is beginning to bite particularly in mass markets. Further, the 'market acceptance' seems to be reasonably steady but new entrants to the market and imitation are beginning to be a concern.

Action =

3   *Maturity.* The growth is slowing down now but moderate expansion is still going on. You are happy to maintain the status quo but this will not happen as the competition is squeezing you on profits and there is even more of them.

Action =

4   *Saturation.* You are attempting to hold on. Times are getting worse. Competition is even keener and you are really being squeezed.

Action =

5   *Decline.* The market is very difficult. You may have to cut and run. More new products are required as a matter of urgency. The competition is challenging you on price and on products.

Action =

How Many Products Do We Need?

One of the crucial points of living with the product lifecycle as discussed above is the acceptance that, as products (either a single product or a complete range) move into the maturity stage of their cycle, it is necessary to have others in the pipeline to take their place. We have already seen that it is possible to modify and relaunch a product and in doing so to 'kick off'

BOX MKT4.10

Product portfolios

Drucker suggests a mechanism of portfolio analysis of products within the firm. He suggests that all products can be classified into five groups as follows:

1 **Tomorrow's breadwinners.** These are either modifications or improved versions of what we've got as our staple diet or new products.
2 **Today's breadwinners.** These may exist today but they really are the innovations of yesterday.
3 **Yesterday's breadwinners.** These are old hat but eat up all that they earn in promotion, etc.
4 **'Problem children'.** Difficult to live with perhaps but better parental control could make the difference between a healthy child and a potential deviant.
5 **'Also-rans'.** Thank you and goodnight time as these products, like some national football teams, have never come up to expectations.

Source: Adapted from Drucker, 'Managing for Business Effectiveness'

---

the lifecycle once again, but in the long term new products will be needed and the safest strategy is therefore to have a portfolio of products at different stages of development. Please refer to Box MKT 4.10.

One of the problems involved in operating product portfolios is that, however detailed the screening and testing phases, we can never be quite sure that, when eventually launched into the market, a product will perform in the way that our researches predict. We can see from the PLC and from Drucker's analysis of product categories that all products must be kept under constant review to establish their present, and hopefully their future, level of contribution to company profits. Marginal products can only lower the level of a company's profitability so it is absolutely essential that its portfolio should be carefully reviewed and controlled. One of marketing's most widely accepted tools for doing this, and for considering the implications in marketing and organizational terms of various courses of action is the Boston Matrix (see figure 4.4).

One of the advantages of the Boston Matrix and, indeed, also of the PLC is that it is a visual tool which can produce a useful picture of a company's product strengths and weaknesses and of the directions in which cash is likely to flow between the various products in the current portfolio.

Stars are usually seen as the best products to have, however, as we saw when examining the product lifecycle concept, these products also need high levels of investment to ensure their continued success and their eventual progress to the status of mature product or 'cash cow' – when

Stars	Problem children
High market share, high market growth.	Typically new products which have not yet reached their potential.
Investment is needed so that they can mature into cash cows where profit is highest	Profit from cash cows is invested in selected ones as market growth is high in an effort to develop them also into cash cows
Cash cows	**Dogs**
High market share, low market growth.	Low market share, low market growth.
Equivalent to mature stage of product lifecycle. Investment is at maintenance level and profit is available to invest in stars and selected problem children	Little chance of any growth – needs to be reviewed regularly so that a decision can be made about when to withdraw them from the market

Figure 4.4 The product portfolio matrix developed by the Boston Consulting Group.

they should be providing funds to subsidize their successors. However, that does not necessarily mean that they deserve no further investment themselves. A product at the 'mature' stage of the PLC or in the 'cash cow' sector of the Boston Matrix may actually be a brand or market leader, in which case it will require ongoing investment if it is to maintain this position in the long term. This means that there must be a careful balancing act between the needs of the product in a leading position and the need to invest in new products for the future.

This highlights the dangers of relying too heavily on what are some of the most popular and well-known tools of the marketing manager and, as Mercer[6] warns: 'Marketing techniques should be the servant of the marketeer. They should be used as an aid to the creative decision-making processes, and can never be a substitute for them. Although they may frequently offer helpful insights, they almost never offer definitive answers in themselves.'

The product portfolio, or the product mix, is the total number of products manufactured by any company. In larger companies, this mix will be grouped according to what are known as product 'lines'. These are groups of products which are closely related to each other and it is possible that the products in any one line may be balanced according to the different quadrants of the Boston Matrix. The relationship between products in any line may be that they are similar, such as chocolate bars, or that they are sold to similar customers, for example, camcorders and accessories. The number of different product lines carried by a single

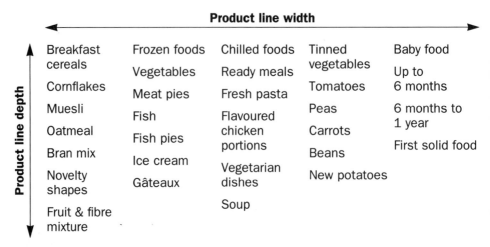

Figure 4.5 Possible product range for a manufacturer of food.

company will be referred to as the 'width' of the product range, while the number of products in a single line will be known as the product line 'depth' (see figure 4.5).

A company may add to its product mix in a variety of ways in order to obtain the best possible level of products to offer:

■ It can add to the number of product lines it carries, that is, it can extend its product width. This may be a desirable strategy if it wishes to have a broad base of operation. However, it also means that it runs the risk of entering markets in which it has no experience.

■ Product lines may be extended downwards by the addition of products which are cheaper than those already on the market. If it is decided that this strategy is the one to follow then it must be very carefully done as there is always the risk that these new products might harm the image of the originals. Fashion designers have successfully introduced ranges of more basic garments, for example.

■ Alternatively, it may prove possible to extend a product line upwards into a more expensive bracket; however, it is likely to prove time consuming and costly to achieve the desired jump in image.

■ Another way of extending a particular product line is to fill in any obvious gaps but, if this strategy is to be successful, there must still be sufficient space between the various products in the line to allow them to be clearly differentiated. If this is not the case then the new product may simply take sales from those on either side of it.

The most advantageous overall portfolio can only be fashioned through a well-organized system of marketing information gathering, regular product audits and effective marketing planning procedures. Performance levels of all products in the portfolio need to be constantly monitored and it must be possible to review costs, sales and profits product by product and on a regular and well-determined time basis.

In addition to adding products to its mix, the sensible company must also be prepared to delete them if they contribute very little to the overall levels of profit obtained – products in this position may well, in Boston Matrix terms, be 'dogs'.

It should also be noted that, even if the perfect product portfolio is achieved, it may not actually last for very long. The dynamic state of today's markets means that complacency must never become a state of mind and that all a company's products must be constantly monitored against the state of their markets and the activities of the competition to ensure that they still deserve to retain their place in the current portfolio. You should now tackle Activity MKT 4.2 on the product 'portfolio'.

ACTIVITY MKT4.2

TO DROP OR TO HOLD?

Activity code
- ✓ Self-development
- ✓ Teamwork
- ☐ Communications
- ☐ Numeracy/IT
- ✓ Decisions

The managing director was arguing for an elimination of product X and he was encountering opposition from the development section and from some of the marketing team.

The argument seemed clear cut. The real profitability came from other products in the mix and this product, a potential star, had never really shone brightly.

The opposition thought otherwise. A lot of time, money and effort had been put into development. It was not sentimentality but the product had not had an opportunity to shine. With a little more time and some promotion, it would run.

The sales manager threw in another argument. 'Look, it may not be brilliant but it still fills a hole in my product mix. If we don't sell it, I can name two firms that will jump into this space. Once they are in they can make further inroads along the whole of the product mix.'

The MD was not convinced. 'The time (both managerial and sales) taken up with this product is disproportionate to its value. I'm not doing a cost-accounting job on you, but the production costs, the warehousing and the physical distribution must all come into the reckoning.'[1]

The opposition went on the attack. 'The product is okay; it has not had a chance to grow. The introduction was mishandled by my predecessor,' said the marketing chief, 'and penetration remained low through a lack of promotion. We should repackage it and go for growth rather then remove it.'

The MD had more doubts now but he was not convinced by the opposition's views. He would reflect on it.

1 Analyse what is going on here.
2 Note the arguments for elimination and for holding the product list and weigh their importance.
3 Give a view/recommendation based on the evidence in this scenario.

Source:
1 See Anderson and Nix, *Effective Accounting Management*, for a discussion on this subject

What Makes Our Product Different?

One of the problems with products, unless they can be patented, is that they are seldom unique. The new 'Battery Manager' introduced to the market by Innovations is both unique and patented. It is the first product said to be capable of recharging most ordinary batteries and thus of extending the useful life of a normal dry cell battery by up to ten times. Not only will it save considerable sums of money for the battery-buying public but it will also, hopefully, help to reduce the enormous numbers of batteries consumed and jettisoned every year, thus having a beneficial effect on the environment as well as on the profits of the company.

Not many products, even new ones, come into this category. In order to create markets for their products, manufacturers need at least to seem to be offering something which is different from anything else on the market. This is done through packaging, image building and branding, all three of which are key elements in getting the better of the competition.

The subject of packaging is dealt with in detail under the heading of 'promotion' in Unit Five. It is a vital element both in developing high recognition levels for products and in creating the desired brand image. Expensive perfumes would never seem to smell the same if they were placed in plain brown cardboard boxes in dark bottles. At the other end of this scale, The Body Shop has made a virtue out of plain plastic refillable bottles which contribute enormously to its caring and environmentally conscious image.

Cigarette packaging also contributes largely to recognition and differentiation factors with its proliferation of distinctive and well-known packs like those of John Player Special and Marlboro. Additionally, branding in the field of cigarettes is very strong. Marlboro still holds the memory of the cowboy in 'Marlboro country' and John Player Special benefits from its links with the glamour and power of motor racing. These images are even more extraordinary when placed against the fact that there is little actual difference between one cigarette and another – they are the result of deliberate image building and branding policies.

Branding is particularly important where there is this little difference between the products of different companies. The petrol giants attempt to compete strongly in this area, where one of the longest ever running campaigns is the Esso tiger and, even in the area of poultry, Bernard Matthews is able to claim that his 'bootiful' turkeys are superior to any others. In the car market, differentiation may be achieved through style as well as speed (Porsche and Jaguar) or through performance (miles to the gallon) or reliability (Japanese cars).

Products may also achieve their aim of being different through added value, which may be through the service element bundled with them which may consist of variables like *speed of delivery* (overnight parcel deliveries), *installation* (washing machines or industrial equipment), *speed of response to service calls* (computers and photocopiers), *frequent traveller bonuses* (hotel chains and airlines) and *pre-sales services* (fitted kitchens and double glazing).

It may also be well-trained personnel that differentiates one company from another. In the case of airlines, it is often the caring and competent service given by cabin staff that is emphasized in the advertising, while all McDonald's staff are trained to be courteous as well as fast when they are serving customers.

With consumer goods, the most used form of product differentiation is probably branding which is then strongly linked to advertising, packaging and image building. The method used may be *family branding* where a very well-nurtured brand name becomes the platform for a wide range of products (Bird's Eye, Heinz) although each product is the subject of separate marketing effort (fish fingers, frozen ready meals, baked beans, soups). In other cases it may be the name of the company which is pushed in a much more generic fashion (Bang & Olufsen) or, again, it might be the individual brands which are promoted, to the extent that they may actually be in competition with each other (Procter & Gamble, with Ariel, Bold and Fairy).

Yet another approach to branding is that adopted by large retailers, particularly supermarket chains, where 'own brands' sell in competition with, and alongside, heavily branded products. When carried to its fullest extent, this 'own brand' policy may extend to the elimination of competing products in retail outlets – Marks & Spencer and St Michael being the best example.

The whole question of product differentiation is an important one and is closely linked to the additional marketing tools of segmentation, targeting and positioning. These are dealt with in Unit Two.

How Do We Manage Our Products?

All companies need to manage and control their products and services very closely. They need to adopt different and appropriate strategies at different points in the lifecycle of each product and they need to balance their product portfolio in line with, for example, the teaching of the Boston Matrix, the pressures of the market and the objectives of the company.

Decisions of this nature will have a far-reaching influence on the future growth and success of the company and they need to be made, most of all, in the light of product/market opportunities. Please consult Box MKT4.11.

BOX MKT4.11

Product/market strategies

- *Market penetration.* Involves a company in seeking to sell more of its existing products in its existing markets. Activity in this area would involve increased advertising and promotion linked to attempts to increase the scope of distribution, thus making the product(s) more widely available. This is likely to be the cheapest option for growth, particularly in a growth market, and it is also the least risky as the company will be operating in product/market areas with which it is familiar. In a mature (or saturated) market this will be a more difficult area to approach as success will involve taking market share from the competition.

- *Marketing development.* By adopting this strategy a company will be attempting to increase sales by taking its existing products into new markets. This may involve either moving into new geographical areas (including international markets if the home market is mature or close to saturation) or new market segments. Choosing this option is likely to prove both more expensive and more risky than market penetration but it has the merit of allowing the company to operate with familiar products.

- *Product development.* Adoption of this strategy means a more long-term approach than either of the first two as it will include the time taken by a company to develop new or improved products to sell in its existing markets. This is both a more expensive and a riskier path to follow, but it does fit in with lessons taught by the product lifecycle and it also allows the company to operate in familiar markets.

- *Diversification.* In this case, increased sales are sought through the development of new products for new markets – the riskiest most expensive and most long-term option of all.

Source: Adapted from Ansoff, *Strategic Management*

Where a company has a variety of products in the same or similar markets, or a number of brands on the scene at the same time, it is likely that the system for managing products will include the use of product (or brand) managers – positions which are held to be extremely fast moving and extremely stressful and are therefore usually held by young and aspiring marketing people. This situation may also involve the use of a separate sales force for each product or each brand.

The work of the product manager will include the co-ordination of all advertising and promotional activities as well as product improvements and, depending on the company concerned, he or she will also be involved in the preparation of marketing plans and the setting of sales and profit targets. This pattern of product management is often found in companies in the areas of detergents, cigarettes and chocolate bars where there are many products in a company's portfolio.

One of the main reasons for this approach is that it will ensure that concentrated attention is given to every product or brand and that, for example, the needs of established products are not buried under those of this year's 'stars'.

Services as 'Products'

Many writers on marketing will say that the marketing of services is exactly the same as that of products and that, in fact, all that is needed is the substitution of the two words. However, there are some very great differences between the two. As we have seen earlier in this unit, products are actually made up of both tangible and intangible attributes which together make up the whole offering. Additionally, some products also carry a heavy service element, for example, after-sales service and advice is a large part of the total offering made by computer companies.

In these cases there is both a physical and a more intangible manifestation of what is being offered for sale but, in the case of pure services this is not so. One of the main differences is that prospective customers cannot see what is being offered before they decide to purchase – they are unable to 'try it for size' – and they must rely heavily on the person who is selling it to them. This is particularly so in the buying of financial services or when taking advantage of the service being offered by a solicitor or an accountant. All we have to rely on then is the personality of the individual in question and the possibility of personal recommendation from someone who has already experienced the quality of what is received.

Also, in the case of services, we have what is known as 'inseparability', when the production and consumption of the service take place at the same time – for example, when a meal is eaten in a restaurant or a holiday is taken in a resort new to the consumer. Additionally, the purchaser of a service does not have it to keep as is the case with a product – the benefit of the holiday is only felt while it is taking place.

Services are not only intangible, they are also perishable. The customer can only make use of them once without paying again and, so far as the provider is concerned, if a theatre seat is empty at a particular performance or a hotel bedroom is empty on a particular night, it cannot be held in stock in the same way that a product can – the revenue lost has gone for ever.

Services are subject also to 'variability'. Quality-control systems can ensure that products coming off a production line are not sub-standard and, even if the quality system fails occasionally, the product can be repaired or replaced, but this is not the case with services. The variability of services comes through differences in the people providing them which is one of the reasons why banks and hotel chains have invested heavily in customer-care programmes in recent years.

Services can be marketed just as effectively as products can but care must be taken to ensure that sufficient allowance is made for the special conditions outlined here.

How Do We Begin to Price Our Products?

When beginning to think about the question of setting prices for products, whether they are new or whether they are well established, it is important to remember that, in marketing terms, price may well have a low level of relationship to cost – although it is naturally accepted that, in most cases, price levels must be above cost levels. Price has been described as: 'The amount for which a product, service or idea is exchanged, or offered for sale, regardless of its worth or value to potential purchasers. Although a monetary equivalent or value can be imputed, prices can incorporate goods exchanged e.g. cars traded in or similar deals.'[8] The marketing department's detailed involvement with price is essential because of the prime role played by price in the exchange concept which is one of the principles to be found at the very heart of marketing and also because of the department's close involvement with both customers and the sales effort.

Pricing is also a vital part of the whole marketing process, it may determine whether or not a new product is accepted onto the market and it may also be a factor in determining the volume of sales achieved for the company in the longer term. In highly competitive markets, high prices may result in lower sales unless the marketing department can reduce the effect of price through adding value to the product or convincing the public that the higher price is worth paying through concerted efforts in the area of image building. It is one of the most important tasks of marketing management to 'sell' the price level of a proposed product or service to its proposed market.

Price, along with cost and sales volume, is one of the main variables which determine profit. This means that the higher the price that can be raised without affecting either costs or sales volume then the higher the profit will be – which is where marketing again comes in.

How Pricing is Linked to Company Objectives

One of the key decisions affecting the marketing of a product is price. Before deciding where to set a price, a company needs to know what it wants to achieve in the marketplace. If a product has been carefully designed to fit into a certain position, either upmarket or further down, then the price levels of its products will reflect this and will actually play their part in that positioning process.

The clearer a company's objectives, the easier it will be to determine the levels at which prices should be set. Kotler[9] tells us that a company can pursue any of six major objectives through its pricing:

1 *Survival.* This can only be a short-term measure as, when survival is the prime objective, a company might price its offerings so that it is just covering variable costs along with some fixed costs – a situation which it obviously cannot contain in the longer term. At most, this situation will allow the firm to survive through a period of recession, intense competition or extreme change in its marketplace.

2 *The maximization of short-term profit levels.* Again, this cannot lend itself to the long-term advantage of any company as it would be pushing short-term financial performance to the detriment of its long-term position. In this situation the company might also be ignoring the messages of its market with regard to the likely reactions of customers and competitors. A company might adopt this position in the short term if it had cash-flow problems.

3 *The maximization of short-term revenue.* By estimating the likely levels of demand for its products, a company might set a price which it hopes will produce the highest level of sales revenue. This course is often adopted in the belief that the achievement of maximum possible revenue levels in the short term will eventually lead to maximum levels of profits in the long term as well as growth in market share.

4 *Maximum growth in unit sales.* Other companies might price at a level aimed at achieving the highest possible sales volume. This is because they hope that sales levels will be high enough for the achievement of economies of scale in production and distribution thus leading to a high level of long-term profit. This strategy is known as **penetration pricing** and can be successful in a market which is extremely sensitive to price. A low price may also help to discourage price competition.

5 *Skimming the market.* Innovative new products lend themselves to a skimming strategy so that the best possible financial benefit is gained before competitive

offerings are launched into the market. The high price will emphasize that the product is a superior one and the price will be lowered as sales begin to slow down in order to take advantage of segments positioned lower down in the market.

6 *To equate products with quality.* If a company wants to have a name for high quality then it may price its offerings higher than other similar products to achieve this. Naturally, the quality and reliability of the product will have to match the price.

Now refer to Activity MKT4.3.

ACTIVITY MKT4.3

PRICING

Activity code
- ✓ Self-development
- ✓ Teamwork
- ✓ Communications
- ✓ Numeracy/IT
- ✓ Decisions

Pricing aims are shown below. Determine a pricing policy to meet these aims and make a comment justifying your actions.

Aim	Possible pricing policy	Comment
'Quick buck'		
'Market entry and/or increase market share'		
'Steady rate of return'		
'Recoup costs in the immediate term'		
'Portfolio pricing' to give the overall product range an edge		
Discounting as a promotional feature		
Market-led pricing		

Factors Influencing Pricing Strategies

Companies must not only fit their strategies for pricing products into the list of their own corporate and marketing objectives, they must also fit them into the practical aspects of their areas of operation and into the other areas of the marketing mix with which price is linked: product, promotion and place (or distribution). Apart from this, general considerations from the wider environment in which the company operates need to be taken into account when price levels are the subject of decision and review. It is useful to look at some of these areas in rather more detail:

- *Product-related factors* include the product's position in the *product lifecycle* where either a skimming or a penetration strategy may be adopted in the early stages and modified as the product matures; the extent of the *product range* which might mean that, where a product spans several market segments, a differently priced variation may be offered to each segment (adaptations of basic models of cars designed and priced to appeal to people who like sporty cars, for example, Ford's XR2 and XR3 models); and the relationship between *product quality* and *image* where premium pricing might be advantageous.

- *Promotion-related factors* where the type and extent of promotional activity is linked to company objectives and to marketing objectives, for example, where *low promotional expenditure* and *low price* are linked together, the product is likely to be a basic one like sugar or potatoes.

- *Distribution-related factors* reflect the way in which products are distributed and sold, for example, where a large number of retail outlets is vital to the meeting of marketing objectives then special prices and promotional offers need to be made available to retailers and wholesalers.

- *Factors outside the company* which affect the levels at which it sets its prices would include levels of competitive activity, the economic situation and interest rates, social factors, prices charged by suppliers and the nature of the market, for example, whether consumer or industrial.

Methods of Setting Prices

Given that Kotler's[10] 'three Cs' of pricing – *customers, cost* and *competition* – have been taken into consideration along with the other factors examined above, a company should be in a position to begin to set an actual price.

There are a variety of methods of doing this. One of the most basic is **cost plus** pricing, where the manufacturer (or the retailer where appropriate) adds a fixed percentage mark-up to the cost of each unit produced. The percentage level at which the mark-up is set will depend on the type of product, the type of industry and the type of market in which the product is offered for sale.

Break-even pricing is also a popular method which involves an analysis of the number of units needed to cover fixed and variable costs at different levels of production. Once this has been done, the level of profit required is decided and production levels and the sales effort are organized accordingly. The biggest drawback of this method as well as of cost plus pricing is that they allow for little attention being paid to market considerations.

More forward thinking companies use the buyer's **perception of value** as a means of arriving at price levels rather than their own costs. To do this they use the elements of the marketing mix other than price to develop a perception of a suitable price in the eye of the likely purchaser. For example, marketing research methods might be used to find out how much individuals would be prepared to pay for a particular type of product (which might, at this stage, still be just a concept). The company would then work out the cost of producing the product in line with sales estimates to see whether a viable level of profit might be achieved at the proposed price.

In other cases, a company might price its products according to the **going rate**. It might be that a small company must set its prices at the same level of larger ones in the same industry if it is to succeed. Where competition for a particular contract is concerned, for example, for large building projects, it may be that **sealed bid pricing** will be the norm. This means that a company must price to beat what it thinks the competition will offer and in relation to how much it wants the contract rather than in relation to its own estimated costs and its profit objectives. Criteria for pricing are shown in Box MKT4.12.

Using Price as a Marketing Tool

The pricing structures used by companies need to reflect all the areas discussed above and they also need to take account of its marketing objectives and promotional activities.

- *Promotional pricing* involves the short-term reduction of prices to boost sales in the short term in the hope of long-term advantage. A variety of types of promotional pricing are available:
  - *loss leaders* require the dramatic reduction of prices on one or two items in order to attract customers into a retail outlet which might be a supermarket or a department store;
  - *interest-free credit* can be used to stimulate sales during times of economic recession or during July and January sales in department stores;
  - *extended guarantees and service* contracts can add extra sales to consumer durables or to office products;
  - *cash discounts* can help to clear high stock levels.

BOX MKT4.12

Criteria for pricing

Crissy and Boewadt[1] provide us with a useful checklist for pricing criteria and suggest when a high or low price (however so defined) should be applicable. The criteria are shown below with the implications for price.

	Pricing implication	
Some criteria	*Low*	*High*
■ *Promotion*		
◆ effort	Little	A lot
◆ contribution to line	A lot	A little
■ *Product*		
◆ type	Commodity	Proprietary
◆ obsolescence	Long life	Short life
◆ versatility	One use	Many uses
◆ lifespan	Short	Long
■ *Market (overall)*		
◆ coverage	Intensive	Selective
◆ share	Big	Small
◆ change (e.g. technology)	Slow	Fast
◆ phase	Mature	Young
■ *Place*		
◆ channels	Short	Long
■ *Production*		
◆ manufacture	Mass	Customized
◆ type of	Capital-intensive	Labour-intensive
■ *Service*	Little	Much
■ *Profit*		
◆ return	Longer-term	Shorter-term
◆ turnover	Fast	Slow

Source:
1 Adapted from Crissy and Boewadt, 'Pricing in perspective'

- *Discriminatory pricing* is often used to allow for different prices being charged according to market segment or to customer group:

  - *pricing according to customer group* means that different groups might be charged different prices for the same thing e.g. pensioners or students can obtain cheap rail tickets through the use of discount cards;

  - *pricing according to location* allows for different prices being charged even though they cost no more to provide, for example, cinema and theatre seats are priced according to how they are placed which allows for customer preferences on location and on price.

- *Product line pricing* involves the development of strategies and price levels for a whole line of products. In the case of clothing this may involve the use of price points which allow for, say, a line of skirts which sell at £20, £30 and £40. Additionally, if the differences between the cost levels of different products in a single line is small then customers are likely to buy at the next level up from that of their original intention. This will most likely not be the case if the price difference is a large one.

- *Essential product pricing* may be used where the purchase of a particular product means that it is essential for the buyer also to purchase an ancillary product, for example, cameras need films and razors need razor blades. In this case, the basic products may be priced low and the essential additions may be where the manufacturer actually makes the profit.

- *Two-level pricing* allows for a basic fee to be charged with the addition of a variable usage charge, for example, a monthly charge is made for telephone rental with additional charges according to the number of calls made.

The Box MKT4.13 gives a context to pricing within the enterprise.

BOX MKT4.13

Market and organizational considerations

Pricing: a new product

In the market or capitalist economy, the marketplace is king.

The demand for products will be conditioned by the market size and the needs/wants of the potential customers. The buying behaviour of these customers, from psychological needs to consumer desires, will have an impact on price. The size of the market population will be important as well: a mass market may mean volume sales with cheaper prices while a focused industrial market will probably mean a far narrower clientele and usually a higher pricing structure. Disposable income of consumers will be a critical component in higher-priced 'luxury goods' while essentials like food need to be bought almost irrespective of income.

The demand for other goods in the market may impact on pricing policy. The competitors' goods may provide a going rate; the potential for product alternatives or 'substitution' must be taken into account. Demand may be derived through a close dependency on a primary product, for example, car security locks will depend on the number of cars on the road. There is a cross-elasticity factor whereby the demand for goods can be influenced by the demand for other goods. For example, new curtains may be related to new furniture, and so on.

So the reaction of the competition, the 'inner' value of the product to the customer, the sensitivity of demand to different prices, the potential survival rate of the product and any legal constraints or ceilings on price should all be considered.

Within the organization, the cost accountant will have a considerable input into pricing strategy.[1] Other organizational considerations revolve around the product and the overall mix. For some examples of issues see below:

Some marketing considerations	Price implication
Is the new product part of a series and completing the range of the portfolio?	Cross-subsidies possible on pricing from portfolio.
Are there seasonal slumps and does the product 'iron them out'?	If so, it is an 'additional' tool, so pricing may not be critical if slack capacity etc. of production is being met.
Can we use existing distribution routes?	Again, new routes will be costlier and should be reflected in price.
Can we go 'piggy back' on existing products?	Again, like existing distribution channels, this will allow cross-fertilization between the products, so price may not be critical assuming it is in line with the 'piggy'.
Do we need a new image to promote this product?	If it is not consistent with existing imagery, the cost of promotion may be significant and may need to be reflected in pricing. There may also be an image of price for all company goods.
How much promotion is required, e.g. advertising?	These costs will have to be met either from the product itself or from the range. Relates also to potential volume sales expected.

Some marketing considerations	Price implication
Can we give some 'added value' through guarantees, service contracts etc.?	This may allow the price to float up a little or separate contracts, e.g. electrical goods, can be used to give larger service guarantees.

So, hitting the 'right price' is a complex matter involving marketing and other organizational variables, particularly costs.

Source:
1   See Anderson and Nix, *Effective Accounting Management*

It is possible to say that pricing is based upon basic economic theory and that, for this reason, marketing people need to have a knowledge of the principles of supply and demand as a sound basis for the development of successful pricing levels and strategies.

However, economics alone cannot ensure success in pricing, and a knowledge of marketing principles, markets and customers is also essential so that pricing strategies can be evolved to meet company objectives in matters of market share and volume sales. In addition, separate strategies need to be developed for products at different stages in their lifecycle and in different types of market. If economics can provide a base, then that base needs to be built on with the tools and techniques available to marketing management. We will continue to develop these tools in the final two units, particularly with a focus on the techniques associated with the other parts of the mix.

Notes
1 Bloom, 'Product redefinition begins with the consumer.'
2 Kotler, *Marketing Management*, 2nd edn.
3 Kotler, *Marketing Management*, 7th edn.
4 Ansoff, 'Strategies for Diversification.'
5 Booz, Alan and Hamilton Inc., *New Products Management for the 1980s.*
6 Mercer, *Marketing.*
7 Hedley, 'Strategy and the business portfolio'.
8 Cannon, *Basic Marketing.*
9 Kotler, *Marketing Management.*
10 Ibid.

Unit Five

Distribution and Communications

Learning Objectives

After completing this unit you should be able to:

- understand the role of logistics management within the overall marketing mix;

- distinguish between materials handling and physical distribution management;

- choose appropriate methods of promoting products and services;

- consider objectively the question of evaluating the success of communications campaigns;

- apply the generic skills.

Contents

Unit Five

❝ There was once a miraculous product. According to its manufacturers this product could do the most marvellous things:
make you breathe more easily, soothe your throat, improve
your performance in sport and work, aid your digestion,
freshen your breath, give you an air of sophistication and
glamour and make you popular with the opposite sex.
   The product is still around, but the claims made on its behalf
have been toned down a little since the 1960s. The product is
the cigarette. ❞

M. Jones, 'The fire eaters'[1]

Overview

This unit is concerned with telling customers what you have to offer and
deciding how to make it available to them. Consequently we examine the
various methods of getting the goods out to the customer. This also has an
impact on the decision-making area of physical distribution. The elements
of this 'communications menu' between firm and customer is then touched
upon alongside the 'communications mix'. Insights are given into the
practical workings of advertising, sales promotion and public relations
which are all covered in depth in a separate volume of this series.[2] (See
figure 5.1.)

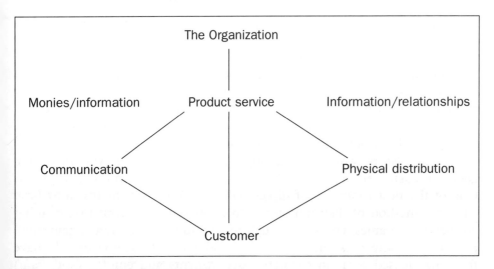

Figure 5.1 Outline diagram of Unit Five.

The Role of 'Place' in the Marketing Mix

The first two variables in the marketing mix are concerned with product/ market decisions and with pricing decisions, that is, with deciding what product or service to offer for sale and what price to charge for it. In some ways, although marketing research will have been undertaken and the competitive environment examined, these are internal decisions: they are concerned with what happens *inside* the company, although the external context should always be noted. In contrast, the final two elements of the marketing mix are concerned with what happens *outside* the company: with physically making the goods or services available to customers (place) and with persuading them to buy in the first place (promotion). The 'place' and 'promotion' involve relationships and communication networks, as developed in our preface.

From an operational point of view, logistics or physical distribution management entails the practical integration of all of the organizational efforts which are applied to the movement and storage of its products. From a strictly marketing point of view, it means making the goods (plus any necessary services, for example, installation) available to customers at the right place, at the right time and in the form in which they are required.

Physical distribution management also covers:

- channel decisions and management;
- logistics;
- wholesaling and retailing;
- customer support and service levels.

However, the actual decisions about which distribution channels and methods should be used are strategic ones and are therefore going to be made at board level in accordance with the company's overall corporate plan. They should also be made in the light of marketing information and the company's declared marketing objectives and, additionally, they should be linked closely to the question of competitive advantage. From this point of view, it might be important to match the number of outlets available to the competition, or to try to achieve deeper penetration in vital areas, or to aim for a wider geographic spread of outlets.

It might also be worth considering *different or additional* ways of getting goods to customers, for example, through direct sales and/or mail order. One of the best examples of direct selling is Avon Cosmetics; they have chosen a method of distribution which is far removed from that of other cosmetic companies who sell through retail outlets – although certain more prestigious companies such as Estée Lauder and Lancôme usually have their own leased areas in cosmetics departments and employ (and train) their own consultants. Direct selling and supply also takes place in industrial markets where, say, a new computer system is to be installed and meetings occur over a long period between sales people and personnel involved in the decision-making process.

This approach is justified when the size of the likely order is large enough to support it, for example, in the case of the computer system mentioned above or in the case of Avon Cosmetics where the chosen sales/distribution system differentiates the product from all others. Additionally, in the case of cosmetic companies with their own space in large department stores, only outlets which are likely to produce a large (and therefore profitable) volume of business would be deemed acceptable. See Box MKT5.1.

BOX MKT5.1

Making and breaking companies

The Palladium Cinema at Midsomer Norton, near Bath, has closed. Established in 1913, its life lasted some eighty years.

Competition is always around the corner. Television first, then videos and perhaps more salubrious cinemas have taken their toll.

The key difficulty according to Ken Steel, the owner, has been *distribution*. The local towns and cities get the best films from the distributors up to a month, if not longer, before his cinema. Consequently, his potential clientele goes elsewhere. With a break-even position of 100 customers every night, his actual position was nearer 30 customers per night. This has occurred in spite of a growing market in UK cinema attendance almost doubling since 1985 to 100 million in 1993.

The demise has been caused by distribution and timing. Because customers could not (or would not) wait for the film to come to their local cinema, the audience numbers fell and this, in turn, meant that the distributors would not circulate the films to Mr Steel. This vicious distribution circle could not be broken.

Source: Adapted from Harrison, 'The last picture show ends in tears'

What Methods or Channels of Distribution are Available to Us?

Where most fast-moving consumer goods are concerned, such as toothpaste, potato crisps, breakfast cereals, magazines, the value of any individual sale is not large, and volume sales are relied upon to produce acceptable levels of profit. Therefore, sales need to be made through a large number of different outlets if the necessary volume is to be achieved. It would be both practically impossible and far too costly for manufacturers themselves to set up and service these outlets. Imagine, for example, Cadburys trying to set up their own outlets for selling chocolate bars to the public.

Additionally, in the case of these low profit margin, high volume products, the outlets through which they are eventually made available to consumers need to be able to spread the cost of selling them over a range of products from a variety of manufacturers.

Stern and El-Ansary[3] tell us:

> *Intermediaries smooth the flow of goods and services. ... This procedure is necessary in order to bridge the discrepancy between the assortment of goods and services generated by the producer and the assortment demanded by the consumer. The discrepancy results from the fact that manufacturers typically produce a large quantity of a limited variety of goods, whereas consumers usually desire only a limited quantity of a wide variety of goods.*

This is where wholesalers and retailers come in – as part of the **distribution chain** as **channels of distribution**. Now please refer to Box MKT5.2.

BOX MKT5.2

Wholesalers and distributors

Wholesalers and distributors are both links in the overall distribution chain, and their purpose is to provide a link between producers of goods and small or widely scattered retail outlets which are uneconomic to service individually.

- *Wholesalers* deal mostly with retailers such as corner shops and small grocers. They stock a variety of products from different manufacturers, mostly in the ranges of fast-moving consumer goods (although there are also electrical wholesalers) and these are sold either through the wholesaler's own sales force or through self-service warehouses.

- *Distributors* are usually held to be wholesalers who deal with industrial goods and sell them to small businesses and tradespeople, for example, in the building trade.

- *Agents* usually sell products for more than one supplier on a commission basis which is dealt with through a formal contract. In many ways, they function as extensions of the supplier's own sales force but they may operate in areas which it is not economic to cover with permanent staff.

- *Cash and carry* is the most basic form of wholesaling and essentially, it is a supermarket for retailers.

Source: Adapted from Mercer, *Marketing*

Manufacturers thus have the choice of either dealing directly with the individuals or organizations who purchase their products, or of reaching customers through one or more intermediaries. The choices made will depend on the size of the company, the type of merchandise and the characteristics of the marketplace in which it is being offered for sale.

From figure 5.2 we can see that the function of distribution channels is to move products from manufacturers to consumers in an appropriate manner and that the use of intermediaries reduces the number of individual transactions that the manufacturer has to make. This decreases the overall costs of distribution, both through the reduction of the number of sales which have to be made and through reducing the number of points to which physical deliveries have to be made.

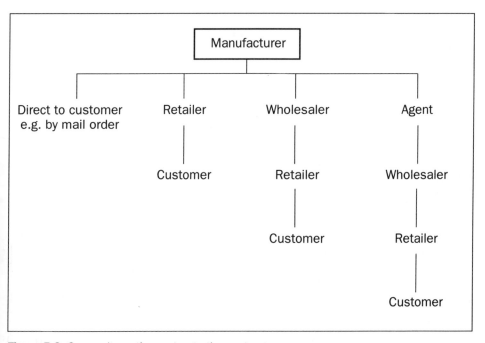

Figure 5.2 Some alternative routes to the customer.

The more intermediaries there are then the *longer* is the distribution chain held to be:

- The use of a direct marketing channel means that goods go straight from the manufacturer to the user. So far as consumer goods are concerned, there are four main methods of selling direct: *mail order* (catalogues like Freeman and Littlewoods, or direct sales through advertisements, such as collectors' items from the Bradford Exchange which are advertised in colour supplements); *door-to-door* selling (like double glazing or Jehovah's Witnesses); *party plan* (Tupperware, lingerie and wigs); and the *manufacturer's own shops* which may, or may not, be *franchises* (The Body Shop, Thornton's Chocolates).

- Products may be sold directly to retailers by manufacturers, in which case there is a *single-stage* distribution chain (supermarket chains like Sainsbury and Tesco buy in huge quantities direct from manufacturers like Heinz or Procter & Gamble who deliver into the supermarkets' own regional warehouses). Alternatively, the distribution chain may go through *two stages,* where products are sold by manufacturers to distributors (in the case of industrial goods which are then sold on to builders' merchants or small tradesmen) or wholesalers (in the case of consumer goods like food or small electricals which will then be sold on to small retailers).

It should also be noted that large manufacturers may make use of different lengths of distribution channels for the same products, for example, Heinz may sell baked beans both to supermarket chains and to food wholesalers. Please refer to Box MKT5.3.

BOX MKT5.3

Distribution channels in the service sector

The idea of marketing channels can be applied in a wider sense than simply that of moving physical products from producers to consumers. Producers of services (like hairdressers and health centres) and of ideas (like campaigning organizations) need to take decisions about making themselves available to their target audiences.

> Hospitals must be located in geographic space to serve the people with complete medical care, and we must build schools close to the children who have to learn. Fire stations must be located to give rapid access to potential conflagrations and voting booths must be placed so that people can cast their ballots without expending unreasonable amounts of time, effort or money to reach the polling stations. Many of our states face the problem of locating branch campuses to serve a burgeoning and increasingly well-educated population. In the cities we must create and locate playgrounds for the children. Many over-populated countries must assign birth control clinics to reach the people with contraceptive and family planning information.

Marketing channels are also used in 'person' marketing. Politicians need to find methods of getting their messages over to their constituents and to the public at large by the use of channels which might vary from party political broadcasts on television to surgeries in individual constituencies and coffee mornings for faithful supporters.

Source: Adapted from Kotler, *Marketing Management*

How Do We Decide Which Channels to Use?

As was stated in the introduction to this unit, decisions about distribution methods and chains are strategic ones and, additionally, as well as affecting every part of a company's operational structure, they are also vital because of their place as one of the elements in the marketing mix – the four Ps.

Decisions made about distribution directly affect both the *pricing* and the *promotion* elements of the overall mix. Price levels will be affected by the choice of channel according to the number of *stages* in the distribution chain because a profit has to be allowed for at every stage, thus adding to the ultimate price to the consumer.

The promotional and selling aspects of the organizational task will also be affected by channel decisions. The size and shape of both sales force and promotional budgets will be greatly influenced by whether goods are sold direct or through intermediaries. Additionally, decisions regarding distribution chains need to be strategic ones because they are long-term commitments. It costs time and money to establish relationships with distributors and wholesalers on a national level so that arrangements once made may not lightly be changed.

At the same time, the company has to balance up the estimated costs and benefits of different approaches to distribution. Dealing directly with customers leaves the organization in full control of all its sales and distribution activities while, on the other hand, it can reduce distribution costs by dealing with intermediaries. However, if it does this, then it loses control over some elements of the operation. For example, wholesalers may be persuaded to stock certain products but it may be more difficult to ensure that they make an effort to move your products on into the hands of retailers rather than those of your competitors. For this reason, trade promotions (which are dealt with in the promotion section of this unit) and incentives are a vital part of any organization's sales and distribution operations.

The example of Polygram can be seen in Box MKT5.4. Thereafter, tackle Activity MKT5.1 which concerns channel selection.

BOX MKT5.4

Distribution channels

Polygram, the film to music company with the expensive CDs, is now looking to alternative channels of distribution for its middle- and lower-priced CDs. The new channel will supplement existing retail outlets which range from specialist music shops to garages. The new channel will not take up valuable shelf space which can be used for selling the more expensive versions of the CDs.

Polygram will have both pop and classical CDs available through this new channel.

The method is to sell CDs via the daily delivery of milk to your doorstep!

ACTIVITY MKT5.1

KEN COLLEGE

Activity code
- ✓ Self-development
- ✓ Teamwork
- ☐ Communications
- ☐ Numeracy/IT
- ✓ Decisions

Jim Mo is the Principal of Ken College in Bath. The college is a new venture started by Jim with financial backing from an old friend. Jim's background is in financial management and consultancy. British by birth and Kenyan by adoption, Jim has a Euro-African vision of business.

His early working life revolved around financial consultancy audit and management for large partnerships based in London and in Nairobi. Involvement in small and medium-sized businesses to financial appraisal, investment analysis and capital funding projects occurred in this ten-year period. In addition, he had experience of management consultancy, particularly training. The years were getting by and he was reasonably comfortable as a professional accountant, but he yearned for the financial independence of being his own man.

The skills and expertise of a financial accountant are easily transferable, so he started his own firm. At first he looked at an import–export agency between Kenya and the UK but lack of capital inhibited such a programme getting off the ground. There was some success, but the mainstay of the income came from financial management. Even then, the big audit firms had a stranglehold on the compulsory company audits and managed to have the profitable spin-offs in other financial consultancy owing to their presence in the market. Indeed, some of their financial services could be seen as loss leaders or at least were easily absorbed into the enormous audit fees. Competition was tough – very tough.

On a flight back from Africa during this tough period, he flicked through a business magazine and found an interesting article. Here, competition was not bad; quite the reverse as it could lead to great success since energy and commitment were required to get above your rivals. He was refreshed in mind and reflected further.

He was certainly envious of those large accountancy firms and he realized that their size inhibited innovation. However, his one-man band could not compete on the same stage as a centre of excellence because of resource constraints. It was excellent – clients had encouraged him to, but he could never compete in international finance with these big boys without institutional backing, or without an international reputation acquired from writing innovative work in the fashion of the American business guru Professor Porter. The writing would have to wait but the institutional backing could not. He would act on his return.

Jim, an active, fast-thinking man, decided to look around for some institutional backing for his financial consultancy. He had a competitive edge with his unique experience, contacts, knowledge of developing countries and external funding to these countries, particularly in Africa. He tried to get some pump-prime funding but to no avail. He was shrewd enough not to go to the high street banks with their rates of interest which verged on usury in some cases.

'Perhaps the idea itself is flawed,' he reflected. 'Let's look at the facts. Unique knowledge and experience of Africa, UK and financial management, coupled with a vision of enterprise.' 'Correct,' said his friend, Ala. 'But you are taking a production-oriented view. It is not just what you can do; this must be tailored to what the marketplace wants. Indeed, the market dictates and your strengths must dovetail into these opportunities. Forget "minimization of weaknesses" which many texts advise – go for your strengths related to an opportunity.' 'Mm,' Jim concurred. The issue was opportunity.

Needs must, so Jim continued with financial consulting, and did some part-time teaching at a private college. He was a natural teacher with good communications skills, a pleasant manner and a rapport with the students, underpinned by practical exposure to finance and accounting at a senior level.

During a financial exercise his thoughts moved back to some earlier ideas which had occurred to him on the way into town by underground train. 'I teach two separate groups of some fifty students. That's a hundred in all, each of whom pays fees of around £5,000. Now they do about ten subjects including mine – so that's around £500 per subject per student and there are a hundred students. That makes quite an attractive sum (£50,000). They pay me £21 per hour for four hours' work, which is £84, and no extra for marking – although they allow me a one-hour tutorial per week, so that makes £105. Call it £100 per week for thirty weeks. That is £3,000. So six students pay my salary. Apart from their fixed costs of the building and the variable costs of admin. and advertising etc, the mark-up here must be colossal. More importantly, these overseas students – often from Africa – end up paying full fees for a qualification which is at best only partly recognized in the UK and in their own country. It's not on.'

Armed with a sense of indignation, a need for money and a desire for fairness, Jim now knew where he was going. A fellow African businessman, a friend of a friend, agreed to put some capital into the project, which both saw as viable.

Jim's first step was to go back to finance. The professions surely needed some college to prepare their respective students. Market research showed this to be the case, but arguably the market was saturated with such specialist colleges. Professor Porter was right, thought Jim, but the playing field at the beginning of the game needs to be a little more level. His exposure to the private business college was the way forward. It would include both finance and business. Good premises were obtained in a reasonably well-to-do part of Bath where students from abroad could come to learn both finance and business studies.

Jim looked first at the product. A degree or equivalent qualification could be bought in for a price from an overseas college, but this would be self-defeating as students wanted to come to the UK for a British qualification, and many of these qualifications from 'universities' were virtually worthless. To attempt to get a British-validated degree would mean a tremendous expense on resources, library to computing, more qualified full-time staff and probably bigger premises. A 'franchise' was possible but, again, the resources were limited at this time. The college would become a 'feeder' for the larger institutions preparing overseas students for a British education.

The next issue was: how to reach the target market, or what channels of distribution could he use? Jim started to thumb through his old marketing notes. What channels were open to his Bath-based college targeting overseas students? Equally important what guiding principles could be exercised in the choice of channel?

The channels are as follows:

- *'Retail'*, that is, an existing college based overseas.
- *Wholesale.*
- *Distributors,* who could buy in his 'goods' and sell them on to the customers.
- *Agents.*
- *Direct selling* via visits, exhibitions, personal selling and brochures etc.

The real choice was between agents acting on his behalf and direct selling. It may not be a straight one versus either but the 'mix' had to be appropriate and guidelines for channel selection also had to be thought through.

1 Advise Ken College on some criteria of channel selection.
2 Give the pros and cons of using agents and using direct sales.

Channel decisions have to be made in the light of the *product*, the *market* and the *company* which is involved in each case, and these decisions involved in producing the overall marketing mix itself:

- So far as *the market* is concerned, industrial products will probably need to be distributed through different channels than those used for consumer products, even if the actual product itself is the same, for example, light bulbs could be categorized as industrial products or consumer ones, depending on the end user. Where the market is closely concentrated into a small geographical area then it may well be preferable and more economical to deal direct with customers, but once it spreads far beyond this then the use of distributors or wholesalers may be the only answer.

- *The product itself* also plays a part in the making of distribution decisions. Small, high-volume items like chocolate bars or paper tissues are likely to have longer distribution chains than heavy, bulky products which may be difficult to transport and, in the latter case, it may be a retailer who makes a sale but the product may be delivered to the customer direct from the manufacturer. For example, expensive suites of furniture may be bought from a sample seen in a department store, the manufacturer will not actually produce the item until the order is received, then it is delivered to the customer up to three months later. In contrast, perishables like fruit and vegetables need to be delivered quickly and, while in transit, they need to be kept in suitable physical conditions.

■ *The type of company* is also important. A small, struggling company may need to use intermediaries because it cannot afford to run the fleet of vans or the number of sales people which will be needed to deal directly with customers.

Now tackle Activity MKT5.2.

ACTIVITY MKT5.2

MAIL ORDER

Activity code

✓ Self-development
✓ Teamwork
☐ Communications
☐ Numeracy
✓ Decisions

Assume that you are a marketeer in the mail order business.

Read Box MKT5.5 on agents and mail order.

From the following facts derive a marketing view of where your business should be going.

■ Since the 1970s market share has been falling.
■ The sector is losing out to the established retail outlets in the high street, or to the warehouses at the edge of towns.
■ Credit policies, the rationale behind the catalogues for most people, are easily obtainable elsewhere.
■ Many agents are no longer agents (see Box MKT5.5).
■ Launching a new catalogue is expensive.
■ There is a 'dated' flavour about their image, perhaps reminiscent of harder times for many people and of living on 'tick' or hire purchase.

These three factors influence whether or not it will be either necessary or desirable to use intermediaries for distributing products, but decisions about the actual channels to be used and the number of stages in those channels still have to be made. Companies need to think about the following:

- *The types and numbers of intermediaries* to be used, for example, whether to use retailers or wholesalers or both. Additionally, it is necessary to think about the level of distribution needed to achieve marketing and sales objectives, for example, is it vital to achieve *intensive distribution* through persuading every possible outlet to stock the item? (The competitive situation will also influence this decision.) In other cases (those perhaps of expensive cosmetics or high-priced china and crystal like Wedgwood or Waterford) *exclusive distribution* may be the right answer where a few, carefully chosen, upmarket outlets reflect the image and cost of the products themselves. However, in many cases, something between these two extremes is likely to provide the best answer through the use of *selective distribution* where the costs of servicing large numbers of outlets will be balanced against the need to secure an adequate and viable part of the available market.

- Which channels are more likely to reach *target markets*? For example, would the exclusive outlets mentioned above be appropriate, or would it be preferable to have a wider spread of middle-of-the-road outlets?

- What sort of *bargaining position* will the manufacturer be able to achieve? For example, in an exclusive, carefully chosen outlet, such as a car dealership, the manufacturers should be able to expect a good deal of effort to be put into the sales of their products. However, if the product is simply a new type of breakfast cereal on sale in a supermarket, then the position will be completely different.

- Which distribution pattern will, in the long term, produce the *highest possible level of sales at the lowest possible level of cost?* Ultimately, whatever the answers to the other questions asked about physical distribution and different channels, this should be the deciding factor. Please refer now to Box MKT5.5.

BOX MKT5.5

Distribution: agents and mail order

In January 1993, Sears Roebuck decided to abandon their famous catalogue. With huge losses (almost $838 million, third quarter) radical 'surgery' appeared to be inevitable.

The catalogue had helped rural America keep up to date with clothing, jewellery and farm tools since 1896.

A shopping revolution may be under way, with better access to 'real' shops accounting for heavy after-tax losses over the last few years and up to $175 million lost in one year alone.

Mail order in the UK seems to be following a similar pattern. Credit is available from most retail outlets and customers have the convenience of seeing what they are buying before parting with their money.

The distribution system traditionally relied on agents who would promote the catalogue to friends and workmates. A weekly payment would follow to clear off the purchase. Perhaps over-generous pricing as far as the companies were concerned did not help, as cheaper alternatives could be bought in most high streets. The agents began to be the purchasers and the network system – initially a basis for an agent having a catalogue – meant that the circle of selling began to crumble. Littlewoods are now shedding labour and GUS is seeing its market share slipping by 10 per cent to 30 per cent over the last ten years.

A specific target policy of hitting the consumer more directly has been employed by Next, but it may be reaching a different segment of the population. With rising incomes and greater access to retail outlets coupled with freer credit, this type of distribution may have seen its best days. Yet there will be some market left – particularly in depressed areas or people with depressed incomes in times of recession – but this may be in relative decline as well. We can say that the agent in this case with his or her commission looks to be a dated form of distribution.

How Might We Cope with Conflict and Competition?

It is important to remember that, however much effort you put into choosing exactly the right channels of distribution and the right intermediaries, yours is not the only company interest that they are dealing with. They have their own interests at heart as well as yours. For example, there have been occasions when car manufacturers have been in conflict with their dealers over terms and conditions, and even The Body Shop has had to oppose franchisees in court. There may also be conflict involved when you sell some of your products direct to supermarkets and some of them through wholesalers.

Additionally, there may be conflict between dealers or franchisees who consider that others are poaching their exclusive areas. In cases like this it may well be up to the manufacturer (or franchiser) to arbitrate. Other ways of coping with motivation levels of wholesalers and retailers who also will be selling your competitors' products may be through discounts and promotions.

Coping with the Mechanics of Distribution

Unfortunately, the making of channel decisions is not the end of the distribution story – there still remains the physical movement of goods from one place (the factory, warehouse or regional depot) to another (the customer, retailer or wholesaler).

This is the area of **logistics** or **physical distribution management** to which, these days a **systems approach** is frequently adopted. This means looking at the complete operation of moving finished products from the factory to the customer as one whole task, or system, rather than as a series of small and unrelated tasks which may be dealt with by different departments. Only by adopting this approach does it become possible to handle physical distribution in the most economic way.

In some companies, the distribution system comes under the control of the marketing department, in others it belongs to the production department and, in still others, it is a separate entity under the control of a physical distribution manager who may also actually be in charge of the system by which components or raw materials are brought into the factory.

Elements which make up the physical distribution system might include:

- transport (including decisions about whether a company operates its own fleet of vehicles or uses carriers);
- stock control (including ordering new supplies of raw materials and controlling stock levels of finished goods);
- packing and materials handling;
- order processing;
- warehousing (including making decisions about the number and location of warehouses).

Looking at this breakdown, it can be seen that logistics management or physical distribution management can actually be divided into two parts. The first part (*materials management*) deals with the purchasing of parts and materials, their delivery to the factory (including elements like 'just in time' if this system is adopted) and covers everything to do with the movement of the product until it finally rolls off the end of the production line in its completed state. Once the product is completed the *physical distribution* element takes over to mastermind the journey of the product to its final home. Please refer to Box MKT5.6 for some relevant research findings.

Communicating with Your Market

Most of us have heard that if we make a better mousetrap, then the world will beat a path to our door – but will it? Presumably, the aim behind the production of the better mousetrap is to sell it – preferably to as many people as possible. However, if we simply make our mousetraps and then sit waiting for customers, how many are we likely to get? No matter how brilliant our products might be, we can hardly expect floods of customers unless they have some means of finding out what it is that we have to offer.

BOX MKT5.6

The physical distribution system

A research project carried out by the Centre for Physical Distribution Management breaks the functions of the task down into extremely detailed areas of work. The list comes from a close examination of the work actually carried out by physical distribution managers:

- *Transportation* covers: the use to which vehicles will be put, for example, carrying finished products to regional warehouses; specifying the types and designs of vehicles to be used, such as refrigerated vehicles which may be needed for perishable goods; whether or not to use independent carriers for some or all of the work; direct or indirect deliveries, for example, straight to customers or firstly to regional storage points; load and route planning; purchase or lease of vehicles.
- *Materials handling* covers: the movement of material round the factory; storage; all movement and handling systems.
- *Packaging* involves: the safety of goods in transit; packaging for individual items.
- *Warehousing and location* covers: warehouse size and layout; location of depots and warehouses so as to give the most economic national distribution.
- *Stock holding and control* involves: necessary levels of stocks of finished products and materials; physical control of stocks.
- *Processing* covers: design and operation of admin. systems related to materials and stocks; drop size and cost analysis.
- *Control and analysis of costs* involves: audit of costs, allocation of costs; analysis of profitability of individual customers.
- *Strategic and general issues* covers: service levels and their costs; policy formulation; keeping abreast of relevant legislation; supervision and motivation of distribution staff; decisions re use of own fleet versus use of contractors.

Source: Adapted from Cannon, *Basic Marketing*

Even more than that, the onus would seem to be on us to tell them, rather than on them somehow to find out because, after all, we chose to make the product in the first place.

The answer is that we do need to find ways of communicating with our markets so that we can be sure of selling enough 'mousetraps' to produce an acceptable level of profit. This is where we come to the area of *marketing communications*, that is, the *promotion* part of the marketing mix and the final element in the four Ps of marketing. In this unit we will take a broad overview of the subject which is dealt with in detail in a separate book in this series, *Effective Marketing Communications*. Please refer now to Box MKT5.7.

No matter how much research we carried out before deciding to go ahead and produce a particular product, no matter how much that research showed that the market wanted the product, we still need to tell

---

BOX MKT5.7

Mass production, mass markets and mass media

Ever since Henry Ford installed the first production line, firstly large batch production and then mass production became more and more important as mass demand for products and services developed and increased.

The continued growth of mass markets fed demand which, in turn, kept the production lines running. Development of the production process has continued, as demand has continued, with the introduction of automated production processes, computer-aided manufacturing (CAM) and the use of robots by car manufacturers.

Mass demand and mass production led to the development of mass media to allow communication between producers and their markets. First came newspapers, then magazines and the introduction of colour printing for large circulation magazines. These were closely followed by radio, then television as communications and promotional media.

The initial capacity for mass production brought prices down (the Model T Ford was the first car that the American middle classes could afford) and led to mass demand and consumption which, in turn, led to the development of mass media.

Any one of these would not be possible without the other two and, in today's highly competitive markets, effective methods of mass communication are vital for business survival.

Even with industrial products, the nature of the communications mix used today is far more extensive than in Henry Ford's time.

This is why today's students of marketing need to understand and appreciate the complexity of the current communications situation.

Source: Adapted from Foster, *Mastering Marketing*

---

people when it becomes available and where they can go to buy it. Luckily, the modern world of marketing has a ready-made system of communicating with markets – there is a whole **menu** of communication methods available (both **personal** and **impersonal**) from which to choose an appropriate **communications mix**. This varies according to the market, the product and the stage it has reached in its lifecycle, the customer, the budget, the competition and our overall corporate and marketing objectives (see figure 5.3).

The broad areas of the **menu of marketing communications** are (and these will be looked at in turn):

- advertising – both media and non-media;
- sales promotion – including merchandising and packaging;

	Personal	Impersonal
Paid	Face-to-face selling Telephone selling Exhibitions	Press advertising Broadcast advertising Posters Sales promotion Leaflets Brochures Catalogues
Unpaid	Press receptions Seminars Tours of factory Open days Charity events	Press releases News stories Newsletters

Figure 5.3 Personal and impersonal methods of communicating with customers.

■ public and press relations;
■ personal selling.

Box MKT5.8 summarizes the main types of options open to the marketeer.

However, communication with markets is more complicated than simply deciding where to advertise and whether or not to include public relations in the communications mix. The act of communication, in marketing terms, also includes putting across the atmosphere and the image associated with the product because these are part of the intangible product aspects which go towards building up the whole offering made to the market. So, it is not just the choice of media which matters, it is the choice of message as well – plus the way in which that message is presented.

The whole purpose of marketing communication is to move potential customers from a state of ignorance about a product or service to a state where they will actually take action and buy. We use the process of marketing communication to send messages which will help us to achieve this objective and, above all, we hope to be able to create messages which will be powerful enough to overcome the obstacles placed in their paths by everything from the customer's own inertia to the weight of the

---

BOX MKT5.8

The communications menu

Advertising
National newspapers
Regional and local newspapers
Consumer and leisure magazines
Specialist press
Trade and technical press
National and local television
Radio
Cinema
Posters
Trade directories
Local directories
House magazines
Audiovisual sales aids
Catalogues (mail order)
Leaflets and brochures
Vehicle livery
Display signs
Taxis
Waste bins
Direct mail
House styles and logos

PR/publicity
Press releases
Press conferences
Charity sponsorship
Press receptions
Speeches
Annual reports
Lobbying
Seminars
Tours
Publications
Community involvement

Sales promotion
Competitions
Lotteries
Packaging
Demonstrations
Free samples
Money-off coupons
Merchandising
Send away gifts
Extra quantity in pack
Free gift in pack
Banded packs
Self-liquidating offers
Loss leaders
Point-of-sale material
Displays
Discounts
Trading stamps
Collect coupons, choose gift
Exhibitions
Interest-free credit
Trade-ins
Charity promotions
Trade shows

Personal contact
Sales calls
Formal presentations
Telephone selling
Sampling
Trade fairs
Sales force incentives

---

promotional activities of the competition. Branding also plays an important part in this process of communication by providing strong visual and emotional links between the product (for example, through its packaging) and the promotional activities (for example, advertising) which are designed to sell it. (See figure 5.4.)

For each situation with which we are faced, we have to select a different collection of communication methods: we have to choose the right **communications mix** from the overall **communications menu**. There is no single 'best' way of putting together the 'right' communications mix. Every one of the available possibilities has its own advantages and disadvantages which need to be weighed up against cost and against predictions of their likely level of effectiveness.

Also, it is important to keep in mind the fact that the process of selling is a multi-stage activity – placing advertisements designed to inform and create awareness may be the first stage, a sales promotion campaign offering interest-free credit for a limited period may be the second stage, but it may not be until the third stage, of personal selling, that the sale is made.

The process of deciding upon the most desirable communications mix must begin with what should be the marketing department's bible – the current marketing plan. It must also be closely linked to the established

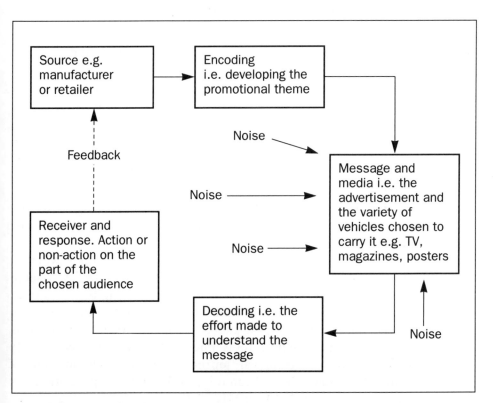

Figure 5.4 The process of communication.

Source: Adapted from Kotler, *Marketing Management*

marketing mix. Then, with these provisos in mind, it is necessary for the planners to begin to ask themselves a series of questions such as the following.

- *Who are our customers?* What kind of people are they? Where do they live? What kind of newspapers and magazines do they read? What do they like to watch on television? When do they listen to the radio?

- *Whose needs do we hope to satisfy?* Are they leaders or followers? Are they innovators or adapters? Are they family men and women? What are their leisure interests?

- *What are the benefits of our product or service and how will it offer satisfaction to our customers?* Are they looking for safer driving? Would they like to do the ironing faster? What are the benefits of a quiet weekend in the country?

- *What factual information will we need to supply and what will be the emotional appeal involved?* How will we describe and convey both the tangible and intangible aspects of what we have to offer?

- *How can we most successfully communicate with our customers and potential customers?* What type of media will be most suitable? Do we need a 'pull' strategy?

- *What is the best way of reaching the various links in the distribution chain?* Should we put most of our efforts into a 'push' strategy? Should we advertise in the appropriate trade press?

Working through these questions in a structured manner helps promotional planners to work out how many different selling tasks they need to undertake: the number of publics they need to reach and what kind of things need to be said to each of them. This then points to both the communications mix and the promotional message it will carry.

Whatever the elements of the mix which is eventually chosen, one thing is vital: the various parts should fit together to make a coherent whole, that is, they should fit in with an overall marketing plan and should all deliver the same message. Perhaps posters need to be planned to carry on the theme adopted in TV and press advertising – as with the Esso tiger. Service promotion is somewhat different from promoting products, so please now refer to Box MKT5.9.

The exact form of the communications mix also depends upon whether the product belongs in consumer markets or in industrial ones. A suitable mix for a breakfast cereal might consist of mass advertising on TV and in women's magazines, posters near shopping precincts and sales promotion (backed up with advertising in local papers). On the other hand, what is appropriate to industrial machine tools might be personal selling, trade exhibitions, PR aimed at technical journals and a small amount of advertising in the trade press. Promoting non-profit organizations is different again, so please refer to Box MKT5.10.

BOX MKT5.9

Promoting services

Although advertising, PR, personal selling and sales promotion can be applied to the promotion of services as well as to products, there are some important differences to be acknowledged when promoting services:

- *Personal selling and employees.* Services are usually produced and consumed at the same time, for example, when eating a meal in a restaurant or having a hair-do and it is at this same time the sale takes place. Therefore, the sale might be made by the person who is providing the service, so that most staff, for example, waitresses or bank clerks, might be described as sales people. It is for this reason that banks, building societies and hotel and retail chains have invested heavily in customer care programmes.
- *Word of mouth.* This is an important point where services are concerned and closely linked to the establishment of customer care programmes. A recommendation from a friend goes a long way when one is considering trying a new restaurant or hairdresser.
- *Tangibility.* Promotional campaigns need to make an effort to present intangibles in a tangible way, for example, airlines use smiling cabin staff to get across to customers the high level of service they provide.
- *Consistency.* One bad experience can sour several years of good experiences as far as staying in a particular hotel is concerned. Customer care programmes attempt to make sure the good service comes as standard.

Source: Adapted from Mercer, *Marketing*

BOX MKT5.10

Promoting non-profit organizations

Individuals working in non-profit organizations often have difficulty in coping with the idea of promotion in connection with the work they do. National Health Service hospitals are more likely to be turning 'customers' away than having to advertise to find them.

However true this may be, all organizations do need to find ways of communicating with the people who use their services. Social services departments need to tell clients when they are open, hospitals need to guide out-patients from one department to another.

Additionally, the government mounts its own advertising campaigns designed to change attitudes or to save lives – most notably the pre-Christmas 'drinking and driving' campaigns which use exactly the same media (television, press and posters) and techniques as commercial campaigns.

Source: Adapted from Mercer, *Marketing*

How Does the Communications Process Work?

In any form of communication, whether visual (like semaphore), audio-visual (like television), aural (like the telephone), or written (like a letter), there have to be at least two parties involved – a *sender* and a *receiver*. Then, in order to make the communication effective, the senders must first know who they want to communicate with, what message they want to transmit and what result they are hoping for.

Additionally, the sender must choose an appropriate medium for transmitting the message (semaphore would not be effective in the dark) and must be sure that the receiver will be able to understand it (even in daytime, semaphore would not be an effective way of sending a message if the receiver has never learned the code). Even when the medium is the right one and the receiver knows the code, there might still be problems if there is so much 'noise' that the message never gets the chance to be heard, or seen.

So far as promotional activities are concerned, companies and individuals are being exposed to hundreds of hopeful messages every day (on the radio as they drive to the station, on posters as they wait for the train, in the newspaper they read during the journey, through evening telephone calls from double glazing companies, and on television as they try to relax before going to bed). This means that marketing people have to accept that their target audience will never all absorb the message, most of them might never even notice it, and, of those that do, only a few will remember it for any length of time.

Nevertheless, we know that advertising and promotion do work when the product, the media and the message are all right and are able to work together to overcome distractions like the news for which the paper is actually bought and the promotional activities being carried out by the competition.

As we saw previously in this unit, transmitting a message to the target audience may be just the first stage on the journey towards a successful sale and it is useful to know that there are several models available to explain and guide this process.

Perhaps the best known of these models is A–I–D–A which covers the four stages of attention–interest–desire–action. In the case of a direct-response advertisement in a *Sunday Times* colour supplement, say, for a limited-edition china figurine, these four stages might involve:

- *Attention*. Rapid page turning comes to a stop as a colourful picture of a ballerina standing on one toe catches the eye. The headline 'Limited edition by well-known artist' invites further perusal.
- *Interest*. 'I need something at the other end of the mantelpiece to balance that dolphin statuette and this looks just as graceful as well as being the same height.' Skimming through the details of the advertisement reveals that the

figurine is one of a numbered limited edition of 10,000 and that it can be purchased by three monthly payments.

- *Desire.* Close examination of the photograph and detailed reading of the available information reveals the fine workmanship involved in producing the figurine and also the story behind it. 'I really like this, I'd like to have it and I can always send it back if it doesn't look so nice in reality or if I decide I can't afford it after all.'
- *Action.* 'There's a coupon which means I don't have to bother to write a letter and there's a Freepost address so I can pop it straight into the post on my way to work tomorrow and I won't even need to queue up in the Post Office for a stamp.'

Now tackle Activity MKT5.3 before consulting Box MKT5.11 to gain alternative perspectives to the concept of advertising response.

ACTIVITY MKT5.3

AN ADVERTISEMENT FOR A MARKETING MANAGER

Activity code

✓ Self-development
✓ Teamwork
✓ Communications
☐ Numeracy/IT
✓ Decisions

In Unit One we examined the role of the marketing manager and now we have just completed the key aspects of advertising. We are going to combine these two themes and ask you (or the group) to design an advertisement for a marketing manager.

The firm is a growth sector in the food and drinks industry and is part of the London Brewing Company. This is a regional position reporting to the managing director. The person will co-ordinate the function for this regional company. The terms and conditions are excellent. You need to derive the specification of the ideal person from the job outline.

Construct an advertisement accordingly.

What all these models have in common is the fact that, although the stages in the process differ, they all start with the need to achieve awareness and end with an action involving product purchase or service use. However, different models are appropriate to different types of

---

BOX MKT5.11

Models of response to marketing communication

The 'hierarchy of effects' model[1]

Awareness
↓
Knowledge
↓
Liking
↓
Reference
↓
Conviction
↓
Purchase

The 'innovation-adoption' model[2]

Awareness
↓
Interest
↓
Evaluation
↓
Trial
↓
Adoption

Sources:
1   Adapted from Lavidge and Steiner, 'A model for predictive measurements of advertising'
2   Adapted from Rogers, *Diffusion of Innovations*

---

product and to the ways in which different products are perceived by their purchasers. This means that promotion professionals need to decide which is the appropriate model to adopt in a particular product/market situation and design their communication activities accordingly.

What is Advertising?

Advertising is perhaps the most visible method of communicating with customers and potential customers and can be seen as:

- any paid form of non-personal presentation of products, services or ideas by an identified sponsor who may be the *manufacturer*, the *distributor*, the *retailer* or any combination of all three.

If advertising is the most visible of the available methods of communicating with markets, then the most visible form of advertising itself is probably TV commercials, because these are placed before us in our own homes more or less as part of the leisure activity of watching television. However, it is interesting to note that the amount spent on press advertising in a normal year is more than double the amount spent on television.

It is also useful to note that it is not only commercial organizations which use mass advertising – colleges advertise for students (the De Montfort University in Leicester has recently been using national television for this purpose); political parties use press and posters to put their case across to the electorate (particularly when there is an election on the horizon); charities advertise for funds (and so that they can acquire new names and addresses to add to their mailing lists); and campaigning organizations use press advertising to present their case.

Media advertising covers the list below.

- press
- television
- posters and transport
- cinema
- radio

Press advertising further breaks down into the following categories:

- national press;
- regional and local press;
- consumer magazines and periodicals;
- trade and technical publications;
- directories including trade and professional: Yellow Pages and local directories, such as Thomson directories.

Advertising is an effective marketing tool, but whatever the opinions of the public, marketing professionals have to be prepared to accept that it is not all powerful. Advertising on its own cannot brainwash the public into buying products they do not want and have no use for. Over a period of time it can help to change attitudes, for example, TV commercials by the Health Education Council have no doubt helped to change public attitudes towards smoking. However, it is unlikely they would have been effective on their own, without the very real message conveyed by the results of research into the links between lung cancer and smoking (particularly passive smoking).

Attractive and persuasive advertising may indeed influence a trial purchase of a product but, if the product does not then live up to the claims made for it by the advertising, or if the consumer simply does not like the taste (if it is something like toothpaste or a food product), then no amount of money spent on advertising will induce a repeat purchase and, for the majority of consumer products, it is repeat purchases which are essential to long-term commercial viability.

Again, advertising never stands on its own – it should always be viewed as a part (even though a very important part) of an overall marketing communications strategy which, again, has to be seen as part of the complete marketing mix. Please now tackle Activity MKT5.4.

ACTIVITY MKT5.4

ADVERTISING: FOR AND AGAINST

Activity code
- ✓ Self-development
- ✓ Teamwork
- ✓ Communications
- ☐ Numeracy/IT
- ✓ Decisions

This activity concerns the ethics and the utility of advertising.[1] It can be used as a basis for a seminar or group debate with some core arguments (shown here) both for and against advertising. It can also be used as a report for individuals to take a view on the merits of the whole process.

The case against
- It manipulates people into spending money on things they don't need and can't afford.
- If less money was spent on advertising, goods in the shops would cost less.
- It encourages envy and snobbishness.
- There is so much advertising that people are pushed into paying out for things they would not buy otherwise.

The case for[2]
- 'The consumer not only has the power to choose but exercises it ruthlessly.'
- 'The consumer has spending power nowadays for many goods and services above the necessities of life. Industry responds by offering a wide variety of such products. ... People have to choose.'

- 'The consumer can pick and choose what advertisement s/he wants to consider.'
- 'The process of advertising ... achieves no more than an interest to try the product and, if that product does not live up to expectations, it is not bought a second time.'
- 'The special value of advertising is its cheapness and rapid spread of product information.'
- 'Consumer attitudes ... are the consumers' own choice and industry and advertising have merely responded to their needs and wishes with products, services and communications. The communications have not created the attitudes; and to restrict the communications will not change the attitudes.'

Source:
1 Adapted from Wilmshurst, *The Fundamentals and Practice of Marketing*
2 Produced by the Advertising Association

When and Why Do We Advertise?

Whether or not we choose any form of advertising as part of our communications mix depends on a variety of things:

- *What is the product?* Mass-produced consumer goods lend themselves to mass advertising because potential markets are usually large and well spread throughout the country and volume sales are desired. On the other hand, specialized industrial products, such as heavy grinding machinery, may have only a very small and scattered potential market, in which case advertising, even in the appropriate trade press, would not be an effective way of achieving sales; other items from the communications menu such as personal selling and exhibitions would be chosen instead.

- *What do we hope to achieve?* If we want to inform the public when our restaurant is open; create and develop brand awareness and brand loyalty; stimulate interest in a new product or reassure individuals who have already bought the product that they made the right choice, then advertising is likely to be the right answer. What we then have to do is choose the most suitable medium, for example, national television or local press.

If, on the other hand, our product is financial services which need to be specifically tailored to suit individual customers, then advertising (with a coupon to fill in for further details) is one of the methods we might employ to establish the initial contact, but we could certainly not expect it to make the final sale for us.

- *What type of market are we operating in?* If we have an inexpensive mass-market product with potential customers in all parts of the country then personal selling is not economic and advertising of one type or another is likely to be the answer. If our market is an exclusive one, as in the case of a luxury product, then advertising may still be an important element in the communications mix but in very specialized types of media.

Additionally, if our product is one where a long distribution chain is involved and the point of purchase is therefore far removed from us, it may be necessary to use advertising as a means of creating demand and ensuring shelf space in retail outlets. Whatever the product, if direct marketing is the preferred area of operation then advertising (in the press or on television) may be the chosen method of achieving sales.

■ *How cost-effective is the advertising likely to be?* Whatever the answers to the foregoing questions, the ultimate decision must be made on the grounds of cost-effectiveness. Advertising should only be used when it is considered to be the most effective and economic method of reaching sufficient numbers of the right target audience.

Please refer to Box MKT5.12.

BOX MKT5.12

Informative, persuasive and reminder advertising

Overall objective: to inform
■ Announcing new products and product alterations.
■ Explaining how the product works.
■ Helping a product in the first stage of its lifecycle.
■ Building an image for the company and the product.
■ Telling customers about new opening hours.
■ Suggesting new uses for an existing product.

Overall objective: to persuade
■ Building brand loyalty.
■ Persuading people to buy now.
■ Obtaining leads for the sales force.
■ Encouraging trial of a fairly new product.

Overall objective: to remind
■ Reminding customers that the product is still available.
■ Reminding people that it might be needed soon.
■ Keeping existing customers 'sold'.
■ Maintaining a product in the mature stage of its lifecycle.

Source: Adapted from Kotler, *Marketing Management*

How Do We Use PR?

PR stands for both **public relations** (sometimes known simply as **publicity**) and **press relations** (sometimes known, now that television and radio have grown enormously in importance, as **media relations**).

The latter involves the tasks of establishing mutually satisfactory relationships with the media and of keeping them supplied with appropriate information which might be in the form of press releases or in the form of comments upon things which are happening around the organization. Public relations involves keeping the public correctly informed about an organization, and its activities and has been defined as:

■ The deliberate planned and sustained effort to establish and maintain mutual understanding between an organization and its publics.

This tells us that public relations activities are not dealt with on a spur-of-the-moment basis – they should be planned and treated as part of the chosen communications mix. As such, they deserve to have just as much skill and attention lavished upon them as any other part of that mix.

Public relations is therefore a much wider activity than simply media relations. The media are just one element, albeit probably the most important one, in the overall task of communicating with the wide variety of groups which go to make up an organization's publics.

These publics include stakeholders such as shareholders, customers or clients, and employees, as well as wider-ranging groups such as local communities; financial institutions; government departments; suppliers; competitors and the general public.

The different groups will have different levels of priority for the organization so far as establishing successful relationships with them is concerned. But an organization that has made planned public relations efforts a part of its promotional strategy will find it easier to launch new initiatives which might have a controversial element to them, for example, the siting of a new factory. The aim is to influence the opinions of the various groups, perhaps to show that the company is aware of its social responsibilities, even to convince its employees that it is a good place to work and so help to improve their motivation.

Public relations employs many of the same media as advertising. As with advertising, it can operate at both national and local level, depending on the objectives in force and the media available. Additionally, there are many occasions when it becomes almost a method of straight promotion, for example, when newly introduced models of cars are road tested and written up by motoring magazines and the national press. In the same way, new industrial products might be reviewed by appropriate technical journals.

One of the advantages of using the press and other media as public relations vehicles is that there are no direct costs involved. That is, no payment is made for the space occupied by a news story about an organization or for printing a press release. However, this does not in any way mean that PR activities are free – there is the cost of producing and sending out the press release, plus the time involved in writing it and also the cost of establishing good relationships with appropriate media staff – editors and journalists. Additionally, if a new initiative is launched at a press reception then this has to be added to the cost and has to come out of the annual PR budget. However, in some companies which do not have a separate PR function, it might come from the overall promotional budget.

One other advantage of the use of PR to achieve press coverage is that the company, or the product being reviewed, appears to have been endorsed by the publication concerned. Everyone knows that advertising copy has to be taken with a pinch of salt but a news article, particularly by a named journalist, has a much more truthful ring to it. However, there is another side to this story. It is possible that the magazine will find the new car lacking in many ways or that the newspaper will add some less favourable opinions of its own to the end of a press release. In this case there is nothing to be done but hope for better luck next time.

Please refer now to Box MKT5.13 which crystallizes an effective action plan.

BOX MKT5.13

Seven steps to successful PR

- *State the problem or aim.* To launch a new product, influence wholesalers and retailers, impress customers, motivate the sales force, build the company image.
- *Carry out research.* To be clear about the present situation, including the problem (if there is one).
- *Identify the groups you want to reach.* Decide who you want to talk to and what you have to say to them.
- *Decide which media will be most appropriate.* It might be TV, local press, a conference, a video or a letter – it all depends on the timescale, the situation and the people you want to reach.
- *Monitor the results.* So that you can be sure that your activities are having the desired effect.
- *Plan ahead.* As part of your communications mix, PR needs to be an ongoing activity.
- *Check the ongoing financial situation.* As with any other form of promotional activity, PR has to be cost-effective.

The steps outlined above are very similar to those involved in planning an advertising campaign – further proof that PR is a genuine promotional activity and a worthwhile part of almost any communications mix.

Source: Adapted from Wilmshurst, *The Fundamentals and Practice of Marketing*

In addition to the cultivation of the media, there are many other effective public relations tools and, as with advertising, the ones chosen on any occasion will depend on the declared objectives of the activity and the group (or public) which it is desired to reach. For example:

- *House journals* may be used for communicating with an organization's own staff and may also be sent to customers, suppliers and the media. Other published material such as annual reports and articles in technical journals written by company executives also make excellent public relations material.

- *Films* may be shown to staff, members of the local community, trade associations and the media.

- *Advertising* can, in special circumstances, be a tool of public relations, for example, in charity programmes. Additionally, corporate (or image) advertising can be undertaken for PR purposes. For example, oil companies may produce TV commercials showing how they care for the landscape when laying new pipelines as an antidote to bad publicity resulting from oil spills, or ICI may show how their activities are helping underdeveloped countries.

- *Joint promotions* with charities are becoming popular. For example, Office Cleaning Services has joined with the World Wide Fund for Nature to help with a campaign to save the British barn owl and American Express joined with St John's Ambulance Brigade in a campaign for the charity's centenary year which involved 'the world's largest party' (held in Hyde Park in the presence of the Queen), a gala performance at Covent Garden and, for a limited period, donations made to St John's every time an American Express card was used.

- *Charity donations and sponsorships* are often looked upon as public relations activities as well as being part of a company's admission of social responsibility. For example, part of the cost of producing the Open University's course for voluntary organizations, 'Winning Resources and Support', was borne by BP whose contribution is acknowledged on all course publicity and material.

The whole question of sports sponsorship as a PR activity is a growing one which has sprung particularly to prominence in the area of television since cigarettes and spirits were banned from using TV as a straight advertising medium. No longer able to advertise directly, manufacturers turned to sponsorship, for example, with the 'Embassy World Snooker Championship' and the 'Benson and Hedges Cup' in cricket. In addition to producing TV coverage on BBC as well as on the commercial channels, sports sponsorship allows substances which may have unhealthy connotations (alcohol and tobacco) to appear in close association with healthy sporting activities.

However, these sponsorship activities do not stop with tournaments – Adidas sponsors tennis players, Castlemaine XXXX sponsors the Australian cricket team, oil companies sponsor motor racing teams, more and more football teams are accepting sponsorship deals and even local youth teams may be sponsored by local companies. In this situation, it is becoming increasingly difficult to know where public relations activities merge into outright promotion. At this point, please tackle Activity MKT5.5.

ACTIVITY MKT5.5

MARKETING OBJECTIVES FOR PR

Activity code
✓ Self-development
✓ Teamwork
✓ Communications
☐ Numeracy/IT
✓ Decisions

When using PR as part of their communications mix, marketing managers need to establish marketing objectives as part of the exercise. Then they can design a series of activities which will meet those objectives.

Expand on the various marketing objectives which PR can actually further in any given scenario.

How Can We Best Make Use of Sales Promotion?

Sales promotion has been defined as: 'The function of marketing which attempts to achieve given objectives by the adding of extra, tangible value to a product or service'.

Advertising can be very effective in creating awareness of a product or a service but this does not necessarily lead to purchase. It has been said that advertising provides people with reasons to buy products but that sales promotion provides incentives. Another difference between advertising and sales promotion is that advertising can be regarded as a strategic activity so far as its role in the overall marketing plan is concerned, while sales promotion is usually regarded as tactical, although advertising might be used to announce sales promotion activities in the short term. Again, sales promotion activities are short term. One reason for this is that they frequently involve some form of price reduction so that, if the promotion goes on too long, it may prove impossible to move the price back to the correct level.

So, the purpose of advertising as a strategic activity is to create awareness, establish a product in its market, build an image and work towards gaining sales for the long-term future of the product/service and the company. As a tactical tool, sales promotion is used as a short-term boost for sales or to encourage trial of a new product.

Sales promotion activities come into three broad categories:

1 *Promotion to the trade.* This type of activity involves dealers, distributors, wholesalers and retailers and is aimed at encouraging these organizations to stock and display the products being promoted. Trade promotions are often referred to as 'pushing the product into the market'. Incentives offered include discounts, sales contests, co-operative advertising, display material.

2 *Consumer promotions.* These are incentive offers made directly to individual consumers, very often in supermarkets. They include demonstrations, free samples, money-off coupons, competitions, special offers.

3 *Internal promotions.* These are directed mainly towards the sales force as incentives and motivation aids. They include competitions, bonuses, sales conferences in exotic locations. The role of the sales force is considered in more detail later in this unit.

Now tackle Activity MKT 5.6.

ACTIVITY MKT5.6

TYPICAL SALES PROMOTION TASKS

Activity code
- ✓ Self-development
- ✓ Teamwork
- ☐ Communications
- ☐ Numeracy/IT
- ✓ Decisions

Your role (group or individual) is to determine a range of typical sales promotion jobs with a commentary on each job. For example, 'encouraging customers to try new products' etc.

Very frequently, sales promotion activities occur at, or near, the point of sale, that is, as near as possible to where the decision to purchase is made. This might be close to the till or in front of a supermarket shelf but, wherever it is, there is competition. There will be several different brands of baked beans on the shelves in Tesco (including their own) and there will also be a great number of breakfast cereals to choose from. It is not until the tin or packet is taken from the shelf and put into a trolley that the purchase decision has been made – and even then shoppers frequently change their minds, put the product back and take something else instead. Unless loyalty to a particular brand is paramount, decisions at the point of sale can be made or changed by a shelf sticker giving details of a special offer or even a display card reinforcing the message from last night's TV commercial This does not only apply to products sold in supermarkets – the decision to buy one washing machine or TV set rather than another might be made because of a strategically placed showcard offering interest-free credit on a specific model.

The problem here is that all companies want their products displayed as prominently as possible. Most of them organize sales promotions and offer incentives, many at the same time, to the extent that retailers (and wholesalers) are inundated with display material and requests for extra shelf space. Retailers in particular are becoming extremely choosy about which promotions they will support with the result that significant amounts of expensive display material may never get used, so that a promotion might receive significantly less exposure than hoped. 'Premium offers' as noted in Box MKT5.14 may give some edge to the marketeer.

BOX MKT5.14

Premium offers

- *Free gifts.* These come in a variety of forms. They may be in the packet (plastic dinosaurs in breakfast cereal packs where children want to collect the whole set, thus ensuring repeat purchase). They may be attached to the pack (ballpoint pens attached to magazine covers). The gift may be the pack itself (instant coffee packed in storage jars which are attractive enough to make people want to collect several of them).
- *Free, sendaway offers.* Here, a free gift is offered in exchange for proof of purchase (usually several proofs of purchase). Again repeat purchase is encouraged, the offer appears generous and many people, after having bought sufficient packs, never get around to sending for the gift, thus reducing the manufacturer's costs.
- *Self-liquidating offers.* In this case, consumers are required to send money as well as proofs of purchase although usually a fairly nominal amount (a CD for £1, perhaps). The advantage to the manufacturer is that the money sent actually covers the cost of buying the merchandise which has been bought at a big discount.

A decision regarding whether or not to run a sales promotion campaign has to be made as carefully as any which are involved in developing a communications mix. The decision-making process involved might cover the following:

- List, in order of priority, the marketing problems being faced by the product or brand.
- Decide on the budget available for solving the problem.
- List, and cost, the available solutions, for example, extra advertising, product refinement, different pricing strategy.

- Estimate the likely level of effectiveness of each solution.
- If the results of the previous two activities indicate that sales promotion is likely to provide the most effective solution to the problem and there is sufficient money available to pay for it then a promotion is indicated.

However, it should be noted that it never makes sense to run a promotion simply because your competitors are doing so. It may make sense for the other company but not necessarily for you since their situation may be very different from your own.

Please now refer to Box MKT5.15.

BOX MKT5.15

Typical sales promotion objectives and activities

Objective	Promotion
To increase consumer awareness	In-store raffle/displays/free draws/competitions
To increase product penetration	Free gifts/money-off coupons/sampling/ refund offers/banded packs/reduced prices
To increase repeat purchase	Competitions/money-off coupons/refund offers/self-liquidating offers/free storage jars as packs
To increase brand loyalty	Free gifts/personality promotions/coupons/ buy one get one free/twin packs/refund offers/re-usable containers
To increase frequency of purchase/or amount bought	Competitions/banded packs/in-store promotions/free gifts/shareouts/giveaways
To shift high stocks	Free offers/in-store raffles/merchandising/ tailor-made promotions
To attract customers to premises	Free gifts/samples/money-off coupons/tailor-made promotions
Trading up to larger sizes	Consumer choice coupons/refund offers/multibrand schemes
To increase distribution	Tailor-made promotions/trade competitions/sample distribution/sales force incentives/discounts
To encourage display	On-pack offers/banded packs/premium offers/heavy price cuts

One of the biggest advantages of sales promotion is that its effects are immediate, sales can be expected to rise almost as soon as the special offer becomes available. However, once the promotion ends sales fall equally rapidly, often below the level they were at before the campaign. This is because, during the period of the special offer, shoppers often stock up (particularly if entry to a competition or access to a promotional offer requires the coupons from several special packs) so that it is a long time before more supplies are needed. 'Packaging: functions and goals' is discussed in Box MKT5.16 which ends this section before we tackle expenditure on communications.

BOX MKT5.16

Packaging: functions and goals

Functions
- *To identify the product.* By standing out from the competition it gives products an identity and attracts the attention of potential customers. Attractive packaging helps to persuade individuals to pick up the product to examine it more closely.
- *Declares the amount of product being offered.* For example soap powders and yoghurts all have the amount of contents displayed on the pack. The purchaser knows how much she or he is paying for the stated amount.
- *Offers protection.* Helps to protect products during the distribution process, while in storage, on the shelves and while being carried home.

Goals
- *Attraction.* To attract attention; to improve the appearance of a boring product like soap powder; to use colour in a positive way, for example: yellow = sunshine/health/warmth; green = quietness/nature; red = excitement/heat.
- *Economy.* To use just the right amount of packaging to enhance and protect the product without appearing wasteful of resources.
- *Convenience.* Well-packaged goods are easier for shoppers to handle, to pack and to transport home. If packed in standard, say, square packs or tins, then they are easier to stack, to transport and to move around.

Labels
- *Style.* Need to blend with the packaging being used.
- *Communication.* Must identify the product, specify the ingredients and give usage instructions.

Source: Adapted from Foster, *Mastering Marketing*

How Much Do We Need to Spend on Marketing Communications?

This is a crucial question, because the amount we decide to allocate to our communications budget will largely dictate what kind of promotion we can carry out. Television advertising is expensive and so are the production costs involved. Unless we can measure our budget in hundreds of thousands of pounds, mass national TV advertising is not an option.

Unfortunately, there is no simple answer to the question of how much we could, or should, spend on promotional activities but, there are many ways in which budgets are arrived at in reality:

- *Arbitrary methods.* More often used than might be expected these, so called, methods involve an organization in deciding how much it can afford, or is willing, to spend. Although the rough guess involved may be based in some measure upon experience, it makes no allowance at all for the state of the market, or competitive activity, or even for the nature of the task to be carried out.

- *Percentage of sales turnover.* On the face of it, this seems to be a sensible approach as it is at least based on something concrete. However, even this approach has its problems. If the chosen method involves a fixed percentage of the previous year's turnover then there is no real allowance for increasing costs, and the budget will go up and down according to changing levels of turnover, without any reference to what is actually happening in the market. Additionally, allocating a percentage of anticipated turnover is difficult to do in practice, and budgets might suddenly be cut if sales do not reach the level estimated.

- *A unit percentage.* This method of budget allocation is used most often with high-volume consumer products and involves setting aside a fixed amount for each unit produced, say 5p, although this would involve cutting expenditure if production was to be reduced for any reason, perhaps falling sales. This may happen at the very time when increased promotion is needed to counteract diminishing sales or increased competitive activity. It also takes no account of the product's position in its lifecycle.

- *Setting budgets in relation to the competition.* Matching the spending levels of the competition might seem to be a sensible thing to do but this method actually ignores the fact that, although we might be able to see how many advertisements they place, we can never truly know what goes on in their minds. Nor can we really know how effective their activities are. If our product is a new one, then we may need to spend considerably more than a competitor whose product is well established in order to gain a place in the market.

- *The target method.* In this case, the overall objective is set, then the cost of the promotional spend estimated as being necessary to achieve it is allocated as the budget. The objective might be sales volume or the generation of a particular level of sales leads. We would then have to estimate the amount of advertising, or other promotional activity needed to reach it. This method has the advantage of taking note of the management principle of first setting objectives, then planning activities designed to attain them. It can also be flexible in its approach.

The final method listed above, being task-based, would seem to be the most advantageous method to adopt, but even this has many disadvantages as there will always be a variety of ways of achieving the same objective, some of them considerably more expensive than others. In fact, probably the best method to adopt is a *composite* one where a variety of factors is taken into account.[4]

In this case, we will be taking note of: what we can afford, the task we want to carry out, the amount being spent by our competitors, our experience of the market, and what we have learned from previous communications campaigns. The ultimate decision will, of course, depend on additional factors such as the organization's commitment to a marketing-based approach to business, the personal opinions of the managing director and the success of the marketing department (or the communications manager) in bidding for a share of company funds.

Managing the Communications Task

Being able to manage the communications task in any organization also involves being able to develop and plan communications and promotional programmes, right from the very beginning. There is a staged series of seven practical steps involved in tackling this activity which, of course, needs to be closely linked to the organization's declared marketing objectives and marketing plan and also to the balanced marketing mix which has been developed for the company's offerings to the market. The steps are:

- identifying the target audience;
- setting the communications objectives;
- designing the communications message;
- selecting the communications mix;
- allocating the budget;
- deciding on the promotion mix;
- measuring the results.

These tasks are very wide-ranging, as is the whole marketing communications process and, if success is to be achieved in the long run then careful co-ordination is essential.

An important element in the task of managing communications is the selection of appropriate media. In many cases this is done by an advertising agency but the system also needs to be understood, and agreed, by the individual responsible for the management of the communications task.

Once the objectives for the campaign have been set and the budget agreed, the choice of media is the next step.

The first question to be asked is: *What kind of media would be appropriate?* The choice would be made from the available menu of media and the individual items considered might be: broadcast media (radio and television), press advertising (including PR) in newspapers and/or magazines, posters (either static or on buses and trains), exhibitions (either trade or consumer), and direct mail which lends itself to detailed targeting.

The second question narrows the choice to: *Which would be the best medium?* For example, if newspapers have been chosen from the original menu, which newspaper(s) would be the most appropriate choice? Narrowing the focus still further, the next question would concern the *size of space to be booked and the frequency of insertion.* The final step in the exercise concerns the budget again and looks at the previous question in terms of: *How much space will the agreed budget cover?*

What should have happened during the course of this exercise is the narrowing down of the available choices to those which will (within the agreed budget) reach the maximum possible number of the chosen target audience, although production costs do also need to be taken into account, for example, colour reproduction obviously costs considerably more than black and white.

Communications managers can also do a variety of things to improve the efficiency and effectiveness of the promotional campaigns they plan and execute. They can attempt to negotiate better positions for their messages, either in the press or with regard to poster sites, they can pre-test their communications messages through research, or they can compare one copy theme with another by carrying out trials in different geographical areas. They can then post-test the same advertisements and attempt keener media buying, possibly through the use of computer scheduling.

Evaluating the Results of Communications Programmes

Having invested large amounts of time and money in a variety of methods of communicating with customers and potential customers, it is essential that communications professionals attempt to evaluate the results of their work in order to ascertain whether or not campaigns have been successful in terms of meeting the objectives set for them and whether or not they have been cost-effective.

With advertising, if a campaign has been mounted to inform, or to raise awareness, then consumer surveys carried out before, and after, the campaign could be structured to measure the percentage rise in awareness

surveys of this type can measure how many people remember a particular advertising campaign.

Direct response advertising, where individuals are invited to order merchandise directly or to send for further details, is easier to evaluate – the number of orders received is easy to record, as is the number of requests for brochures. It is then easy to measure the number of enquiries which result in firm orders and to work out the cost of converting enquiry to sale.

The results of sales promotion activities are also easy to measure and to cost. The number of coupons redeemed can be counted, as can the number of entries to competitions and the level of sales before, during and after sales promotions have been carried out. The number of enquiries/sales resulting from demonstrations can also be checked. It is essential, too, to examine results against the costs incurred, for example, to look at revenue lost because of price reductions against that gained through extra sales. Similarly, it is necessary to balance out the costs of dealer incentives, the cost of special display material and the cost of any special activity on the part of the sales force as well as any advertising costs incurred in publicizing the promotion.

So far as being able to measure the results of communications campaigns is concerned, probably the most important aspect is to know what you really set out to achieve. This is one of the principal reasons for drawing up measurable and achievable objectives for every communications campaign undertaken. Thus, if the main objective is 'a 5 per cent increase in awareness' of a particular product, then measurement of awareness levels both before and after the campaign will ascertain whether or not the objective has been met.

One of the best-known models within the communications industry is DAGMAR, which expresses the concept of working towards objectives for us as Defining Advertising Goals for Measuring Advertising Results. The model may apply specifically to advertising but the principle definitely applies to all methods of communication.

Face-to-Face Selling

Selling involves the personal presentation of products and services to potential customers and is important in both consumer and industrial markets. The type of sales force a company has, its size and the way it is organized, depend on the product, the market and the company, in the same way that other methods of marketing communication do. The sales force might be divided into geographical regions, by product or by market.

Again, as with other promotional activities, the approach adopted and the objectives set are affected by the nature of the task in hand. In some cases, where a company has a great deal of strength in its chosen market, the main objective will be to keep existing customers happy and to try to ensure that they do not slip away to the competition. On the other hand, if what the company wants is rapid growth, then the sales force must be trained and motivated to win new accounts.

Additionally, the type of marketing strategy adopted will influence the role and task of the sales force. If the strategy is one of 'pushing' products into the market through concerted sales efforts aimed at wholesalers and retailers, and with the use of strong selling techniques, discounts and dealer incentives, then the task will be very different from that where a 'pull' strategy uses mass advertising to persuade individuals to buy.

Personal selling is likely to be the most important part of the communications mix in industrial markets and consumer durables, for example, expensive hi-fi equipment or non-standard products, like fitted kitchens or life insurance. The activity is also different from all other methods of marketing communication because it is the only one where a personal relationship is established between the seller and the buyer. This means that the sales person is more in control of the message which passes to the receiver because questions can be answered and objections to purchase countered on the spot.

The size of the sales force will depend on the volume of sales and the size of the available budget. Once the size of the sales force has been established, the next step will be the allocation of territories and the setting of sales targets both for areas and for individual sales people.

Sales objectives are usually quantitative:

- sales levels;
- profit levels;
- market shares.

They are also qualitative:

- frequency of customer contact;
- level of customer service to be achieved;
- level of coverage of an area.

Face-to-face selling is the most effective way of achieving sales, but also the most expensive. Having sales people out on the road making cold calls is seldom a cost-effective way of operating. It is advantageous to use advertising for obtaining sales leads or, perhaps, to do this by telephone. This means that personal selling – although very often a large sales department exists in its own right – is still just one part of an organization's chosen communications mix. Box MKT5.17 outlines the core job of a sales person. Activity MKT5.7 should then be tackled as it pulls together the direct sales effort and the overall communications mix.

Notes

BOX MKT5.17

The core job of a sales person?

From selling milk on the doorstep or selling shoes in a shop to selling computer hardware to manufacturing companies, there may be no such thing as a 'typical' sales person.

Yet there may be similar key roles for all sales people, with the degree of emphasis on the roles altering according to the customer, product and type of selling.

The job may be broken down into: administration, sales promotion, physical selling and customer/client service/goodwill.

- *Administration/self-management.* The sales/marketing manager may be in charge, but the reality of many sales jobs is that the individual sales person has a high degree of personal responsibility for self-management. Such duties include: route planning/coverage, balancing effort and volume, maintaining a sales 'kit' etc., preparing reports on customers and competition, attending meetings, reporting 'overdues'/credit difficulties and maintaining an up-to-date prospect list. A self-analysis of reasons for gaining or losing sales can be quite enlightening as well.

- *Sales promotion.* This relates to the whole communications mix in marketing.[1] Depending on the level or type of communications, the development of new accounts, the distribution of literature, samples and catalogues, training of 'middle men', giving presentations on proposals, calling on agents' sales people etc. can all be involved. This is a very important part of the job and helps to ease the actual sale.

- *Selling.* Regular contact, selling and demonstration, handling questions or objections through strong selling or product skills, estimating customer needs and knowing company policy on price and discounts etc. can all be involved in making that sale.

- *Service.* Handling adjustments, returns, difficulties, complaints, letters of praise, special orders and maintaining customer loyalty are key roles not only after the sale but as part of a marketing philosophy for the whole organization.

Source:
1 Anderson and Kleiner, *Effective Marketing Communications*

ACTIVITY MKT5.7

THE LONDON BREWING COMPANY

Activity code
- ✓ Self-development
- ☐ Teamwork
- ☐ Communications
- ☐ Numeracy/IT
- ✓ Decisions

The London Brewing Company has some 7,500 employees and sales of almost £800 million per annum. As the name suggests, it was founded in London, and the head office remains there. Times have moved on, though, and given its national and increasing international market, it should perhaps be renamed 'the UK Brewing Company'.

The company moved out of London into geographical 'divisions' after the Second World War. With acquisition and the removal of some of the fiercest local competition through a policy of attrition, the six geographical divisions became regional companies responsible for their own costs and profitability. Increasingly each of the regional companies has been given fuller autonomy. Apart from the corporate plan, capital/investment projects and the overall marketing plan, each company is virtually independent.

The focal point of each regional company is a brewery, so there are six breweries altogether making over forty-five different beers and lagers. On the retail side there are 4,221 tenanted public houses, thirty-two shops specializing in selling wines, beers and spirits, and eight 'inherited' inns-cum-restaurants, all in East Anglia. The pubs and inns are controlled by the regional companies while the shop side is controlled by a specialist company based in Stevenage, Hertfordshire. Each of the companies has a regional board of directors, whose chairperson is on the main board in London.

The typical regional company of The London Brewing Company has the following sales organization, reflecting both the customers in the market and the geography of the area. There is a 'tied' market to restaurants and bars belonging to the regional or national firm. Apart from their own outlets, there are the so-called 'free trade' customers who own or rent their establishments and are not honour-bound to take beer from a particular brewery. The third group is the 'take-home' trade from their own specialist shops and grocer-cum-liquor stores to large hypermarkets. As these large hypermarkets tend to have bulk buying at their HQs, the breweries use national account managers to sell into these firms. If the firm happens to be in the territory of a regional brewery, that brewery sells in the whole of the potential stock of London Brewery, not only its own regional beer, to the hypermarket.

In addition, a small team of merchandisers are involved in soft (non-alcoholic) drinks and in selling packaged snacks such as crisps and peanuts. The sales teams in each region also 'sell' wine and spirits to their own establishments and attempt to push their own brands to other establishments (restaurants, public houses, inns and small corner shop liquor stores). The 'hard' drinks are sold centrally by London to hypermarkets.

The sales team is divided into: sales representatives, tele-sales/order takers, merchandisers (who help with displays in small shops/outlets etc.) and administration. The representatives cover specific customers. So one rep would be responsible for the 'tied' customers in his or her geographical region and so on. This means that another rep may visit the establishment for food (peanuts/crisps) or the publican/innkeeper can phone in his or her order. The 'hard' drinks are outside the control of this team as London serves the non-tied outlets while two specialists in wine and spirits cover each of the regional breweries.

Tele-sales are based at the regional HQ alongside the sales administration people. The merchandisers are based here as well (around one or two per brewery) and they back up the main sales team of some eight reps per brewery.

The market trends are as follows:

- The 'tied' trade is increasing at the expense of the 'free trade'.
- More lager is being sold compared to beer.
- Canned beer is sold in retail outlets alongside canned lager; little bottled beer is sold at these outlets.
- The 'take-home trade' has increased some three-fold over the last ten years. This has been at the expense of the inn/pubs trade to a great extent.
- Premium bottled lager is selling well in all outlets.
- The restaurant business is good for wine and spirits.
- The pubs (tied and free) tend to sell more beer than spirits or wine, although the sales of white spirits and white wine have grown considerably of late.

1 Comment on the sales organization.
2 How would you alter this format, and what criteria should exist for the reorganization of the direct selling effort?
3 Make meaningful comments on the 'communication mix' for this organization's current marketing initiatives.

1 Jones 'The fire eaters'.
2 Anderson and Kleiner, *Effective Marketing Communications.*
3 Stern and El-Ansary, *Marketing Channels.*
4 Broadbent and Jacobs, *Spending Advertising Money.*

Unit Six

Strategic Evaluation

Learning Objectives

After completing this unit you should be able to:

- understand the different approaches adopted by market leaders and followers;
- accept the concept of the marketing audit;
- choose appropriate ways of evaluating a company's planned marketing activities;
- appreciate how the task of evaluation is linked to the marketing information;
- apply the generic skills.

Contents

Unit Six

> " We must note that the questions to be asked in any process of evaluation are of at least two logically discrete kinds. Some of them are empirical which ... explore the relative merits of a project in terms of its costs, its effectiveness and so on. For questions of this kind we are looking, therefore, for relevant empirical data. Other questions however are asked in the process of [evaluation]. ... These are the questions about ends rather than means, which ask whether the purposes of the activity are for the right purposes, whether the experience ... is of value whether [it] is good in itself, rather than merely effective in achieving its ends. "
>
> *A.V. Kelly,* The Curriculum, Theory and Practice [1]

Overview

The final unit pulls together the main threads of the book and returns to our model which we first examined in the preface. We examine various methods of developing effective marketing strategies and programmes. In turn, these are analysed and evaluated. The trend towards globalization is also noted. We then turn to evaluation and audit. The marketing performance of the organization is gauged according to various methods, including our initial model of marketing. (See figure 6.1.)

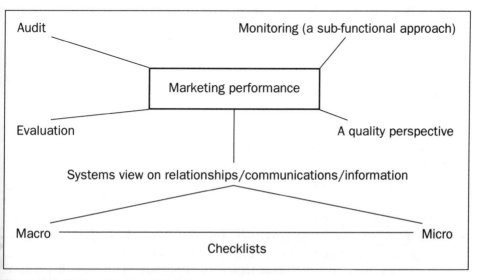

Figure 6.1 Outline diagram of Unit Six.

189

Marketing Strategies and Marketing Policy

We have already looked (in Unit One) at the concept of marketing planning, that is, at the stages which have to be gone through in order to produce a working document for the marketing department to follow during the period for which the plan has been drawn. However, the contents of this plan do not only affect the marketing department, they affect the whole company. The production department will be involved through the declared product policy as will the accounts department through pricing and ordering and the sales force through the promotional plan which has been produced. So an 'action plan' is required to 'operationalize' the paper plan.

The **marketing plan** is the instrument through which **marketing objectives** will be attained and the marketing objectives will have been developed from the **corporate objectives** which, in turn, should be developed from the company's **mission statement**.

The mission statement really should tell us *why* the organization is there – in its purest form it is a vision of what the organization is, or what it is hoping it will be one day. In fact, what the mission statement is trying to do, is to answer the most basic business question of all which is 'What business are we in?' and, even more than that, 'What business *should* we be in?'

In marketing planning, as well as in corporate planning, the mission statement has to be the starting point of the whole process because it sets the boundaries within which all other organizational plans have to be framed. So, if the mission statement gives a company its reason for existing, its marketing strategy then provides it with a means of travelling in that direction.

So far as timescales are concerned, the mission statement is the thing which looks furthest into the future. For example, the mission statements of Japanese companies have been known to last for thirty or forty years. Strategies then establish long-term intentions for pursuing the company's mission while policies/programmes or tactics define the short-term actions which will be taken to put the strategy into effect. A strategic overview is illustrated in Box MKT6.1.

Many people have problems when they begin to try to distinguish between *objectives*, *strategy* and *tactics*.

■ *Objectives* set down where the organization is trying to get to as described in its mission statement. They also act as a measure against which its strategy and activities can be assessed.

■ *Marketing strategies* have been described by Weitz and Wensley[2] as a process through which companies make decisions about where to place their efforts, about which markets and market segments to operate in and which products they want to set in those markets. Strategies should ideally be written down so

---

BOX MKT6.1

Some answers to the question of what business we are in

Companies very often define their businesses according to the type of product they make or what manner of service they supply, for example: 'we make washing machines'; or 'we supply spare parts to auto dealers'. In a classic article in *Harvard Business Review* in 1960, Theodore Levitt[1] said that this was what he called 'marketing myopia', and that the best definitions of businesses where those that defined markets and customers rather than products.

His argument emphasizes the fact that businesses should be looked on as *customer-satisfying processes* rather than *goods-making processes*. One of the most quoted examples of this form of myopia concerns the American railways who saw themselves as being in the *railroad business* rather than in the *transportation business* – a mistake which is supposed to have caused their downfall.

Careful definition of the business a company is in, that is, neither too narrow nor too wide, can open the eyes of its management to a viable future course to take.

Source:
1   Levitt, 'Marketing myopia'

---

that all the necessary people are aware of them and they should cover all four areas of the marketing mix. Strategies are characteristically long-term and are therefore only subject to major change if there is some great alteration to the marketing environment in which the company operates or if there are compelling reasons why it should institute a change of direction.

■ *Tactics and policies* are the detailed short-term activities which have been determined by the declared strategies and which will be followed in meeting them, such as, the types and extent of advertising or sales promotion. Unlike strategies, tactics and policies will be altered in response to stimuli like changes in market conditions, fluctuation of interest rates and levels of competitive activity.

According to Peters and Waterman in *In Search of Excellence*[3] the companies which turn out to be most successful in the long run adopt a 'tight-loose' approach to the implementation of strategy. This means that the actual strategies are tightly defined at board level but that they are kept to the fundamentals of the business, such as the overall product range. Management is then informed of the strategy and 'loosely directed'. This

---

BOX MKT6.2

Variables affecting decisions about marketing strategies and policies

---

All the elements of the marketing mix are variable and any declared marketing mix will be different from any other because the balance between those elements differs for every company and every product or service. Even companies operating in the same product/service areas will balance the variables differently. There are five main areas of variability and all are concerned with strategies and policies.

1 *Product-related variables* relate to the product range and the product mix, the stage in their lifecycles reached by current products, development of new products, ascertaining the wants and needs of customers and potential customers.

2 *Market-related variables* are concerned with the marketing mix, the advisability of moving into new markets, the segmentation of markets.

3 *Price-related variables* deal with all aspects of pricing, including discount structures, trade terms, strategies – whether skimming or penetration.

4 *Promotion-related variables* cover all aspects of the communications mix which must be appropriate to all aspects of the marketing mix and the company's strategy.

5 *Distribution-related variables* relate to all decisions about marketing channels.

Source: Adapted from Foster, *Mastering Marketing*

---

means that they are allowed a large amount of autonomy regarding the implementation of the strategy and the tactics and policies which are used to put it into affect. Decisions concerning marketing strategies and policies are affected by many variables. Please consult Box MKT6.2 on these factors.

As far as marketing strategies are concerned we need to take account of the following features:

■ They need to be consistent with the organization's overall objectives. For example, if the declared aim is to operate in the high-volume end of its market then it should not be looking at small numbers of high-quality outlets for its products.

■ They need to be attainable: there is no point in wasting the time involved in developing strategies which the organization is in no position to carry out. For example it must have the financial resources to fulfil its plans.

■ There must be specific targets to work towards, such as a certain percentage of market share. If there are not targets then it becomes impossible to measure progress in any sort of meaningful way.

■ There will always be an element of compromise involved, because some corporate goals will conflict with each other. For example, there may be conflict between short-term profit objectives and long-term survival or between profit and social factors like the wellbeing of the staff or environmental pollution.

■ Different marketing strategies may be needed for different product groups or different market segments, for different markets or for different competitive situations and for different stages in product/market lifecycles.

What are the Available Types of Strategy?

Broadly speaking, firms can only be either followers or leaders. **Market leaders** usually have the largest share of their total markets, most often, in excess of 50 per cent. Additionally, they are likely to be consistently first onto the market with new products or with new developments of existing ones.

For example, Procter & Gamble introduced the first biological washing powder, Ariel, which has remained the market leader. They were the first to introduce a liquid version of the product and the now familiar concept of the 'washing ball' which is filled with liquid and placed inside the washing machine. They were first to counteract the environmentalists with a condensed product utilizing a very much smaller pack which was then pushed as being considerably less wasteful of resources. They were also first with 'refill packs' and now, first with a special 'Ariel for stains' which uses a new type of washing ball.

Those companies which are not leaders must always be followers of one sort or another and, here again, there are choices to be made. Pepsi-Cola, a follower for many years of the dominant market leader, Coca-Cola, eventually mounted a challenge through its 'taste test' campaign which increased considerably their market share at the expense of the leader.

Other companies are content to be followers. They might never match the share levels of the leaders but they may have a considerable part of the overall market as they will usually be offering their products at a price lower than that of the market leader. For example, another washing product is unlikely ever to catch up with Ariel. However, one advantage of being a follower is the avoidance of many of the risks involved with developing and launching a completely new product. The second brand onto the market may have had the chance to produce a product which is superior to that of the market leader and will also be able to take advantage of the demand for the product which has been created by the innovators and risk takers.

Another advantageous way of being a follower is to establish a particular niche, for example, by operating at the extreme top end of the market, and thus avoiding outright confrontation with the market leader. This is a strategy which is particularly useful for small and/or new companies.

Where Should Market Leaders Aim Their Efforts?

In some ways, it might seem that, once our product has become the market leader, there is nowhere to go. However, there is always 'down', and this is what is likely to happen if we simply stop trying to do anything positive. This is likely to be the case particularly when a unique product has established a dominant position fairly rapidly. McDonald's were not the first hamburger outlets but they are now the market leaders through being more aggressive and better than the competition. They were not even the first into the UK market but they outperformed, and took over from, Wimpy.

According to Kotler[4] there are two main strategies open to market leaders – they can try to expand the total market and thus increase their own sales, and/or they can defend their market share against market 'challengers'.

Expanding the total market

This is in the best interests of even dominant companies because, if the total demand increases, then they are likely to get most of the advantage which comes from the extra sales. A company with this strategy in mind should first turn to the product/market possibilities described in Unit Three. Most products have the capacity to attract new users if the right approach is adopted. For example, a leisure centre might be able to attract individuals who never exercise or play sports if the activities on offer can be made to appear sufficiently attractive or sufficiently beneficial – to improve health. (Further penetration of the existing market is the first box of the Ansoff Matrix as described in Unit Three.)

Again, using the same example, it may be possible to expand into new market segments by introducing sessions tailored specifically to the needs of retired people or into new geographical areas by offering special prices to individuals coming from more then five miles away. (The second box of the Ansoff Matrix involves selling existing products into new markets.)

Additionally, it is often possible to expand the total market by discovering new uses for existing products. If a product which has been developed, for example, for kitchen use, to clean gas hobs, is discovered to perform excellently when it comes to putting a shine on the chrome parts of cars and motor bikes then the manufacturer is on to a very good thing. Information about alternative uses for products very often comes from customers, so it pays manufacturers to monitor customers' uses of their products on a continual basis through their ongoing research activities. It is also useful to note that, in industrial markets, the majority of suggestions for new ways of using existing products do come from customers.

It is also often possible to persuade individuals to use more of a product than they do. If customers can be convinced to use more of a particular product then the market leader also stands to gain. For example, it may be possible for the manufacturer of an anti-dandruff shampoo to convince customers that the effect will be greater if they wash their hair twice a week instead of once.

Defending themselves against competitive activity

Market leaders need to be constantly looking behind them for the efforts of their competitors and, again, a good example is the 'war' between Coca-Cola and Pepsi-Cola. A company in this position would be wise not to sit back and rely on the fact that it has held a dominant position for many years. It can diversify into additional product areas or pay extra attention to the pricing, promotion and distribution elements of the marketing mix.

Additionally, Ariel keeps its position as market leader by continually 'attacking' the competition through the addition of refinements as described above.

Is it Acceptable to Remain a Follower?

If the overall objective is to sustain profit levels in the long term, then the deliberate acceptance of a place as follower can be an attractive strategy. As stated earlier, followers avoid many of the risks taken by innovators and leaders. Additionally, if the market leader is in a very strong position then any direct attempt to challenge its place would be likely to activate counter-attack, perhaps through price cuts or increased distribution and promotional activities, which would be difficult for the challenger to cope with.

However, being a follower does not mean having to accept that one's product is second best. The level of market share achieved may still be considerable and there may be product attributes which appeal to a distinctive area of the market and, again, the market share will need to be defended against other firms and against new entrants into the market.

How Might a Market Leader be Challenged?

A follower not content to remain a follower needs to think carefully about the right course to follow. A strong follower with a good product, perhaps one which compares very favourably with that of the market leader, might choose to make a direct bid for the leadership position by taking away market share – as did Pepsi-Cola – particularly if there are only the two big players in that market.

BOX MKT6.3

Some strategies for going after market leaders

Any company which wants either to make an all-out challenge to a market leader, or simply to increase its own market share must have a detailed and carefully constructed strategy if it is to have any chance of success because the market leader is likely to be more capable of withstanding a long period of intense competition.

The challenger could choose to sell its products at considerably lower prices than those of the market leader. If the quality of the challenger's product is equal to that of the market leader then the price-conscious area of the market is likely to change brands.

Alternatively, the challenger might attempt to: produce an innovative product which would move customers away from the market leader because of its novelty, provide better customer and after-sales service, look for innovative ways of distributing their products, reduce production costs to enable better pricing structures and so on.

On the other hand, if there are several companies in the market apart from the leader, then the one which is most ambitious might begin by trying to take sales from one or two of the weaker ones. Alternatively, a sensible approach might be to choose to go after a market segment, or a geographical area, where the market leader is at its weakest. Some strategies for going after market leaders are discussed in Box MKT6.3.

Finding a Niche

Small companies in markets where there is a strong leader and perhaps also one or two strong followers are still able to compete and to prosper through finding a niche which is large enough for them to make profitable and yet small enough for the market leader not to need.

Niche marketing is an ideal approach for a small company wanting to enter a crowded market because it is possible to achieve success in this way and also because the cost will be considerably less than that of trying to make an impact across the whole spread of the market.

For example, a small company capable of producing high-quality garments might be able to specialize in producing exactly what is wanted by Marks & Spencer. This is a strategy followed by some companies in this country. However, it might prove to be a risky one in the long term, if reliance is placed totally upon one customer.

Niche marketing was one of the success stories of the 1980s, particularly in retailing with the advent of the Sock Shop, Next, Tie Rack and Knickerbox who were all really also innovators. However, since the recession, their long-term success has perhaps become more problematic. One of the largest niches ever occupied must be that developed so dramatically by The Body Shop, but even this success story is showing signs of slowing down since the development of similar products by retail giants such as Boots and Tesco.

What are the Chances of Going Global?

The idea of operating in a global market is an attractive one – a single product or product range backed by a standard advertising and promotional campaign lays out an enticing vision of enormous economies of scale and increasing levels of profit for the company which is both willing and able to take the necessary risks. However, the reality might not be so appealing!

The marketing concept emphasizes the fact that customers and markets are not all the same, that different marketing mixes and different marketing programmes need to be developed for different markets and even for different segments within the same market. It seems unlikely therefore that markets as far apart, both geographically and culturally, as (say) Greenland and Nigeria will be content with the same products and the same advertising campaigns.

Products which embody the American way of life appear so far to have been able to cross national barriers with great ease, as the product itself is increasingly bundled with intangible elements which make it even more attractive – Coca-Cola, McDonald's and Levi's are all global names. On the other hand, Nestlé is much more likely to adapt its products to suit the tastes of the different countries in which it operates.

However, the world is still becoming smaller and we have many positive examples of globalization in front of us, particularly the international marketing successes of Japanese products. It is becoming clearer that companies wishing to do something other than stagnate cannot afford to concentrate for ever only on their own home markets even if they are extremely large. Additionally, the internationalization of trade has grown to such an extent that successful national companies can find themselves challenged in their own home markets by imported products which are cheaper than their own as well as being technically superior, again coming quite probably from Japan.

Another facet of the global scene is the emergence of trading blocs so that we now have three developing mega-markets: the USA/ Canada/Mexico; the European Community; and the Pacific Rim countries.

BOX MKT6.4

The international product lifecycle

International product lifecycles operate in a way which is similar to that of domestic products. The operation of this effect can be looked on as a warning to companies that globalization of their operations is perhaps the only way to guard themselves in the long term against being attacked in their home markets by overseas-produced versions of their own products.

In the first state, a manufacturing company which is successful in its home market will look for additional outlets for these products and so turns to exporting, that is, sending finished products into overseas markets.

In the second stage, foreign production starts either legitimately through a licensing arrangement or a joint venture or by foreign manufacturers simply copying the product.

In the third stage, the foreign producers begin to compete with the original company in overseas markets. They compete on price through lower manufacturing costs.

Finally, the copycat producers begin to produce sufficient volume for them to take advantage of economies of scale as well as lower personnel costs and they begin to export into the original company's own home market and to undercut their prices.

Source: Adapted from Paliwoda, *International Marketing*

In future, it will become more vital for long-term success for companies to have access to these geographical areas as is evidenced by Japanese car production plants in the UK which are poised to use this route as an entry to European markets. Please refer to Box MKT6.4.

Another characteristic of the companies which operate in a truly global sense is the way in which they source and manufacture their products. For example, lower labour costs have led companies to base their manufacturing in areas like Taiwan and Korea, a fact which is particularly true of computer companies and ship building. Taking this policy even further, we have automobile manufacturers like Ford who make engines in one country, chassis in another and assemble their cars in yet another. It is true to say that companies which operate globally plan their activities and put them into operation on a worldwide basis. However, it does not mean that only enormous corporations are able to operate globally – it is still possible to operate a strategy of niche marketing on a global basis.

Companies do not jump straight from domestic markets onto a completely global scene. They may well begin by exporting their domestic product and some may never move beyond this stage. For example, distillers of Scotch whisky remain exporters rather than moving towards

---

BOX MKT6.5

Options for entering overseas markets

Any company wanting to get involved in overseas operations usually starts by exporting their finished products to areas which are either geographically or culturally close to home. Even here they have a choice – they can export directly or indirectly. The latter is the safest place to start and the operation is usually carried out through independent middle men. Indirect exporting is less risky because the expertise of the middle men is available and it is also cheaper because there is no necessity for the company to set up its own export operation.

The next step is often licensing which, again, is less costly and less risky than other routes to international markets. In this case, the licenser enters into an agreement with a licensee for the latter to produce the former's products or use their trademark etc. in return for a fee. Coca-Cola's use of franchising for production facilities in overseas countries comes under this heading.

A stage closer to globalism might then be a joint venture where a production facility would be set up in joint ownership between foreign companies and local investors in order to produce products for the overseas market.

The final stage would be setting up a wholly owned production facility in a foreign country. This activity has definite advantages for a company which is experienced in international markets. This route would ensure lower production costs in the longer term and also allows the investor to keep control of their investment.

However, the route eventually chosen depends on several different factors, for example, some countries will allow foreign investment only in the form of joint ventures. As with everything else in marketing, each situation needs to be weighed up against costs and benefits before final decisions are made.

---

producing on a worldwide scale. The next stage may be a licensing agreement or production in one other country from which there may well be additional expansion into other viable international areas.

The subject of international marketing is dealt with in detail in another text in the *Effective Management* series, *Effective International Marketing*. In the meantime, please refer to Box MKT6.5.

Indicators of Performance: Towards Evaluation

As well as developing marketing strategies and planning marketing programmes, marketing managers also need to develop systems for feedback, evaluation and control. Marketing programmes are expensive to implement and, no matter how detailed the pre-project research, marketing research can never be a crystal ball. Therefore, part of every company's detailed marketing activity should consist of checking the levels of success achieved by its strategies and policies. It needs to do this so that every success can be recognized and built upon for the future and also so that problem areas can be identified in time for remedial action to be taken.

One important use of the marketing plan surfaces here: its use as a measure for evaluating performance. The annual marketing plan should contain objectives and forecasts, so it is valuable as a means of checking whether sales are moving to the required level. The marketing plan can be used as a means of control in four different areas as follows.

Analysis of sales

Most organizations keep sales records, these can be obtained from the sales force although the sales force may deal with only part of the selling effort, or they can be recorded through logging orders as they come into the firm. In either case, these figures need to be made available to the marketing department as part of the organization's marketing information system (see Unit Three).

Sales thus recorded can easily be compared with sales forecasts and targets and it can also be useful to relate sales to type of outlet, for example, supermarket chain or large wholesaler where the distribution channel takes this form. Industrial companies also need to relate sales to order levels and customer type. They can also be related to the targets set for individual sales territories and reasons can then be sought for any serious variance. For example, sales might have fallen because of increased competitive activity or because one particular sales person consistently fails to meet targets. Sales are usually tracked in terms of **sales variance**, that is, the amount by which actual sales vary from the targets, which can then be used to build up a detailed picture.

Analysis of market share

If companies only look at their overall sales levels then they know how they are performing relative to their sales forecasts and targets, but this tells them nothing about how they are performing in relation to their markets and their competitors. It is entirely possible that, although a company's sales are growing, it is still losing market share to more aggressive competitors. This is of course another compelling reason in favour of a marketing orientation which ensures that they are looking outwards into their markets rather than inwards at their own concerns.

Even knowing *how* it is performing in its markets is not enough for the truly marketing orientated company – it is equally important to know *why* something is happening. For example, if market share is increasing then the company must be doing well in relation to its competitors, but is this because of the new advertising campaign, because of the new discount structure or because a close competitor is having problems?

Analysis of sales costs

Sales costs are monitored to ensure that the amount spent on achieving sales is not too high for the company to bear and the cost looked at here is the actual cost of the marketing, promotional and selling effort in relation to sales levels, that is, what it actually costs to make sales.

Financial analysis

In this case, what is being looked at are financial ratios such as the company's gross profit, net profit and return on investment. Where possible, it is also useful to consider this analysis in relation to other competing companies.

It might seem strange to be examining these ratios in relation to a company's marketing effort. However, marketing managers can still contribute towards improving overall financial performance by taking action to reduce stock levels or by increasing sales without increasing expenses.

Qualitative Methods of Evaluation

From a marketing point of view, it is vital to keep track of sales levels and the cost of selling the company's products. However, marketing managers do not only have to deal with hard financial measures, they also have to deal with the softer qualitative areas like image and customer perceptions and satisfaction levels, so here, we might be looking at methods of evaluation which involve research. These methods are perhaps less direct than the financial ones which are in use but they are no less essential. Useful areas to concentrate on are as follows:

- *Research.* This might be achieved through the use of ongoing customer panels which can track levels of satisfaction and changes in attitude over a long period. Interviewing can be used to check levels of awareness of a product before, and then after, a special advertising campaign. Depth interviews and focus groups can also be used to uncover attitudes and preferences.
- *Customer questionnaires.* In industrial markets, some companies use postal questionnaires to check on customer satisfaction levels. This is a method which can also be used in consumer markets where names and addresses of customers are actually known. For example, hotel chains could use postal questionnaires to check on satisfaction levels as applied to the level of service received and the helpfulness of the staff. Hotel chains also leave questionnaires in guest rooms hoping that they will be completed and handed in.

BOX MKT6.6

Actions marketing managers can take to improve profitability

Improving profitability very often means reducing costs, but care has to be taken to ensure that reducing costs does not mean pulling out of so many activities that the marketing effort becomes ineffective.

In a difficult situation, it can be best in the long run to do nothing. If budgets have been allocated in the most sensible manner, and all pointers suggest that the communications mix is the best that can be arranged, then cutting back on expenditure might be a short-sighted action.

It is worth looking at the efficiency of the sales force to make sure that territory is being covered to optimum effect. It is even worth checking with customers to find out how often they like to receive service calls from sales people – it is possible that calls are being made too frequently. While examining this area, it makes sense to check on the number of new customers being added to the list and also on the number of customers being lost. Averages are also a useful measure to apply through the average number of sales calls per day, average revenue per call, average cost per sales call and so on.

Advertising effectiveness is a difficult thing to track. However, useful measures are cost per thousand levels for all media used, number of enquiries received from each advertisement, cost per enquiry.

Being *effective* is better than simply cutting costs.

- *Customer complaints.* Complaints can be logged and collated so that management has the opportunity to introduce systems to overcome the problems which lead to large numbers of complaints about specific products or specific service areas such as after sales.
- *Lost orders.* Management needs to know if orders are lost because products are out of stock or do not meet customer needs. Continual requests for products which are not stocked can lead to changes in retail buying policies.

Now refer to Box MKT6.6.

Auditing the Total Marketing Effort

As emphasized above, ongoing evaluation of marketing activities should be an essential part of the work of the department. This is monitoring on an operational level: looking at detailed activities and cost levels. It is also essential to the long-term health of any organization's marketing effort that the whole function of the department should be evaluated.

The marketing environment in which companies operate is volatile and fast changing and much of what happens is beyond their direct control so that strategies and programmes can become obsolete almost without warning, for example, if a close competitor launches a new product. Additionally, the total effectiveness of a company in its chosen marketplace cannot be judged only by sales figures and research into the effectiveness of advertising campaigns. Good results might be a function of a growing market rather than a perfect marketing strategy.

Kotler[5] tells us that there are five major attributes of marketing orientation which can be measured in order to gauge a company's overall marketing effectiveness. The exercise takes the form of a questionnaire which asks the respondent to consider the attitudes of the company towards different areas of marketing. A sliding scale is used to measure the company's attitude towards different areas of marketing philosophy. The areas covered are:

1 *Customer philosophy.* The first section examines a company's attitude towards customer orientation and thus to the whole concept of marketing as a philosophy of doing business.

2 *Integrated marketing organization.* This section considers whether or not an organization's sales and marketing efforts are co-ordinated at the top and also whether or not the marketing effort operates in co-operation with other departments like R&D and production.

3 *Adequate marketing information.* Here, the exercise looks at whether or not the company carries out marketing research on a regular basis and also asks how much it actually knows about its markets and customers. This really covers the extent and effectiveness of the marketing information system.

4 *Strategic orientation.* Now the question asked is about the extent of formal marketing planning and the quality of the organization's marketing strategy.

5 *Operational efficiency.* Here, what is looked at is the operation of the marketing effort and the capacity of management to ensure that it is efficient and effective.

Low scores in any area mean that this is something which needs attention and thus, management is given the opportunity to take corrective action.

Perhaps the best known of all marketing evaluation tools is the **marketing audit**. This is well known to students of marketing because it is the first step in case-study analysis and, in the real world of business, it should also be the first step in any marketing planning exercise.

In fact, the marketing audit is the 'where are we now?' section of the marketing plan where it sets out to examine the current marketing set-up of the organization and the environment in which it operates.

Just as the annual financial audit is a snapshot of where an organization is in financial terms on a particular day – usually the last one of the financial year – so the marketing audit sets out to build a picture of where it is in marketing terms at the time the audit is carried out. The marketing audit will show up areas which need attention and identify the internal and external factors which will reveal whether or not the company can survive in the marketplace (see figure 6.2).

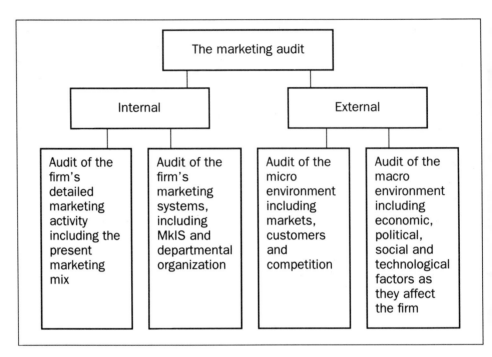

Figure 6.2 Outline of areas covered in a marketing audit.

Source: Adapted from the Open Business School, *Marketing in Action.*

For the benefit of the company and for that of the individuals carrying out the audit it is more efficient if the material for the audit is collected on an ongoing data basis, that is, through the marketing information system. The actual audit should be a management function, although on occasions an outside consultant might be used. The collection of data may be done by junior staff but the analysis should be done by managers.

As well as being a way of judging the marketing health of a company, a marketing audit is a very good way for individual managers to familiarize themselves with all areas of marketing activity. The areas looked at should include:

- *Products* (with data from production and R&D departments as well as from marketing).
- *Sales and distribution* including packaging and logistics and the operation of the sales force.
- *Markets* themselves through data which should come from the marketing information system, including research.
- *Advertising and sales promotion* through the results of levels of effectiveness monitoring which should be carried out as part of the routine work of the marketing department.
- *Financial aspects* of the marketing effort using data from accounts and costings exercises.

■ *Customers,* including who they are, where they are, what their needs and wants are, and what they think of the company and its products.

ACTIVITY MKT6.1

THE KEY AREAS OF MARKETING

Activity code
☑ Self-development
☑ Teamwork
☑ Communications
☑ Numeracy/IT
☑ Decisions

Hill summarizes the work of Udell and Pass to illustrate the policy areas selected by industrial producers as being vital to a successful operation.[1] Now, we cannot be expected to arrive necessarily at the same percentage weightings, but the *task* here is to derive the main rankings of what you see as the key areas of marketing within the context of industrial producers.

You can compare your views with that of the researchers in the handbook.

Policy areas

Estimate the number of firms, selecting the policy area as being of primary importance, (i.e. out of 108: 68 and 40 firms respectively)

Product
Product research and development
Product service
Product quality
Average production-selection ratio

Sales etc.
Market research and sales planning
Advertising and sales promotion
Management of sales personnel
Average sales efforts selection ratio

Pricing

Other
Organizational structure
Distribution channels and channel
     management
Financial and credit
Marketing cost budgeting and control
Physical distribution management
Public relations

Give the rationale/conclusions behind your ranking for 'auditing' the function of industrial marketing, then compare with the actual research findings.

Source:
1 See R.W. Hill for commentary on the research findings, *Marketing Technological Products to Industry*

McDonald[6] divides the information required for the audit into three sections:

1 *A review of the marketing environment.* This would include the wider environment in which the company operates and cover areas such as the political situation, social and demographic trends, economic factors like interest rates and recession, and technological trends which might affect the company's areas of operation. Additionally, there would be an examination of the company's closer environment: its markets, customers and competitors. Here, developing trends, for example, an ageing population, would be identified as well as what is happening now.

2 *Review of the detailed marketing activity.* This area covers everything that has to do with the company's marketing mix: products, price levels and strategies, promotional methods and activity and distribution methods. This would include cost levels and would cover everything the company actually does on the marketing scene.

3 *Review of the marketing system.* The final area of review is that of the systems which are in operation and would cover the organization of the marketing effort: the structure of the marketing department; the personnel and their activities and responsibilities; the marketing information system; marketing research systems; review and monitoring systems; and the present marketing objectives, strategies and plan.

It should be emphasized that the collection of the information is a useful exercise and through it, a picture can be built up of the company's strengths and weaknesses in marketing terms. However, the information itself has no intrinsic value – it is the conclusions that are drawn and the actions that are taken as a result of the analysis which are important to future success levels. It is successful planning for the future which matters above all else. The details of marketing planning are dealt with in Unit Two.

Evaluation/Audit: A Quality Perspective

The need for quality across all functions and disciplines of management has become a byword of the 1990s. Given our *relationship* vision between the firm and its employees, between the state and its regulation and the firm, as well as between the organization and its customers or end users, quality is a key aspect of such interactions. We will develop this quality theme for evaluative purposes.

A series of self-explanatory boxes summarizes the following:

- 'Quality: the concept' (Box MKT6.7).
- 'Quality: a customer perspective' (Box MKT6.8).

BOX MKT6.7

Quality: the concept

Quality is the degree of excellence required to meet customer needs and wants.

So quality is very much part of the philosophy of marketing as it ensures that the product or service conforms to customer expectations. The aim is ultimately a defect-free product or service. Yet quality is not just about error detection; it is a broader concept encompassing high performance and a customer-orientated state of mind in all those concerned with a product or service.

BOX MKT6.8

Quality: a customer perspective

The organizational objectives tempered by local conditions give some context to which quality indicators or 'norms' are expected. A self-analysis can determine whether we are meeting these 'norms'.

However, the key aspect of any marketing organization is the customer. So we need the views of the customer which must be fed in to the established quality 'norms' of the organization, and a facility must exist to modify these norms in accordance with the views of the consumers.

The opinions of consumers researched en masse for developing products can be analysed to assess the existing quality of customer care being given by the organization. The information can either be quantified or qualitative, 'hard' statistics or 'soft' attitudinal issues.

Thereafter, we can examine quality through the process of consumer audits (Box MKT6.9) which gives performance standards to gauge some evaluation of quality.

BOX MKT6.9

Quality and consumer audits

> To err is human. To err twice is a mistake – not to be tolerated.
>
> Bert Stephens, then President of Boca Raton Hotel and Club

The consumer audits of the Boca Raton Hotel and Club, a five-star resort with some 920 beds south of Palm Beach on Florida's east coast, have passed into the legends of the sector.[1] There are lessons here for us all – irrespective of nationality or industry sector.

The staff clearly differentiates this hotel from others. As a service industry, customer relations must be paramount and this seems to be the case at The Boca Raton Hotel and Club.

Quality on the complex is based on a vision of standards:

- Job tasks are noted.
- Procedures are written up on how to do the job.
- 'Standards of expectation' are derived.

Training, ongoing communications systems and 'error' detection consolidate the process. The consumer audit is a critical component of this vision and practice of high-quality standards.

The guests are asked to use a 'guest comment card'. The hotel is rated on a scale, the staff (name) are rated, as are the room, dining facilities, sport and leisure facilities and personal services, from the beauty salon to child minding.

Every three months a separate questionnaire goes out to previous guests to give both individual and collective responses to the whole quality process. A harder edge comes from reviewing any rebates given to guests.

Other indicators in this quality audit include the costs of errors, employee turnover/wastage, and performance approach linked to the established performance standards.

The approach looks somewhat proceduralized with key standards and key behaviours. It almost looks like scientific management in its task analysis, but there seem to be 'soft' as well as 'hard' standards which mollify this task edge. It is also more quality assurance than total quality, but there are clear messages here for the marketing organization.

Source:
1 Basic information from Pearson, 'The Boca Raton Hotel and Club'

The final box on quality gives us a keen insight into the various eight dimensions of quality which can be used by the marketeer. Again, the external (customer) frame of reference needs to be set alongside the internal 'marketing organization' vision to give a complete view of quality and its evaluation. Please now refer to Box MKT6.10.

BOX MKT6.10

Quality: the final marketing frontier?

Quality control – sorting out defects – and quality assurance – attempting to remove the defects because they are a problem – are the bread and butter of operations managers. The Japanese trade invasion, with goods based on reliable quality, has swamped western markets in recent years.

Much of the Japanese strength[1] has been based around their approach to quality. As the Japanese adapted western technology to their ends since 1945, western business is now increasingly adapting total quality management (TQM).

Lamb[2] cites an interesting example of the US glassmaker, Corning, and its approach to total quality. She refers to the work of Garvin who sees some eight dimensions of quality:

- reputation
- performance
- features
- reliability
- conformity to standards
- service
- durability
- aesthetics

Corning went TQM in 1983. In spite of initial training of some 28,000 in the basic quality principles, the initial training results were not particularly positive. Attitudes seemed to be the answer, with no positive 'role model' appearing from management and a cynical labour force.

Interestingly, the customer orientation of this strategic vision is based not only on market research but on 'internal' attitudinal research amongst the labour force. The individual employer who works day in and day out on any project knows the wrinkles of a job better than anyone. To tap this knowledge a quality approach may also be linked to some incentive scheme for employees to reinforce positive attitudes to quality.

Sources:
1   See Anderson, *Effective Personnel Management*
2   Adapted from Lamb, 'The quiet revolution'

Evaluation/Audit: The Training Model Approach

We started by looking at the variables associated with the marketing initiative in the preface. We will also conclude with this model. You will recall that the model has macro and micro dimensions. If we blend these two themes, we can derive a useful checklist and gauge our marketing initiative. At this point, please refer to Boxes MKT6.11 and MKT6.12; the plans-cum-audits in these boxes also help us to initiate the action by providing a frame of reference. Finally, they summarize the main themes contained within the book.

BOX MKT6.11

Macro plans and audits

The 'plan of campaign' can also act as a useful checklist for auditing which marketing actually happens within the organization and within the specialist marketing department. We can refer to the variables on the marketing initiative (see Box MKT6.2).

Wider external environment
The interaction of political, economic, sociological and technological factors provides a context to the 'macro' environment of the organization and its marketplace(s). These variables influence the market, providing both opportunities and constraints. Examples include:

- **Political** Legislation can inhibit a marketplace, for example by the control of pornography and television advertising. The political stability of a country, region or area can certainly influence the market. For example, certain countries in Latin America have had a revolutionary tradition since post-colonial times and this must have an impact on business stability in the long term.
- **Economic** The amount and quality of skilled labour in one area compared to others can provide a wealthier market. The movement of labour in the EC can be cited here. Price inflation can inhibit any consolidated marketing effort and savings can be wiped out as in some Latin American states or in Eastern Europe in the early 1990s.
- **Sociological** A greater ecological awareness can mean that products such as car exhausts must be altered to take account of the environment. The ethnic mix of a population can lead to cultural trends in eating, for example, that can be exploited.
- **Technological** Energy changes, information technology (IT), improved communication systems and so on make information and knowledge more readily available to everyone from competitor to customer. Change can have a drastic effect on the products; for example, the market for riding whips declined sharply with the advent of the motor car industry.

The competition
Trends and potential changes in these competitive trends must be built into an intelligence system. Some of the principles of internal planning can be used to gauge the competitive marketplace. A balance is required between keeping an eye on the opposition and developing your 'own' product or service.

The customer
The make-up of the customer profile, the segmentation being used, the approach to buyer behaviour, trends in buying behaviour and the customers'

views, for example, on consumerism, go to the heart of the whole process. Research is critical.

The organization
The existing strengths and weaknesses, its current product/service mix and how it currently relates to this wider environment as well as the changing scenarios of both internal and external environments complete this overall macro scan.

The suppliers
Their relationship to the organization: how they dovetail into the product, its quality, cost and so on.

BOX MKT6.12

Micro plans and audits

The marketing initiative came from within the organization relating external opportunities in the marketplace to internal strengths. Further, we have advocated not only a marketing department charged with this responsibility, but a marketing organization imbued with the philosophy of marketing.

The marketing organization
The marketing objectives (short- and long-term) need to be 'translated' for everyday consumption by employees. A working quality approach to service is a good benchmark of this philosophy in practice. A widespread understanding of the business awareness and realities right across the organization (and not only amongst managers) may be another indicator of this approach. Perhaps, above all, there needs to be a customer orientation from all employees and not just 'direct' staff such as salespeople and marketeers.

The plan
Evidence must exist of a coherent plan based upon external opportunity and internal organizational capacity. A programme of implementation and appropriate goals and 'milestones'[1] and budgets needs to be in place alongside some organizational structure and marketing leadership.

Detailed 'mix'
This could be based on the four Ps or the seven Ps (see Unit One). Assuming the four Ps the following issues may be helpful:
- *Product.* Type, stage, development/decline, mix, the portfolio, potential additions/deletions etc.
- *Place.* Methods of distribution: the means of distribution, alternative channels, back-up service via the distribution network, role of middle men/agents etc.

- *Promotion.* Publicity campaigns linked to sales promotion tactics. Advertising type and form linked again to the product portfolio and to any personal selling initiatives.
- *Price.* The method of calculation. The going market rate and pricing linked again to the product portfolio through discounting or whatever. The options open for pricing management need to be noted.

Tactics

An expansion of the 'mix' to give detailed tactics by product with set goals and timescales needs to be in operation.

Review/monitoring

The whole marketing plan and specific tactics must be constantly monitored via external and intelligence or research feeding into the organization.

Integration

It is critical that the marketing initiatives do not start and end with the marketeers, for an integrated strategy towards the marketplace involving all departments is an essential part of the *marketing organization*.

Source:
1 We discuss these benchmarks and their use elsewhere. See Anderson and Barker, *Effective Business Policy*

Notes

1 Kelly, *The Curriculum, Theory and Practice.*
2 Weitz and Wensley, *Strategic Marketing.*
3 Peters and Waterman, Jr, *In Search of Excellence.*
4 Kotler, *Marketing Management.*
5 Ibid.
6 McDonald, *Marketing Plans.*

Conclusion

We are not going to summarize the book in this conclusion. Instead we are going to reiterate that marketing is the business. Further, that business exists in turbulent external environments and the marketing organization must come to terms with such changes. Looking outward is not enough – the marketing organization must also develop a culture of enterprise within the firm. Sound information, good communications and, above all, sound relationships, can mean that the customer culture pervades the whole of the organization, making it able to adapt to the often fickle tasks, needs, wants and aspirations of its customers. For at the end of the day:

> *[Marketing means looking at the] ... whole business seen from the point of view of its final result, that is from the customer's point of view. Concern and responsibility for marketing must therefore permeate all areas of the enterprise.*

> Drucker, *The Practice of Management*

Bibliography and Further Reading

Anderson, A. H., *Effective General Management* (Blackwell, Oxford, 1994).

Anderson, A. H., *Effective Labour Relations* (Blackwell, Oxford, 1994).

Anderson, A. H., *Effective Personnel Management* (Blackwell, Oxford, 1994).

Anderson, A. H. and Barker, D., *Effective Business Policy* (Blackwell, Oxford, 1994).

Anderson, A. H. and Barker, D., *Effective Enterprise Management* (Blackwell, Oxford, 1994).

Anderson, A. H. and Ciechan, R., *Effective Financial Management* (Blackwell, Oxford, 1994).

Anderson, A. H. and Chansarkar, B., *Effective Market Research* (Blackwell, Oxford, 1994).

Anderson, A. H., Dobson, T. and Patterson, J., *Effective International Marketing* (Blackwell, Oxford, 1994).

Anderson, A. H. and Kleiner, D., *Effective Marketing Communications* (Blackwell, Oxford, 1994).

Anderson, A. H. and Kyprianou, A., *Effective Organizational Behaviour* (Blackwell, Oxford, 1994).

Anderson, A. H. and Nix, E., *Effective Accounting Management* (Blackwell, Oxford, 1994).

Anderson, A. H. and Woodcock, P., *Effective Entrepreneurship* (Blackwell, Oxford, 1994).

Ansoff, H. I., 'Strategies for diversification', *Harvard Business Review* (September–October, 1957).

Ansoff, H. I., *Strategic Management* (Macmillan, London, 1979).

Argenti, J., *Practical Corporate Planning* (Allen & Unwin, London, 1980).

Atlas, J., 'How Madison Avenue knows who you are and what you want: beyond demographics', *The Atlantic Monthly* (October 1984), pp. 49–58.

Backman, J. and Czepoel, J. (eds), *Changing Market Strategies in a New Economy* (Bobbs-Merril Educational Publishing, Indianapolis, 1977).

Bain, L. E. and Kurtz, D. L., *Contemporary Marketing* (Dryden Press, New York, 1980).

Bennett, R., 'Using research in training', *Journal of European Industrial Training*, 3, 5 (1979).

Bloom, R. H., 'Product redefinition begins with the consumer', *Advertising Age* (26 October 1981).

Booms, B. H., 'Marketing services by managing the environment', *Cornell HRA Quarterly* (May 1982).

Booms, B. H. and Bitner, M. J., 'Marketing strategies and organization: structures for service firms', in *Marketing of Services*, eds J. H. Donnelly and W. R. George (AMA, Chicago, 1981).

Booz, Allen and Hamilton Inc., *New Products Management for the 1980s* (Booz, Allen and Hamilton, New York, 1982).

Broadbent, S. and Jacobs, B., *Spending Advertising Money* (Hutchinson, London, 1984).

Business Technician and Education Council (BTEC), 'Common skills and experience of BTEC programmes' (BTEC, London, n.d.).

Cannon, T., *Basic Marketing: principles and practice* (Cassell, London, 1987).

Christopher, M., Payne, A. and Ballantyne, D., *Relationship Marketing* (Butterworth-Heinemann, Oxford, 1993).

Clewitt, R. M. and Starch, S. F., 'The shifting role of the product manager', *Harvard Business Review*, 53 (January–February 1975), pp. 65–73.

Cravens, D. M., *Strategic Marketing* (R. G. Irwin, Holmewood, Ill., 1982).

Cravens, D. M., Hills, G. E. and Woodruff, R. B., *Marketing Decision Making: concepts and strategy* (R. D. Irwin, Holmewood, Ill., 1980).

Crissy, W. and Boewadt, R., 'Pricing in perspective', *Sales Management* (15 June 1971).

Crosier, K., 'What exactly is marketing?', *Quarterly Review of Marketing* (winter 1975).

Davis, M. P., *The Effective Use of Advertising Media* (Hutchinson, London, 1988).

DeLozier, M. W. and Woodside, A., *Marketing Management: strategies and cases* (Charles E. Merrill, Columbus, 1978).

Department of Employment, *Glossary of Training Terms* (HMSO, London, 1977).

Dickens, J., 'The fresh cream cakes market: the use of qualitative research as part of a consumer research programme', in *Applied Marketing and Social Research*, ed. A. Bradley (Van Nostrand Reinhold, New York, 1982), pp. 4–43.

Doyle, P., 'The realities of the product life cycle', *Quarterly Review of Marketing* (summer 1976).

Drucker, P. F., *The Practice of Management* (Pan, London, 1954).

Drucker, P. F., 'Managing for business effectiveness', *Harvard Business Review*, 41 (May 1963).

Duncan, R., 'What is the right organization structure? Decision tree analysis provides the answer', *Organisational Dynamics*, 7, 3 (winter 1979), pp. 59–78.

Eison, I. I., *Strategic Marketing in Food Service* (Lebhar-Friedman Books, New York, 1989).

Festinger, L., *A Theory of Cognitive Dissonance* (Row Peterson, Evanston, Ill., 1957).

Fishlock, D., 'Sparked off by chemical light', *Financial Times* (1 May 1990).

Foster, D. *Planning for Products and Markets* (Longman, Harlow, 1972).

Foster, D., *Mastering Marketing*, 2nd edn (Macmillan, London, 1984).

Fraser-Robinson, J., *Total Quality Marketing* (Kogan Page, London, 1991).

Freeman, R. E., *Strategic Management: a stakeholder approach* (Pitman, London, 1984).

Fromm, E., *Man for Himself: an enquiry into the psychology of ethics* (Rinehart, New York, 1947).

Gorton, K. and Carr, I., *Low-Cost Marketing Research* (Wiley, London, 1984).

Gronroos, C., *Strategic Management and Marketing in the Service Sector* (Svenska Handelshogskolan, Helsinki, 1982).

Haley, R. I., 'Benefit segmentation: a decision-oriented research tool', *AMA, Journal of Marketing*, 32 (July 1968), pp. 30–5.

Hanan, M., 'Reorganise your company around its marketing', *Harvard Business Review*, 52 (November–December 1974), pp. 63–74.

Hanan, M., *Life Styled Marketing: how to position products for premium products* (AMACOM, New York, 1980).

Hannagan, T. J., *Marketing for the Non-Profit Sector* (Macmillan, Basingstoke, 1992).

Harrison, D., 'The last picture show ends in tears', *Observer* (14 February 1993).

Hart, N. A. and O'Connor, J., *The Practice of Advertising* (Heinemann, London, 1986).

Hayes, R. H. and Wheelwright, S. C., *Restoring Our Competitive Edge: competing through manufacturing* (Wiley, New York, 1984).

Hedley, B., 'The fundamental approach to strategy development' *Long Range Planning*, 9 (December 1976).

Hedley, B., 'Strategy and the business portfolio', *Long Range Planning*, 10, 2 (February 1977), p. 10.

Hill, N., *Marketing for BTEC* (Business Education Publishers, Sunderland, 1989).

Hill, N, *Successful Marketing for Small Businesses* (Charles Letts, London, 1990).

Hill, R. W., *Marketing Technological Products to Industry* (Pergamon Press, London, 1973).

Jones, J. A. G., 'Training intervention strategies: making more effective training interventions', ITS Monograph No. 2 (Industrial Training Services, London, 1983).

Jones, M., 'The fire eaters', *Marketing* (March–April 1993).

Kelly, A. V., *The Curriculum, Theory and Practice* (Harper & Row, London, 1977).

Kelly, E. J., *Marketing Planning and Competitive Strategy* (Prentice Hall, Englewood Cliffs, NJ, 1972).

Kiechel, W., 'Corporate strategists under fire', *Fortune* (27 December 1982).

Kotler, P., 'From sales obsession to marketing effectiveness', *Harvard Business Review*, 56 (September–October 1979), pp. 76–88.

Kotler, P., *Marketing Management: analysis, planning, implementation and control* (Prentice Hall International, London, 1991).

Kotler, P. and Andreason, A., *Strategic Marketing for Nonprofit Organisations* (Prentice Hall, Englewood Cliffs, NJ, 1991).

Kotler, P., Ferrell, O. C. and Lamb, C., *Cases and Readings for Marketing for Nonprofit Organisations* (Prentice Hall, Englewood Cliffs, NJ, 1983).

Lamb, C., 'The quiet revolution', *Financial Times* (27 April 1990).

Lancaster, G. and Massingham, L., *The Essentials of Marketing* (McGraw-Hill, Maidenhead, 1988).

Lancaster, G. and Massingham, L., *The Marketing Primer* (Heinemann, Oxford, 1988).

Lavidge, R. J. and Steiner, G. A., 'A model for predictive measurements of advertising', *Journal of Marketing* (October 1961).

Leven, M., 'How to develop marketing strategies', *Lodging* (March 1980).

Levitt, T., 'Marketing myopia', in *Modern Marketing Strategy*, eds E. C. Bursk and J. F. Chapman (Harvard University Press, Cambridge, Mass., 1964).

Lovelock, C. H., 'Classifying services to gain strategic marketing insights', *Journal of Marketing*, 47 (summer 1983).

Luck, D. J. and Ferrell, O. C., *Marketing Strategy and Plans: systematic marketing management* (Prentice Hall, Englewood Cliffs, NJ, 1979).

Luck, D. J., Wales, H. G., Taylor, D. A. and Rubin, R. S., *Marketing Research* (Prentice Hall, Englewood Cliffs, NJ, 1982).

Lucraft, F. and Rice, G., 'Getting involved in change', *Training Officer*, 29, 6 (July–August 1993).

McBurnie, T. and Clutterbuck, D., *The Marketing Edge* (Penguin, Harmondsworth, 1988).

McDonald, M., *Marketing Plans: how to prepare them, how to use them* (Heinemann, London, 1987).

Management Charter Initiative, *Diploma Level Guidelines and Diploma Workshop Report* (Shell UK, London, n.d.).

Maslow, A., *Motivation and Personality* (Harper & Row, New York, 1954).

Mercer, D., *Marketing* (Blackwell, Oxford, 1992).

Morein, J. A., 'Shift from brand to product line marketing', *Harvard Business Review*, 57 (September–October 1979), pp. 56–64.

Moutinho, L., *Problems in Marketing* (Chapman, London, 1991).

Open Business School, *Marketing in Action* (Open University Press, Milton Keynes, 1985).

Paliwoda, S. J., *International Marketing* (Heinemann, London, 1993).

Parker-Jarvis, G., 'AZT: Wellcome's bitter pill', *Observer* (4 April 1993).

Particelli, M. C., 'The Japanese are coming: global strategic planning in action', *Outlook* (Booz, Allen and Hamilton, New York, 1981).

Pearson, J., 'The Boca Raton Hotel and Club', *Lodging* (July 1983).

Peters, T. J. and Austin, N., *A Passion for Excellence* (Random House, New York, 1985).

Peters, T. J. and Waterman R. H., Jr, *In Search of Excellence* (Harper Collins, New York, 1992).

Pettigrew, A. M., *The Politics of Organisational Decision-Making* (Tavistock Press, London, 1973).

Piercy, N., *Market-Led Strategic Change* (Butterworth-Heinemann, Oxford, 1991).

Plummer, J. T., 'The concept and application of lifestyle segmentation', *Journal of Marketing*, 38 (January 1974).

Porter, M. E., *Competitive Strategy: techniques for analysing industries and competitors* (Free Press, New York, 1980).

Rathmell, J. M., *Marketing in the Service Sector* (Winthrop, Cambridge, Mass., 1974).

Renaghan, L. M., 'A new marketing mix for the hospitality industry', *The Connell HRA Quarterly* (August 1981).

Rogers, E. M., *Diffusion of Innovations* (Free Press, New York, 1983).

Ryan, W. T. and Hermanson, R. H., *Programmed Learning Aid for Principles of Marketing* (Richard D. Irwin, Holmewood, Ill., 1971).

Sadler, P., 'Task and organisation structure in marketing', in *Task and Organisation*, ed. E. J. Miller (Wiley, London, 1973), pp. 173–92.

Shama, A., *Marketing in a Slow Growth Economy: the impact of stagnation on consumer psychology* (Preager, New York, 1980).

Shostack, L. G., 'Breaking free from product marketing', *AMA* (April 1977).

Stern, L. W. and El-Ansary, A. I., *Marketing Channels* (Prentice Hall, Englewood Cliffs, NJ, 1992).

Thomas, N. and Pearson, B., *The Shorter MBA* (Thorsons, London, 1991).

Training Commission/Council for Management Education (CMED), 'Classifying the components of management competencies' (Training Commission, London, 1988).

Twedt, D. W., *Survey of Marketing Research* (American Marketing, Chicago, 1978).

Waterman, R. H., Jr, *The Renewal Factor: how the best get and keep the competitive edge* (Bantam, New York, 1987).

Weitz, B. and Wensley, R., *Strategic Marketing* (Kent Publishing, Boston, Mass., 1984).

West, A., *Understanding Marketing* (Harper & Row, London, 1987).

Wilmshurst, J., *The Fundamentals and Practice of Marketing* (Heinemann, London, 1978).

Index